ROS
THE
FASTEST
AUSSIE ON
EARTH

Pete & Delia

all the very best!

Rosco McGlashan 23/1/24

Rosco McGlashan's *amazing* life story by Mark J Read

ROSCO The Fastest Aussie on Earth by Mark J Read
Published by Aussie Invader World Land Speed Record
Copyright © Mark J Read 2023

The right of Mark J Read to be identified as the sole and original author of this work has been asserted in accordance with the Copyright, Designs and Patents Act 1998 and Copyright Amendment Act 2006.

All rights reserved. No part of this book may be reproduced, stored, or transmitted in any form or by any means whatsoever without prior permission in writing from the publisher, nor be it otherwise circulated in any form, including any binding or cover other than that in which it is published here.

Printed and bound by Amazon KDP Australia.
ISBN: 979-8372894372
Language: Australian English
Cover design by Mark J Read.
Images © Aussie Invader World Land Speed Record

ROSCO THE FASTEST AUSSIE ON EARTH

Contents

Foreword by Peter Beck v

Introduction vii

Love, Loss and Life's Lessons 11

Rebel With a Cause 27

Working My Way Up 35

Racing Was in My Blood 45

My Life Changed in Less Than Six Seconds 53

Thrust or Bust 61

Trips, Travels and Tales in The USA 69

My Land Speed Dream Becomes a Reality 77

Friends in High Places 85

Aussie Invader 2 Starts With Sound Advice 91

Construction of a Record Breaker 97

Early Trips, Travels and Tales in Australia 115

The First Record Attempt 135

Return to The Lake 151

Inches From Disaster 163

Aussie Invader 3 – So Near, but So Far 173

The Dynamic Duo 187

False Starts for Aussie Invader 5 201

Later Trips, Travels and Tales in Australia 233

How to Build The World's Fastest Car 243

Build Events and Milestones – Part 1 267

Mongrel Bunch of Bastards 289

Build Events and Milestones – Part 2 295

Aussie Invader 5R in Pictures..................................... 313

The Woman Behind The Man 327

The Final Chapter.. 337

Awards, Honours and Appearances......................... 343

Special Thanks and Acknowledgements 349

Author's Note 351

Foreword
by
Peter Beck

Founder and CEO of Rocket Lab

The number of people who have strapped themselves to a rocket with wheels and let physics and engineering determine their fate is few, and for a good reason. It's a profoundly bold thing to do. I know because I have done it. But those who have undertaken this questionable pastime recognise the unrelenting itch for acceleration that only a rocket engine can offer in a fellow speed worshiper. So, when a straight-talking, unabashedly determined Aussie bloke called Rosco called me in 2008, wanting to build a rocket car to break the world land speed record, I recognised that itch.

There's no shortage of tyre-kickers in the speed world, but anyone who encounters Rosco knows he's not one for empty threats, so I was immediately compelled to support his quest to bend the rules of engineering and set to work on various designs and calculations. It felt good to be in the hunt with a guy like that. You don't come across them often. The ones who look at seemingly insurmountable challenges shrug and simply say, "Better get on with it then."

By the time I crossed paths with Rosco, he was an accomplished, respected and highly capable drag racer and land speed record holder. However, having read the pages of this book, I now have a far deeper insight into the life and times that moulded him. At times brutal, at others inspirational, Rosco's is a story of resilience. Bucking conventional career paths, pushing limits with authority, and beating one's own path are things I'm a fervent supporter of. Still, even I winced at times reading Rosco's wildly tumultuous road to his dream.

Within these pages, it became immediately clear the fire I could see in Rosco when we first met had been burning since early childhood. It made for a white-knuckled life filled with stops and starts. But, most importantly, there have always been more starts after every stall and a spectacular near-death crash. Obsession does that to a person. It fills them with an all-consuming drive that sees them push harder when others call time. Sometimes, this causes havoc to the people in their orbit.

This book shows that's a fate Rosco doesn't manage to escape either. Still, it also reveals his innate ability to bond with people and build exceptional teams driven by a shared purpose. A lot can be learned from how he approaches creating and bonding a team.

Rosco The Fastest Aussie on Earth is a captivating read that draws you into the curious and fanatical world of land speed racing. He's a bloody good bloke who took it on in the face of grim odds.

Peter Beck

Auckland, New Zealand, January 2023

rocketlabusa.com

Introduction

The story you are about to read is of Rosco McGlashan's life, as told to me over many years. Usually, this involved beers, coffee, food, and generally good conversation. It's an incredible story of a man obsessed with speed, thrills, and living on the edge.

When we met, he would often tell me bits of his life in a series of fantastic stories of things he had done or had happened to him in the past. Sometimes, we would talk about something on the land speed car we were building or what we were doing at the time. This would lead to a story and a fantastic tale that you thought, *Wow, that's just unbelievable!* Most people would have a few of these stories in their lifetime. Rosco had hundreds.

I realised I had to write these stories down before they were lost forever. So, you're about to read the true story of one man's life, who has become a motor racing legend in many people's eyes. It's a story of highs and lows, good and bad, and triumph over adversity, but most of all, it's a story of the human spirit and endeavour of someone who never gives up.

This is not your typical motor racing memoir. Rosco's early life was undoubtedly challenging and not one of privilege like some in motorsport. He spent time in state-run homes and remand centres, eventually leaving home and school at the age of 12 after a run-in with his family and headmaster. He fought everyone and everything, and at 17, he found himself on the wrong side of the law, in prison and even solitary confinement.

When things could have spiralled down into a lifetime of crime and worse, he finds salvation through his love of speed and raw horsepower. He focuses his fighting spirit and energy on his motor racing and trying to achieve his goal of breaking the world land speed record.

The subject solely dictates the style of this book, Rosco, who is straight-talking and a little bit rough around the edges. I have always felt I should write these great stories as they were told to me, as close to Rosco's own words as I could. I had become the custodian of these great tales and events about one man's journey, obsession with speed, and life's goal to become the fastest man on Earth.

So, sit down, grab a coffee and strap yourself in for a fast ride and one of the most incredible life adventures I believe you will ever read.

Mark J Read

Author and proud member of the Aussie Invader team

e: mark@aussieinvader.com

My Life Portrait Sketch by John Dixon 2014.

-1-

Love, Loss and Life's Lessons

At 18, I was partway through a two-year prison sentence. I found myself in Fremantle Prison's solitary confinement, known as "chokey". It was mid-December 1968, and I'd been in chokey for a week already, with just over three weeks to go. I was given the maximum time they were allowed to put you in solitary, one month.

My cell was one metre wide by three metres long, with enough room to lie down and a tiny table you could eat from, and that was about it. I had one small barred window above my head. It let the sunlight in, but it was too high for me to feel any of the sun's warmth.

I was allowed one hour of exercise a day, and I had just come to the end of my week of bread and water. Yes, that's right, bread and water. Some will tell you it never happened. I can assure you it did. In solitary, you did a week on bread and water, then a week on ordinary tucker. Of course, you wouldn't treat a dog like that, but prison wasn't about good treatment or rehabilitation in those days. It was solely about punishment, and plenty of it.

What I did that got me into Fremantle Prison, and chokey comes later, but I should start this story at the very beginning of my life. A few people who knew this book was being written have told me not to go into early childhood when writing a memoir. It appears most people's early life is quite boring. You will find mine a bit different. Nevertheless, it is key to understanding why I made some poor choices. It will undoubtedly become clear why I was running wild and fighting authority at every chance I got. In fact, I was fighting anyone and anything that stood in my way.

I eventually learned to turn that fighting spirit into something positive, pursuing my obsession of trying to become the fastest man on Earth. My stay in chokey gave me plenty of time to think about my life's goal and plan my land speed and racing ambitions. I had bugger all else to do in my tiny cell. Anyway, here's my story from the beginning.

-ooOOoo-

When the Second World War broke out, Mum was too young to enlist, so she entered the Australian Women's Land Army (AWLA) at 15. The AWLA worked in jobs left by the men going to war. Mum was sent to a tobacco farm in the Atherton Tablelands in Queensland.

Dad was older than Mum and had enlisted. He was posted to Atherton Tablelands for jungle training, and that is where Mum and Dad first met. Dad moved around quite a bit in the Australian Army and was later promoted to Sergeant and bombardier. He was looked at for the elite 1st Parachute Battalion. Still, he was rejected as he had behavioural issues and had been caught drinking on duty. He was later assigned to the 2nd/3rd Anti-Tank Regiment and served in Morotai, North Borneo and New Guinea. Unfortunately, Dad returned from his years of fighting and service pretty screwed up.

Love, Loss and Life's Lessons

I was born Ross McGlashan in Subiaco, a suburb of Perth, Western Australia, on the 23rd of August 1950 to Gavin and Diana McGlashan. Our family consisted of Mum, Dad, my older sister Jill, me, and later my younger sister and brother, Gail and Bruce.

Family life was tough. We weren't financially poor, but emotionally, we were at rock bottom. Mum and Dad were on and off regularly, always fighting, which led to a pretty troubled home life and not a great environment to be raised in. As a young boy, with all this going on, I learnt early in life to deal with shit and stressful situations. I was pretty resilient. In fact, all the kids in the family were.

One of my earliest memories was when I was young, probably about three years old. If I didn't eat dinner, my mum would put me in my highchair on the street. She did this to me three or four times. The first time she put me out there, I remember being embarrassed, and all the kids in the street laughed and made a bit of a joke about it. The following few times this happened, I just shrugged it off, thought it was funny and sat out there, laughing and carrying on. This was the beginning of becoming a rebellious young man.

I started at a kindy in Cottesloe, which was only about 500 metres from the house where we lived. I recall getting dressed and leaving the house one morning to take myself off to kindy. God knows how old I was, probably four years old, and waiting outside for kindy to open up. No one came along, and then I went home in tears and was told it was Saturday. To this day, I still can't work out how a kid at four years of age would have done that, got themselves up, dressed and gone to school by himself. It happened a second time, but I was sharper this time and realised it must've been Saturday and wandered home.

Our house and cars were always filled with cigarette smoke. Dad, who was a chain smoker, would buy a packet of rolly weed, roll his cigarette, lick the paper, and remove the spent butt from the old one. This old butt was still alight, and he would use it to light the new smoke. He would then crush the old butt and place it in the corner of his packet, along with a hundred others, in readiness to construct a new smoke when needed. As kids, we constantly had headaches and complained to both parents without sympathy or resolution. None of us kids ever grew very tall, and the lack of care, food and a poor environment probably didn't help.

My mum was different from my dad. She was innovative and a bit of an entrepreneur in her day. She was always trying to do deals in real estate and flipping houses. She was quite an operator, but this meant all the kids were left to their own devices. Our parents didn't have time for us, except for giving us lots of jobs around our home or Mum's newly purchased house. So, I would be put to work tidying up, sweeping, weeding and painting.

Like most kids who weren't shown much affection or love, we wanted something to care for. I was no different, and we had chickens. I grew very attached to a grey-speckled hen called "Bubba". I used to sneak her into my bedroom at night and fall asleep with her. My parents always punished me for this, but I persisted as most young kids do. Eventually, they stopped me by cutting her head off and serving her to everyone as Christmas dinner. As you can understand, I was heartbroken and didn't have much appetite for that festive meal.

With Mum working a lot, it often fell to Dad to look after us for a few hours or even a day when he wasn't working. This "looking after us" would generally mean him driving us to the local pub. He would booze on with his mates whilst we kids were stuck in the car for hours on hot days. If we were lucky, he or one of his mates might bring us out a drink. He was a bit left-field and not great with the parenting stuff. He was a social guy, but his kids weren't a high priority to him. We got on with it as we didn't know any different. This was our day-to-day life, and it seemed normal to us.

This lack of parental care meant my sister Jill, and I spent a lot of time going backwards and forwards between our home and a state-run home for kids called Wanslea. This home offered foster care for struggling and broken families. Later, my younger siblings Gail and Bruce would also spend time there. Jill and I weren't there together, but we would go there when things were shit at home. It was a safe place for both of us.

Wanslea was next to my school, North Cottesloe Primary, so it was hard to hide that my brother, sisters, and I went to Wanslea. This led to a lot of teasing from the other kids. If you were one of the kids from Wanslea, you were definitely a second-class citizen.

I always remember being hungry at school and never having food at lunchtime. Then, one day, I was caught taking a discarded sandwich from a school bin. I coped crap from the other kids for quite a while but then started snatching their food whilst they were hanging shit on me. After that, I learned to defend myself from people, and attack was the best form of defence.

A nice teacher at that time put me in charge of the morning milk distribution. This involved wheeling several crates of 1/3-pint bottles of fresh milk from the truck drop-off point into our classroom. This milk program must have been an initiative to add calcium to kids' diets or help hungry kids.

When the truck arrived, our teacher would say. "Where is our resident milkman?" I would race out to do my job. The secret benefit was that I could grab three bottles and swallow them in a heartbeat. I'm sure my teacher knew what was going on with me, and I needed the perk. Thank you.

One of my worst times at primary school was being invited to a mate's house after school. I cannot recall how or why, but I got into a fight with him, as kids do, and we parted ways.

The following day, I was called to the Headmaster's Office, and I was at a loss to think why. As soon as I opened the door, he went into a rage about fighting and being one of those Wanslea losers. He beat me with a cane, whipping my legs, arms, back, and finally, my hands. The middle finger on my right hand was split and broken.

He ensured I was banned from playing school football and cricket. I had to leave the premises immediately after the school bell rang. I still have problems with that hand today. It is always a reminder of the abuse I suffered at his hands; this wasn't the only occasion. I hope he burnt in Hell!

I was always into cars from as far back as I can remember. They fascinated me, and I loved anything to do with them and speed. When I was about 10, I was back living with my parents. I started getting into the practical side of cars and tinkering around with them.

My favourite thing was going down the local rubbish tip and poking around in all the gear and bringing home bits to "fix up". My dad often would say, "Get rid of that shit, and get it gone." However, I'd still try and smuggle bits back to work on.

I was down there one day when a hot rod was being unloaded from Claremont Speedway off the back of a truck. I had a thing for going to the speedway and a secret entrance into Claremont Showground. I had loosened some tin behind one of the fences and could pull the sheet out, climb through, and watch the speedway for free.

When I saw the speedway car getting unloaded, I thought, *These guys have got to be nuts. It's absolutely crazy. Why are they throwing this out? Yes, the front wheels are smashed, and it has no engine, but the back wheels, steering, and all the other stuff are there.*

I waited for these guys to leave, raced straight over to it and thought, *How am I going to get this home?* I got the front axle up and resting on the crossbar of my push bike and then tried to get out of the place, which I couldn't.

Luckily, I had a couple of mates who were close by, and I ran around and got them. Then, we pushed it about three kilometres down one of the main streets to my house, managing to put it in the backyard. I was absolutely taken with it, but when Dad came home, he said, "Great bit of gear, son, but when I come home tomorrow night, it's got to be gone." So, the same guys and I returned it to the tip the next day, which was heartbreaking for me as it was something I really wanted to work on.

As it happened, a lady over the road had seen us pushing this car wreck up and down the street, and she said, "I've got a 1940s Ford here that belonged to my late husband, and if you want it, you can have it." This car was a runner, a precursor to the 1953 Ford Customline I bought and started driving at 12.

When we were back home, we were just in the way, so Mum and Dad would send me and my sister Jill to my grandmother's house. She was really strict, and it was so boring. We weren't allowed to talk and had to listen to the clock ticking. We were also told not to walk on her polished wooden door entry, so we had to step over it, and at our young age, we could hardly reach across it. It was nearly a metre wide, and we had to stretch to get across without touching it. A lasting habit I picked up from that experience is that whenever I enter someone's house, I step across their doormat. I don't walk on it, which is pretty strange.

Like many people in those times, we didn't have much, and I learned to steal at a very young age. It wasn't frowned upon but encouraged, especially by my dad. He would put me over a fence at the local council yard, and my job every Sunday afternoon was to steal four big empty Coke bottles out of the bags, one out of each, so they wouldn't miss them. Then, I would hike up this cliff, poke the bottles under the fence, and climb back out myself. Finally, I would walk about five kilometres to the shops and get the money back on the bottles. This would allow me to buy two shillings worth of chocolate with the proceeds. It was a Sunday treat, which I shared with the family.

Dad had me doing quite a few "jobs" like that, putting me through windows of houses and opening them up for him to steal stuff. I put it down to him being a bit screwed up from the war. At a young age, it was ingrained in me to steal and take what I needed or didn't have. It was like a challenge and was something I could do, and I did it well. If it didn't harm anyone physically, why not? I knew it was wrong, but I'm sure the excitement and risk involved in stealing overrode that. I am also sure this adrenaline rush fed into my racing later. I was a born risk-taker and loved it.

When I was 11, I spent a lot of time at Wanslea. Dad worked in the Mount Lyell Chemical Works, a factory that produced superphosphates and acids in North Fremantle. He had a girlfriend there, which added to the family tensions, with Mum and Dad not going too well. So, I got a weekend job at Seawards, a boatyard in Cottesloe, which helped me keep out of the way. I worked all day Saturday and Sunday mornings. The money I got paid meant I could start saving for a car.

Mum and Dad split up and went their own separate ways. Mum left and returned to Queensland, where she was from, and Dad stayed in Perth with his girlfriend. All the kids spent vacations with Mum in Queensland, but we were all living back with Dad most of the time in Cottesloe. Mum paid for people to help look after us. This would mainly involve hiring nannies that Dad would try it on with. They usually didn't last very long.

One day, when I was about 11 years of age, my best mate Rod and I were riding our bikes in Nedlands and went past a car yard full of cars and trucks parked everywhere. Rod and I decided to walk into the yard to look around. Rod opened a truck door, got in and pretended to drive it, making noises as if he was changing gears. I did the same thing in a sports car. We played for about 15 minutes inside the car yard, not doing any harm, just being boys. Suddenly, the cops arrived and arrested us. They called another cop station to come out with a motorcycle sidecar to pick up our push bikes. We were taken into custody in Perth, and the cops put us in the cells.

We were locked up at 11 years of age for being unlawfully on the premises. Luckily for Rod, his dad came within a couple of hours to pick him up and take him home. I spent the next two nights in jail because my old man either wouldn't pick me up or couldn't pick me up.

We both faced court a couple of days later and were charged. We got probation, and my feelings about the law and the police changed dramatically from then on. I was pretty pissed about being locked up at 11 years of age. After that, I rebelled and led a bit of a wild life. I did a few break-ins and stole things I could sell.

The police were pretty shocking with kids in those days. What ended up happening was when you were caught for an offence, some cops would turn around and say, "Right, we got ten of these similar charges on our books. So, you nod your head to all these charges and sign off on them, and we will put in a good word for you at court. The judge will appreciate that, and you'll get off with a reduced sentence."

It was called "wiping the books". Many kids suffered the same fate as I did. They had done one or two things wrong and got charged with bloody ten. I am sure the judges knew what was happening, but the police and the Department of Justice cleared up a lot of cases in one hit.

I spent two stints in boys' remand homes, Longmore and Stoneville and received some hard knocks and worse while staying in these institutions. Standover tactics and abuse just made me even more resentful and rebellious. Finally, however, I started to learn to fight back, getting plenty of practice and becoming very good at it.

Because of Dad's antics, I was pretty independent and stayed out of the way of him and his temper to avoid beltings. I slept on the back veranda of the house on an old ex-army camp bed.

One of the most unusual and frightening nights I remember was when I was about 11 in 1962. I was on the back veranda on a very hot night, and I heard what I thought was Dad walking down the side of the house. It was pitch black, and I was sitting on my bed and looked up, expecting to see him, but this stranger was staring at me. We both looked at each other surprised, and then he turned and walked away without saying anything. What happened next went down in West Australian history. After seeing me, he continued to walk down the side of our house to one of the places behind us. There, he shot two people, then walked across the road and shot two more.

This guy was called Eric Edgar Cooke, a mass murderer in Perth at the time. I was probably pretty lucky, as I think I gave him a bigger scare than he gave me. It was quite an experience; perhaps he would have jumped the wall and entered our house if I hadn't been on the veranda. Who knows what would have happened? The police never interviewed me, and I certainly didn't come forward. I didn't want anything to do with them. Every time I did, they hung shit on me.

At about the same time, I would regularly sneak out and go to local dances and stuff like that. I would often hook up with guys a lot older than myself. I was about 11 or 12, and they ranged from 16 to 18. A couple of them owned cars. I loved the beach and water and would hitch a ride from Perth and go down to Yallingup, probably once a month, to surf with my mates. I would live in the bush, near the beach and surf most days there.

I had saved £40 from my weekend work at Seawards boatyard in Cottesloe and was only 12 and living on and off at Wanslea. I used the £40 to buy my first roadworthy car, a 1953 Ford Customline and traded my 1940 Ford Sloper, given to me by the lady over the road, to do the deal.

The 53 Customline was beautiful. I couldn't stop driving it. I had to hide the car down the side lane next to Wanslea, the home where my sister Jill was living at the time. Every chance I got, I took my baby out and went for a drive. I got better and better and more proficient at driving it. There was no stopping me now.

I started high school midterm at Swanbourne Senior High due to being detained in a correctional boy's home at the beginning of the school year. So, I turned up at 12 years of age, fascinated with cars and motorcycles. School was as boring as bat shit to me. I couldn't handle the discipline and quickly got a reputation as a rebel and troublemaker amongst pupils and teachers. This was only confirmed when my past also became known to them.

After getting out of the correctional boy's home, I was living back with my family, but that was short-lived. My time at the correctional home hadn't left me in a good place, and I was angry and vulnerable. I was only 12, and my dad and I were constantly butting heads.

One night, over dinner, a huge family argument raged with a lot of shouting. We were having tomato soup that night, and I picked up my bowl and threw it. It ran down the wall, and I stormed out of the house, never to return. I left with nothing except the clothes I was wearing.

My younger sister Gail ran down the road after me with a banana, so I had something to eat. She was very upset. I got in my car, drove away, and knew that was the last time I would see my family for a long time.

I followed Donald Campbell's land and water speed records with great interest. He was always on the radio and in the newspapers. I always told everyone who would listen that I would build a car faster than Donald Campbell's and break the world land speed record. This was in July 1963.

There was another highlight when I was briefly at Swanbourne High School. I hooked up with a young sheila, who was also 12. I kept getting notes from her to come and see her after school. Anyway, I finally did and met her down in Mosman Park. She said, "Would you like to have sex?" Not having had sex, this experience was all a bit new to me, but after a few sessions, I started to get the hang of it. Then, one day, I saw her old man running down the back of the house towards where we were. I pulled up my pants, ripped a couple of pickets out of the white boundary fence and shot through. I never saw her again but often thought about this years later. I felt that at 12, she was pretty experienced, and something wasn't quite right there. I hope she ended up having a good life.

One of the first modifications I did on the 53 Customline is something I still marvel at today. I got my hands on an SU electric fuel pump and mounted it behind the back seat in the car's boot. Then, I rigged up a delivery system with a switch on the dash, allowing me to remotely fill the fuel tank on the Customline. What I used to do was late at night, I would pull into a closed garage, flip the protective cover up of their large fuel storage tank, and put my suction hose down into it. Then, I would throw the switch on the dash and watch the fuel gauge of my car rise.

I had to do this when the garage was vacant at night, as the pump would make a lot of noise until it got the fuel delivery happening. Once I had a full tank, I could knock the switch off, pull the suction hose out, coil it up and put it under the seat. I'd put their tank cover back and drive away with a full tank of petrol. No one was any the wiser. I did this for many years and never got sprung once. I never paid for any fuel in those days.

With my stolen fuel, I was regularly driving to Swanbourne High School. One day, after about six weeks of attending school, the headmaster caught me parking my 53 Customline. He was pretty pissed, as I had parked it under a tree in the shade, where he always parked his car. Once he saw it was me, he said, "I knew it would be you, McGlashan! I will report you to the police, and you will go to jail."

So, with my history of dealing with the cops and no family to support me, my mind was made up. That was my last day at Swanbourne High School, and I took off in my car, with the headmaster disappearing into the distance, shouting and waving his fist at me.

I had plenty of stolen petrol and headed east into the sun, reaching a town called Merredin. There were a lot of cops around. I thought, *Nah, this is too heavy shit for me*, so I took a left turn and headed towards a town called Nungarin. There I put my age up from 12 to 16 and started working as a labourer, building wheat silos with a team of guys.

My sister Jill and I in 1956.

Making friends in Queensland.

Teenage surfing years.

-2-

Rebel With a Cause

Having worked for quite a while in tough manual jobs, I decided I wanted to better myself. I was told the only way to get ahead was to get an apprenticeship. So, I decided to head back to Perth and sold my beloved 53 Customline to get some money. It was now 1964, I was 14, and I got a start as a panel beater and spray painter. After three months of working there, it was discovered I was colourblind. After my first paint-matching trial turned out to be blue, it was supposed to be green! I got sacked from that job.

I walked into the building next door and got a start as an apprentice mechanic. After six months, I couldn't tolerate the strict German bosses. Rules and I didn't sit well, so I moved to another mechanical repair shop. One after another, there was always something or someone I didn't like, or they didn't like me. I would still talk about the land speed car I wanted to build with anyone who would listen.

At 15, a friend told me about a job in Melbourne to continue my mechanical career. I purchased an FJ Holden, and it was pretty banged up. I decided to drive to Melbourne with my £350 savings, taking a few belongings with me. I arrived at Norseman, only to learn that the Eyre Highway was underwater and closed to all traffic, so I had to decide what to do. I had three or four days to get to Melbourne to start my new job. I waited until there was no sign of traffic or anyone around, then drove around the barriers, heading towards the Nullarbor and our east coast.

The road was unsealed at the time, and there was dirt from Norseman to Ceduna. It was a very rough dirt track across the Nullarbor. About 100 kilometres east of Norseman was a roadblock with a big fat cop standing there, and he stopped me.

The cop said, "Do you need glasses, or can't you read?"

"Well, I just need to get the Melbourne rather urgently," I said.

"You obviously don't have a driver's licence?"

"No, but I intend to get one in Melbourne."

He told me he needed to check through my car and then asked me how much money I had. I responded that I had £350, which he made me show him. He then took £150 out of it, put it in his pocket, and said to me.

"I'll give you one bit of advice. There is a very good chance you're going to die out there. It's underwater and bloody hot, but the only chance you will have to survive is to stay in the middle of the road. So, regardless of how much water you see, stay in the middle. Do not deviate to the side of the road; the hardest part is right in the centre, but that is where most of the water is."

It was a pretty scary thing to drive, and all you could see forever was water, not knowing how deep it was or exactly where the centre of the road was hiding. There were so many times I thought, *This is it*. I would sneak off the side as the water was getting very deep, and the tyres would start to spin. If the car got bogged down, that would've been it. No one for hundreds of kilometres to rescue me! Luckily, I always managed to keep the wheels turning and get back onto the centre of the road.

Looking back, I can't remember many times I have been that scared. I was just 15 and very alone.

I arrived in Melbourne and Coburg, where my promised job was, and people were protesting. I got there just as Australia's last hanging was about to occur. Ronald Ryan had been convicted of killing a warder, George Hodson, during an escape from Pentridge Prison. The protests were trying to stop him from being hanged. All attempts to save his life failed, and he was the last person to hang in Australia at Pentridge in Victoria.

In Coburg, the mechanics' job I'd come all this way for didn't materialise, so I got a job in a factory a couple of doors down from the jail. There, I found accommodation in Barkley Street in St Kilda, and I quickly learned that it was a tough neighbourhood. At that time, there were gangs, Sharpie's a precursor of Skinheads. I learnt to look for a weapon if two people were walking towards me. The St Kilda Pub was at the bottom of my street, attracting many undesirables and troublemakers, probably a bit like me at the time.

During my stay in Barkley Street, I met up with two surfing mates from Perth, Mick and Alan. They moved into a flat upstairs, where we knocked around together for some time in Melbourne. Unfortunately, the cheap FJ Holden I had bought to drive across from Perth died, so I had to bus it around the city.

A guy in the downstairs flat was selling his FX Holden, so the three of us chipped in to buy it. We drove it around, going to a few surfing spots for a couple of weekends, then travelled south of Melbourne to the Mornington Peninsula.

I decided to throw my factory job in at Cobourg and spend my days surfing. Mick and I left for Frankston, and Alan returned to Perth. We were driving around Frankston when the cops pulled us over and told us that our car had been stolen. Unfortunately, we had no idea or paperwork to prove that we bought it legitimately. You didn't think of things like that in those days. You paid your money and drove it away. The cops were absolute arseholes. They took us down to Frankston cop shop and beat the shit out of us. Both my eyelids were cut so severely I couldn't even see out of them, which took my mind off my cracked ribs.

Mick and I went to court the next day, and luckily for us, Mick's Uncle was a lawyer in Melbourne and appeared for us in court. We saw him speaking to the prosecuting guys, and he must have pulled some strings somehow. Perhaps they owed him a favour? Anyway, we heard the charges, and it was an open-and-shut case as far as the police were concerned.

My biggest problem was having a criminal record, which could have ended very badly. The judge was about to hand down his sentence and asked the prosecuting lawyer whether there were any previous convictions. I was shitting myself, but at that moment, the prosecutor dropped the paperwork, so the judge couldn't see it and said, "No, your Honour, I have nothing here in front of me." The judge ordered that we leave Melbourne within 24 hours, and we were put on a train back to Perth.

Going on a train across most of Australia, I thought, would be a fantastic experience. So, I climbed up between two carriages and sat on the train's roof. Sitting there and looking at the scenery for most of the trip back, some 3,200 kilometres to Perth, was brilliant. No one knew where I was, no one was bothering me, and I felt free and excited about life at that moment in time.

I arrived back in Perth, caught up with Mick and some other guys, and joined the Bombora Surf Club. We went down to

Yallingup one day, probably fifteen guys. It was an absolutely huge day with massive waves and one of the fitter guys in the club, Nick, said: "Who wants to go out and give it a go?" I wasn't a great swimmer then, and Mick wasn't as good as me.

Nick was a tough guy, and other club members declined the invitation to join him, but I thought I needed to prove myself and went with him. Mick came with me. Both of us followed him out across the reef in a massive swell. I couldn't see Nick, and I couldn't see Mick behind me either.

I was shitting myself. The waves were huge, and I had tried to get on three or four waves without success. Finally, I thought, *Shit, I've got to go for the next wave because we're getting pushed up the coast. So,* I just went for it and ended up looking down the face of this monster wave which dropped straight onto the reef. I got on it, and one of the guys said later that it was the biggest wave they had seen all day.

I dropped down the face of the wave. It was like falling down a four-storey building. I wasn't going to stand up, but I grabbed hold of my board with all my might and smacked the bottom of the reef. The board broke into four pieces, and somehow, I washed up on the shore and survived, absolutely terrified but uninjured.

Nick was ahead of us and was already on the beach. Mick Henryon was way down the coast, and the crew ran along the beach and picked Mick up, who was probably over 500 metres away. I shat myself and said, "That's it." I decided to give surfing a break for a while. That day gave me the screaming heebie-jeebies.

The following week, the same scenario happened again, except I wasn't there. Mick Henryon and the crew went to

Yallingup again to surf, and Mick went out there in precisely the same conditions, with massive sets of waves. Unfortunately, Mick drowned and got washed up the coast. So, there's a plaque and statue for Mick Henryon on Yallingup Beach, and I lost one of my best mates. I gave surfing away after that.

I was living a bit of a wild life still, and soon joined a group of guys and took to street racing in stolen cars. I acquired several skills with my different apprenticeship starts. I re-painted them, and we resold the ones we didn't race. We hid their origins by removing their serial numbers and anything that could identify them. Eventually, this lifestyle caught up with me.

One day, while driving a friend's revamped and stolen car to one of my contacts, I was involved in a car chase with the police, but I ran out of fuel and was arrested. I was just 17 years of age and sent to Fremantle Prison on remand awaiting trial. I was charged with Larceny (theft) and two months later appeared in court. I was found guilty and received a two-year sentence to be served at Fremantle Prison in Western Australia.

This was 1967; it was a harsh environment for a young bloke, but I was also pretty wild and tough. I settled into prison life, and it wasn't that bad. I had regular food and a place to sleep, which was better than most of my life up until that point.

During my time there, I had an altercation with a tough standover merchant who was giving everyone a bloody hard time. Prison was very hard for some guys, and they didn't need some arsehole, making it even harder. So, I thought to myself, *I need to pull this guy in line.*

One of our morning rituals was to empty our shit cans into an open drain in the prison yard. I seized the opportunity to square things up with him. I was walking behind him down a flight of stairs. I turned and smashed him across the back of the head as hard as possible with my shit can, sending him flying down the stairs.

I was charged with assault with a deadly weapon. Luckily for him, there was no shit in it at the time. I was sent to Fremantle Prison's solitary confinement section for a month, and he was sent to the hospital! Well, that's why I was in solitary. I decided he needed to be taken down a peg or two, and I was young, fit and wild and didn't give up easily. I hoped he might see the errors of his ways and be nicer to everyone. If not, I'll do it again, and I'm sure he'll eventually get the message.

I was possibly the last person in Fremantle Prison to have done bread and water. I have spoken to a few people who served there, and they say this bread and water didn't happen. It did, and perhaps it wasn't official policy, but I knew what I was being fed, and it wasn't roast beef!

In my tiny cell, if I climbed up the back wall and looked through the small barred window, I would get a great view of the gallows where my late-night visitor as a kid, Eric Edgar Cooke, had been hanged. He was the last person executed in Western Australia on the 26th of October 1964.

About three weeks into my solitary confinement, it was Christmas. I was very surprised when I was allowed to leave chokey early and celebrate Christmas with the other prisoners. We were all given a small tub of ice cream and a bottle of Coke. It was one of the best presents ever. I don't think I've ever eaten anything that tasted that good since.

Unbeknown to me at the time, my apprenticeship had been kept active. Then, with outside assistance, I became the first person in Western Australia to be granted the opportunity to complete my apprenticeship at Barton's Mill Prison Farm in WA. This was unheard of and ground-breaking at the time.

-3-

Working My Way Up

After my release from prison in 1970, I started as a qualified mechanic working for Winterbottom's Motor Company in Perth. This company specialised in selling and repairing British cars and had its own automatic transmission department.

Even in prison, I was still obsessed with cars and speed, reading anything I could get my hands on. I used this time to gain knowledge to build my land speed car. One of the skills I taught myself was repairing automatic transmissions solely through reading books while in prison.

This old boy at Winterbottom's took a shine to me and taught me everything he could. He had decades of knowledge of transmissions, and I was like a sponge. He would get a gearbox and go, "Right, these are the symptoms. Tell me what's wrong with it, and while you're working it out, I'll order the parts we need." He knew exactly what was wrong with it and how to fix it. I got pretty good with automatics with his help.

At Winterbottom's, there was a lovely young girl called Elaine, and she was just 16 years of age, a beautiful and innocent girl. I was 19, turning 20, less beautiful and certainly not as innocent. We had noticed each other and talked several times, and then I asked Elaine out. We went out a few times over the following weeks, and one day her boss called her into his office.

He said, "I hear you're dating Ross?" He told Elaine I had recently been released from prison. She was a bit surprised I hadn't told her, but it's not the first thing you tell someone you want to impress. She was warned off or at least told to be careful of me. I was trying to move on from the prison episode, and we briefly discussed my prison stay. I told her that, as far as I was concerned, it was in the past, and we never really talked about it after that.

Elaine and I were going great, but I decided to leave Winterbottom's and got a job at North Beach Automatics. That job lasted only a short time as I had decided to go up north of our state to work, as the money was far better. Elaine stayed in Perth with her family. She was still only 16.

Around Easter 1971, Elaine turned 17, and she and I had been in regular contact. I wanted her to join me, but her dad wasn't too pleased and said he would come after me if anything happened to her. So, Elaine said goodbye to her family and joined me in Port Hedland. I had scored a job as a Workshop Foreman, managing a mechanical workshop, and Elaine got a job working in a hardware store. We lived in a caravan park and met some good friends there, and Elaine and I got engaged.

After about six months in Port Hedland, we decided to join our friends from the caravan park, who had recently moved on to Darwin. We got a start on a remote Northern Territory station. I was rebuilding CAT bulldozers in a rundown shed without much equipment or help. Elaine was preparing an inventory for the auction of this property. We didn't like Darwin and quickly moved on.

We drove to Mount Isa in Queensland, and the first big workshop I saw there was Barkley Holden, so I asked if they had any vacancies. I told them I was proficient in automatic transmissions, and they asked me to start immediately. The problem for them and us was the lack of accommodation to rent in the area. We were told to go to the newspaper office, as ads go into the office a day before they get published. So, doing this gives you the drop on what properties are coming up for rent.

Elaine and I went into town to the newspaper office. I stayed in the car whilst Elaine went in to view the ads. It seemed like she had been in there forever. When she came out, she was with a tough-looking guy, and he had his arm around her. I immediately jumped out of the car and told him to piss off and take his arm off her. In the ensuing conversation with him, I discovered his name was Joe Vella, light heavyweight boxing champion of Queensland. I am glad I decided to talk rather than fight this time. Joe and his many brothers became great mates.

At 22, I got my first ever driver's licence, and I'd only been driving for ten years without one! I continued my karate, which I started earlier in Port Hedland and had been practising whenever possible. It was pretty new to Australia and Mount Isa at the time. I had a lot of opportunities to gain experience and polish my fighting skills with miners and local troublemakers.

Elaine and I had talked about getting married in late 1972, but with Elaine being just 18, we needed her parents' consent. They weren't too pleased about her marrying me, but they signed the papers. We arranged to be married at a local registry office a few months later.

Whilst in Mount Isa, I was approached to be the Branch Manager of a leading American-based transmission company. I was to run the new repair shop they were opening in Brisbane. I turned down their offer, as we knew little about Brisbane, but we decided to check it out. So, we left Mount Isa and drove there. We arrived in Brisbane and fell on our feet, finding a flat to rent in New Farm, a lovely suburb.

I started at Austral Motors, and the first person I met was the legendary Wally Pushkey. Wally played A-grade rugby league for the Wynnum Manly Seagulls. He owned a fast street car and was involved in drag racing with a V8 bike called *Krazy Horse*. We quickly hit it off, and I met his mates and shared some unbelievable adventures with him over the next few years.

This original V8 bike was built by him and his excellent crew. It had a Ford 292 cubic inch engine and was a prototype for the Chevy V8 bike he later built with the same name. Unfortunately, I never saw Wally's Ford-powered bike run. Still, I believe it now resides in a museum in Wellington, New Zealand.

I got to crew with his team at Surfers Paradise Raceway, where Wally was known as the "Gold Coast Gutsman". *Krazy Horse* had no clutch, so he would launch this bike off a stand that raised the back wheel off the ground. He would then rev it up to about 5,000 rpm and kick the stand away. When the tyre connected with the track, all hell broke loose. The noise and tyre smoke was unbelievable, and this bike would swerve in a massive arc from the right-hand lane into the left. It was mind-blowing to watch. Then, at the three-quarter track mark, this incredible machine would slide back into the right lane again, still with the tyre spinning and fogging up the whole track with smoke.

On average, it would cross the finish line at around 225 km/h (140 mph) with an elapsed time of about 11 seconds. The fastest way down a quarter-mile drag strip is in a straight line. Wally covered about half a mile going from lane to lane. Wally and I shared some great times in Brisbane and New Zealand, where we raced three times together.

About six months later, the American-based auto transmission company that had approached me initially offered me the job again. This time, I accepted it. I started there but quickly became disillusioned by the way they did business. It was terrible, and I became pissed off with the quality of work coming out of their Sydney workshop.

Rebuilt gearboxes were sent from Sydney to our Brisbane workshop and distributed state-wide, only to find many had a problem after installation. It meant we were left having to fix them under warranty. It was a lot of work for us and unjustly gave our Queensland branch a lousy reputation. So, I decided to send the Sydney work to Queensland so we could rebuild the gearboxes ourselves. For various reasons, this strategy didn't sit well with some in the company. I wasn't prepared to compromise on this, so we parted ways.

Meanwhile, the transmission work we performed at the workshop for some of the top race cars was paying off and gave us an excellent reputation amongst the drag racers. So, I decided to start my own shop, Autoshift, with two friends. We started handling Ford and Volvo transmission warranties and doing all transmission work for Skennars Bus & Coachline. In addition, we did a lot of gearbox rebuilds for all major car yards that suffered flood damage. For anyone who does not know, Brisbane is very tropical, and flooding is a regular occurrence there. I made many friends with other motor racing guys, giving us a great work stream.

I wanted to keep my karate going and met Tamio Tsuji, a Japanese Karate master (Sensei). Tamio had visited Brisbane as a trainee on a Japanese Naval ship and loved it. So, he returned and started his own karate school under the Story Bridge. Several of us would get together at a local gym three times a week. Most were football guys and would pay one dollar each for their training and punching bag session. I was practising kicking the punch bag for my karate, so I had to pay two dollars. Apparently, kicking was more expensive than punching, for some unexplained reason!

With the racing side of the business taking off, I also started a specialised racing transmissions business with one of my partners from Autoshift. We called it M.S. Racing Transmissions, and it was on Megellan Street in Lismore. The location made it far more central for our Sydney racing customers. So, Elaine and I decided to move to Lismore, with me driving between our two businesses in Brisbane and Lismore regularly.

Around this time, I had my first opportunity to drive a fast car at Surfers Paradise. At weekends, I was at the track, working on transmissions for clients' race cars. In addition, I was working on a Pro Stock drag car owned by a prominent business guy, who used it as a promotional tool for his racing company.

One day, his driver didn't turn up, and the Pro Stock drag car owner said, "Right, McGlashan, I think you're driving today." I jumped at the chance and proceeded to better the professional driver's best quarter-mile time, so I was the full-time driver from then on. I drove the Pro Stock car for free to get as much experience as possible, hoping to gain a reputation as a good driver. I felt this would help to entice a Brisbane-based sponsor to back my land speed record ambitions. I had many designs for such a car; all I needed was money.

I had hooked up with some great people in Brisbane and was running a bit wild with a few newfound friends. This involved street racing, professional drag racing, drinking, fighting, and generally living as a single guy, which I wasn't. As you can imagine, Elaine wasn't impressed, and we weren't getting along very well. The downturn in our relationship was all down to my lifestyle. We decided the wedding was off and needed a break. Elaine flew back to Perth, as she hadn't seen her family for two years, so it was a good chance for her to catch up with them.

For the next few months, I continued living a single life. Elaine was frustrated at my lack of effort in our relationship. I wasn't taking her calls, and it was all down to me that we were drifting apart. Eventually, she believed the relationship was over, and I couldn't blame her.

Everyone I knew had a Holden V8 Monaro, and there was an unofficial record for a solo drive from Lismore to Brisbane. Local racing legend Max Marr held the record with his time of 2 hours and 41 minutes. I decided I was going to break this record. This was a scary race over the now-defunct Burringbar Mountain Range.

If you were going after a new record, you told an enthusiast at the Stones Corner pub in Brisbane or the Workers Club in Lismore. They noted the time you left and arrived at these points.

My first attempt was 20 minutes faster than Max Marr's record, covering it in 2 hours and 21 minutes. I tried to better it on the return run but came unstuck and crashed, with me going off the edge of a cliff at one of the highest points in driving rain!

I was very seriously injured and taken to the Mullumbimby Hospital. I clinically died and had an out-of-body experience, but I was revived and brought back to life. I can still remember being on the ceiling of my hospital room, looking down at myself and all the nursing staff shaking their heads.

A week later, I was discharged from the hospital but should never have been released. I was still in a terrible way, as the accident had nearly torn my left ear off. I also had head injuries, internal bleeding, a broken collarbone, and a shitload of broken ribs. I was also black and blue all over and a real mess.

I returned to my home in Lismore and decided to take a bath. I ran the water and climbed in but couldn't get out. I was in the bath, sore and exhausted and shouting for anyone passing by to help. I was stuck in that cold water for two days until my dad arrived. He had come over from Perth unexpectedly to see how I was doing and what timing!

My Dad, Gavin, looked after me for a few days, and he decided to call Elaine in Perth and tell her about my accident. So, he gave her my number, and we spoke. It was great to hear her voice, and I apologised for my behaviour and asked her if she would come back and live with me.

Elaine did return, spending three days on a train from Perth. When she arrived in the afternoon, another woman I had met was there looking after me. I tried to tell her it wasn't a romantic arrangement, but Elaine wasn't having any of it. If she'd had the money to return to Perth, she would have gone there and then. The woman quickly left, and we continued our relationship from where we had left off.

Elaine and I married at a registry office in Lismore on the 2nd of July 1973. Elaine was 19, and I was a month off, turning 23. Married life was going well, and we decided we wanted to have a family.

Towards the end of 1973, I was still recovering from my accident, and the travelling between workshops was taking its toll, so we shut up the shop in Lismore and moved back to

Brisbane. I got an offer to go into business with a couple of friends at Stones Corner, a suburb of Brisbane. However, my relationship with Elaine started to head south again.

In early 1974, with no kids on the horizon, we sought medical advice. Tests confirmed Elaine needed an operation and plenty of rest. Elaine was on the road to recovery, but with Elaine resting, I fell back into my old ways and hit the town.

I had bought the newly built V8 motorcycle *Krazy Horse* from Wally Pushkey, which now took a small block Chevy engine. I soon installed my more powerful Pro Stock engine, and *Krazy Horse* was turning in some brilliant quarter-mile times and speeds. The best was 9.1 seconds at about 270 km/h (170 mph). Although I had bettered Wally's quarter-mile times with the new engine, I could never put on a show like Wally. He was definitely the master.

I travelled around Australia and New Zealand, going to race meetings, including in my hometown of Perth, to race at Ravenswood. I loved it there and strongly felt I wanted to return to Perth.

After four years away, that longing to return home got the better of me. I'm sure Elaine knew she would have her family to support her when I was absent and away racing. So, we sold our businesses and loaded up a newly acquired Ford F100 with a towing trailer with all our possessions. I had a speedway hot rod that I had built strapped on the trailer. This hot rod was unique, as it utilised a manually shifted automatic transmission, which I developed and believed was a first in Australian Speedway. The V8 bike was in the truck's tray, and we piled all of our other possessions wherever we could fit them in and headed West, home to Perth.

We started an Auto Transmission workshop in Leederville, and Elaine and I lived in a very basic flat above the shop. The transmission business didn't take off as well as we had hoped, and we struggled to cover the wages. I took a job in Carnarvon at a mine site, with Elaine keeping the shop ticking over. My wages would help support the shop with one or two staff until business picked up, but it never did. We sold the business at a loss and ended up with quite a bit of debt. Elaine flew to Carnarvon to be with me, but the debt from this venture caught up with us, and we were declared bankrupt.

Elaine's health wasn't good; she was in a lot of pain, and she stayed with her mum to recover in Perth after more hospital treatment. So, I left the Carnarvon mine site and moved on to work further up North. I wrote to Elaine and said I would send for her once I had settled there.

Elaine spent time with her mum and reflected on her life and all I had put her through. It was 1974, and we had been together for four years. She was very unhappy and didn't want me or this life anymore. Looking back, I certainly understand why.

We went our separate ways. I was never a great husband and rarely at home. I've always really regretted the crap I put Elaine through. I was too young to be married and way out of control. We eventually divorced in 1977.

-4-

Racing Was in My Blood

I first met my second wife, Dianne, in 1972 through mutual friends. But we didn't get together as a couple until late 1974. This was about six months after I had split up with Elaine. We moved in together in 1975 at my Bayswater property, just outside Perth's Central Business District (CBD). We had a lot of good, fun times together. Dianne had a great personality and was a practical joker. She was always playing tricks on me, and of course, I responded with what I thought were better ones, but let's call it a draw.

My mum helped us secure the house in Mullaloo in 1978, where I still live. So, Dianne and I set up a home there, which is close to the beach. Dianne was a great surfer; I was back into surfing by then. I had a long break after Mick Henryon died. It hit me hard, as he was one of my best mates. I found my love of the water again and would think of him often when catching a wave. So, being in Mullaloo, just a walk from the beach, was an excellent location for Dianne and me to share our mutual love of surfing and beach life.

When I met Dianne, she was a hairdresser but also started to work as a barmaid. I was always concerned about this and wanted to ensure they treated her right. So, I would sometimes go to the bar where she worked and have a drink to ensure she was being respected. We were always out with lots of friends and had a great social life.

We had chickens and a rooster at our Mullaloo home. One day, after the rooster drove us bloody nuts in the early hours, I decided he had to go. I waited until Dianne had gone to work and loaded the rooster in the car. I took it to where she was working and put it behind the bar. Everyone saw the funny side of it, with this rooster running around, squawking and carrying on. Dianne couldn't believe I had done it. When she got over the embarrassment, she saw the funny side of it. Thank God, I never saw that bloody rooster again.

We became parents to our daughter Tenneille, born in May 1979. Shortly after, I decided I needed a more consistent and steady job. I'd been earning money, but it was hand-to-mouth. With Tenneille coming along, I needed a more regular income.

I often drove past the State Energy Commission of WA (SECWA), a government-owned energy company. There always seemed to be a lot going on there. So, I decided to ask and see if they needed workers. I stopped, went to the gate, and spoke to the security guard.

"Who is the big boss here?" I asked.

"We have six main bosses here," the guard replied.

"No, the guy in charge?" I said.

"Ken Kennedy, but you'll never get to speak to him."

"Well, do you mind if I try?"

"No, be my guest."

He let me through, and I walked to where he had said his office was. I walked down the corridor, looking at the names on every door. Finally, I came to Ken Kennedy's, knocked on the door, and went in. There were six guys all holding a meeting.

"Excuse me, I'm here to see Ken Kennedy."

One of the guys said, "I'll be with you in about ten minutes. I'm just finishing this meeting."

He must've thought I already had an appointment to see him. About ten minutes later, he came out of the meeting, and we chatted. I told him I was an expert in automatic transmissions.

He asked, "When can you start?"

"Immediately," I said.

So that was it, and I now had a job. I started working at SECWA in a section where I had to repair heavy machinery.

On my first morning, the guy in charge took me to one side and explained the job he wanted me to do. He wanted me to replace a load of bearings and some hydraulics in a crane, then test it all to check it all worked.

At about 4 o'clock that afternoon, the guy who had given me the earlier task to repair the crane came over to me as I was doing something else.

"Are you having any problems with what I've given you?"

"No, I've done it. It's tested and working fine."

"Shit, it should've taken you about four or five days to do that. You can't be working that quickly."

This was the 1980s, and I was now working for the West Australian Government in a department that hated you working too hard, as it would show the others up. So, the way around that was we would clear a job and then work on our own stuff for a day or two.

I asked the boss, "Is it OK if I bring my motorbike frame in here tomorrow and work on that for a couple of days?"

"Yes, that's fine," he said.

So, that's what happened. After that, I built my first rocket-powered vehicle at SECWA, a motorbike with two small hydrogen peroxide rocket engines. Even better was that the West Australian Government supplied some of the parts and materials!

There were so many funny stories that came out of working at SECWA.

One of the guys I worked with there had also worked at their Midland Workshop. People walked in and out with tools and equipment; for the most part, it was for genuine reasons. But the security guards were told to look for people taking stuff they shouldn't have. So, this led to inspections at the gates when you walked out.

Every Friday, one of the workers would walk out with his lunch box under a cloth in a wheelbarrow. They would stop him, lift the cloth and check his lunch box. Nothing wrong, wish him a good weekend and off he went. It took them a couple of years to work out that he was making wheelbarrows at work and selling them.

Probably the best story in SECWA folklore was about "the ghost". This particular employee had started in one department and was transferred to another. For some reason, he never actually started in that new department. His employment status, or lack thereof, only came to light during a Christmas party a year later.

Several managers were chatting and drinking at the party. This worker's old boss asked one of the managers how he was doing. "I don't know, I thought he worked for you?" was the reply.

It turned out he didn't work for anybody. He was coming in the front gate at 8 a.m., clocking on and walking straight out the back gate. He then proceeded to do the reverse at knock-off time. He had done this for a long while. He was called in the next day and asked to leave. There was no punishment because everyone was so embarrassed, and no one wanted to own up to the fact that he'd been getting paid for doing nothing for so long.

Whilst Tenneille was still very young, I would take her to the beach on days off or weekends. Tenneille was probably 18 months old. I loved my time with her, but settling into being just a provider with a nine-to-five job never sat well with me. I had something missing, and land speed cars and drag racing were always at the back of my mind.

I was starting to pursue my racing ambitions again, and Dianne didn't like it. I completely understand how hard it must have been to live with me, being utterly obsessed with going fast. Dianne and I were great mates but didn't share the same vision of our future or goals and started to lead separate lives.

I was hooked on stories of these rocket car pioneers from the USA in the 1970s. I also wanted to make a living out of racing these machines rather than a career at SECWA. I missed the drag racing lifestyle, excitement and the mateship that goes with it.

I learned early on that a piston engine dragster costs a lot of money to run and takes a lot of maintenance. Great if you have a big sponsorship budget, but a very tough gig if you don't. The owner of the first drag car I ever drove said.

"We win every time we race, and all we get is a $10 trophy we throw in the bin on the way out. It's costing me a fortune. We need to start getting paid to race."

Jet and rocket cars put on a great show at drag racing events and are paid to appear. They weren't expensive to maintain if you looked after them, and boy were they great crowd-pleasers. Yes, the rocket car's hydrogen peroxide was expensive but easily covered by the appearance money they paid you to put on a show for the spectators.

Krazy Horse, or *Krazyhorse* as it was also known, was a real crowd-pleaser and one of the few piston racers you might get paid appearance money with at the time. It was an incredible machine with its Pro Stock V8 car engine shoehorned into a motorbike frame. Riding this bike was challenging, as it didn't have a clutch, but it meant it would leave rubber all the way up the quarter-mile, hitting about 270 km/h at the top end. It spat me off a few times, and when it did, it did it in a big way, but the crowd loved it.

I knew a rocket bike would be a massive draw. I had done my apprenticeship on *Krazy Horse*. Although faster, a rocket bike would be easier to control as there was no engine torque to pull you all over the place. A rocket-powered vehicle wants to go in the direction it's pointed. So, as long as you were straight, you were usually OK, assuming the tyres didn't blow!

The rocket bike was my way back into racing at the weekends, and the racing bug became an itch I needed to scratch. I also had to fulfil the promise I had made myself at age 12, building a car faster than Donald Campbell's and being the fastest man on Earth. I was thirty, and time was ticking, and I couldn't put it off any longer.

When I finished the rocket bike, I started testing it. Unfortunately, I had problems making the rocket engines fire, so I contacted a man in the USA known as "Fearless Fred" Goeske. Fred invited me to join him in California to do some rocket engine "homework". He said he would offer advice on my rocket-powered bike. So, I took some time off work, hopped on a plane, and headed to Thousand Oaks, California, to see Fred. This trip changed my life forever!

-5-

My Life Changed in Less Than Six Seconds

Once I landed in Los Angeles, I headed straight to Fred's house. Fred was a champion drag racer who progressed from conventional drag racing cars to rocket-powered funny cars and dragsters. These cars were fast, bloody fast!

One of the men responsible for these rocket cars and their appearance on the drag racing scene was a guy named Dick Keller. He pioneered the hydrogen peroxide rocket-powered dragster era. He first designed and built the *X-1* in late 1966, a prototype of *The Blue Flame* land speed record car, working alongside Pete Farnsworth and Ray Dausman.

Dick, Pete and Ray formed a company called Reaction Dynamics Inc., and the rocket car era was born. The development and testing of these rocket cars culminated in a new world land speed mile record of 1,001 km/h (622 mph) on Bonneville Salt Flats in October 1970. The car was driven by Gary Gabelich and called *The Blue Flame*. Amazingly, this was the last time the USA broke the world land speed record. The UK's Richard Noble broke it in 1983 with *Thrust 2*, and it has been held by the UK ever since.

Another influential rocket guy was Ky Michaelson, who was also experimenting with rocket-powered race cars from the 60s and worked closely with "Fearless Fred" Goeske. Ky supplied most of Fred's rocket engines.

When I arrived at Fred's house, I couldn't believe my eyes. He had a big fenced-off yard at the back of where he lived, and around the perimeter of his house were 36 full barrels of 90 percent pure hydrogen peroxide rocket fuel. If stored correctly, it was probably OK, but still, it was pretty dangerous. Under the wrong circumstances and at those percentages of purity, it was as toxic as hell. If there were an accident, Thousand Oaks would've probably been poisoned or ended up in space!

We quickly got down to business, and at our first chat, we were trying to fix the issues with my bike's engines. Fred asked me how many silver mesh screens I had in my rocket engine's catalyst pack. These were internal to the engine, and it was impossible to tell by looking at it from the outside. I said I had two, as no one in Australia knew anything about hydrogen peroxide rockets.

I was building this engine from reading library books about German experiments with these propellants during World War II. At this time in 1980, it was before personal computers were widely available and long before the Internet was in every household. There was no online research you could look up; it was all books.

Fred said he used about a hundred mesh screens in his engine's catalyst pack and a hydrogen peroxide (H_2O_2) purity of 90 percent as a minimum. This percentage of purity would create the right amount of decomposition to turn the pure peroxide into oxygen, water and a lot of thrust. The highest percentage of H_2O_2 available in Australia at the time was 70 percent. Still, Fred was most impressed with my rocket nozzle design. He said it was the exact dimensions as a previous engine he had run. As a result, I started to understand these rocket engines. I felt far more confident about getting my rocket bike working correctly now.

We walked out into his suburban two-car garage, where he had a couple of Mexican guys working on lathes and milling machines. Hanging from his garage roof was a rocket-powered go-kart. I immediately got excited and recalled having read some history about these machines. They were fast and powerful, with a very low centre of gravity. Unfortunately, a few drivers had accidents and were injured or killed in these go-karts. It was easy to see why. They would slide under the Armco protective barriers at drag racing venues when the drivers lost control. You probably wouldn't have survived if you hit the Armco. There was virtually no protection for the driver, and you would have been going well over 320 km/h (200 mph) at the time in a small go-kart.

I asked, "Can we get this down, Fred?"

"As long as my ass points to the ground, this is never coming down," was Fred's response.

Not being one to give up easily, I kept on at Fred, and eventually, he cracked. A few days later, he agreed we could go racing. We lifted the go-kart down from Fred's workshop roof with the help of his two machinists. Fred was concerned and a bit pissed that I had talked him into running this rocket go-kart. There was a good chance I would kill myself, and he could lose his NHRA racers licence. He told me that two other rocket karts had killed their drivers when their tyres exploded, and the karts slid underneath the Armco barriers, just as I had recalled.

Fred had a ramp back truck that carried his rocket funny car to various drag strips across the USA. With the help of his machinists, we loaded the kart onto his truck and tied it on. Next, we loaded two barrels of 90 percent pure hydrogen peroxide into the back of his truck. This hydrogen peroxide was manufactured by FMC and of excellent quality. Next, we blew the kart tyres up to 95 psi with nitrogen, checked that all the tooling and brake chutes were in order and headed off to the track. We were going to test the kart at a track in Calle Quebracho, not too far from where Fred lived in Thousand Oaks.

We entered the track through a locked gate and were told to lock it again once inside. The track manager was a friend of Fred's and was doing some tests on his drag-racing "Christmas tree" lights. Fred walked back to talk to the manager, and there seemed to be a heated discussion between them. I wasn't sure what was said, but I understood that the manager was concerned about safety from the arm waving and gestures. Usually, running a rocket car, you need a fire crew on duty and an ambulance. Even though we were testing, we probably should have had these. However, as this was the middle of the week, these weren't present, and we were using highly toxic and very volatile chemicals.

Fred must have won that argument as he came over and told me to prepare. I'd been given strict instructions on how to drive the kart and how the major safety systems functioned. We packed the braking chutes into the two chute cans that sat at shoulder height on either side of the kart. Hydrogen peroxide is a mono-propellant, meaning it's an oxidiser and fuel. Once forced through the silver screen catalyst, it decomposes, and all hell breaks loose!

The blowdown nitrogen tank was filled to 3,000 psi, and the nitrogen (N_2) blows the hydrogen peroxide into the engine, with pressure anywhere from 300 psi to 3,000 psi. A dome-loaded regulator controls this pressure and how much power the engine produces. The more pressure applied, the more power the rocket engine makes. Fred told me to put on his fire suit, gloves, boots and helmet. This safety gear is lined with Teflon to protect the skin from toxic vapours. Unfortunately, Fred was a big guy, and his safety clothing swamped me, so the fit wasn't ideal and made me look like the Michelin Man.

I climbed into the kart and familiarised myself with the controls and running procedure. Fred walked around to the side of the kart.

He said, "I will now transfer the N2 pressure onto the hydrogen peroxide. I'll give you 300 psi."

I yelled back through the helmet, "300, I need more!"

Fred leaned in, and half pulled me out of the kart by the front of the fire suit.

"This thing will kill you deadlier than shit. You've got 300. Let's see how you handle that first?"

I was pissed as the peroxide cost me $350 a barrel, and I would only get two runs per barrel.

The instructions for my first pass were simple. I had to line myself up as straight as possible with the centreline of the track. I had to forget about the Christmas tree and staging lights. Next, I was to look for Fred's hand signals. He was positioned halfway up the track. He raised his hand, which meant go for purge. I stabbed the throttle, and nothing happened except for a loud pressure dump noise. I waited for the next signal, and his hand went up again. I again stabbed the throttle. By stabbing the throttle this time, we were expelling the air in the propellant lines and "cooking" our catalyst pack (heating it up). On this second purge, the kart moved forward, but not startling, and the peroxide vapours were starting to burn my fingers and my eyes. My breathing was now also becoming restricted.

I sat there quite calmly, waiting for both hands to go up. Fred waited until he was confident the catalyst pack was at maximum temperature. Finally, both of his arms went up, and I immediately hit the throttle.

"Holy shit," this kart took off like a scalded cat. I went past Fred, and he was just a blur, and almost immediately, I was at the end of the track and fired both parachutes. I triggered the pitch-up switch, which cuts the engine if the nose goes up, and hit the nitrogen dump switch. Then, I hit the brakes and turned the kart around to point back to where I had just come from.

I could not believe what had just happened. Fred raced down in his truck, taking a few minutes to get to me. I sat in the kart, still trying to take in just how fast this kart was. My heart was jumping out of my chest, and I was astounded at the acceleration of this tiny machine. Then, finally, Fred reached me and jumped out of his truck, shouting.

"You stupid Aussie asshole, you have put both chutes out, triggered the pitch-up, and dumped our Nitrogen storage. Shut that dump down. Shit, it's going to take another half an hour to turn you around for your next run."

"Thank Christ," I replied, hoping my heart would stop trying to escape from my chest.

After a few more runs, I reached 407 km/h (253 mph) in 5.97 seconds over the quarter-mile in this epic little machine. It was just a go-kart but had more horsepower than any modern-day supercar, and my arse was about 100 mm off the ground. The speed and acceleration were just incredible. I knew then that my life had changed forever, and I never wanted to race wheel-driven vehicles again. It was "thrust or bust" for me.

-6-

Thrust or Bust

We returned to Fred's house. We sat down to have a beer, mainly to settle my nerves after all that excitement. I was absolutely taken with this rocket go-kart. I knew then that if I were ever going to be part of motor racing history, it would have to be in thrust-powered vehicles.

After a few beers, we talked about my buying this incredible machine. Fred explained that the Ky Michaelson engine in her was earmarked for another project. But, again, my persistence came through, and Fred decided to sell me this beast. The next day, after doing the deal, I dismantled this machine and found a packing crate for the go-kart's frame and other parts. The engine certainly wasn't leaving my sight. So, it was cleaned, wrapped and placed in an airline carry-on bag.

I was worried it could get damaged in transit if it was in the packing crate. I didn't want to send the engine back by courier. It might have issues being imported. I certainly didn't trust putting it in the hold of the plane. It might get heavy-handed treatment from a baggage handler when he chucked it into the cargo hold. I had no choice but to take it as hand luggage. As I said, the engine wasn't that large, but bloody heavy. It was machined from a solid stainless steel block!

Along with the go-kart, I was given two barrels of 90 percent hydrogen peroxide fuel to accompany it and to have some fun when I got home to Perth. Fred knew the hydrogen peroxide would not get cleared by customs and added "special" labels to these shipping drums. These would "ease" their way out of the USA and into Australia.

We headed south to the San Pedro docks to get my new toy loaded and on its way to Perth. We pulled up at a loading dock and slid the crate and two barrels off Fred's pickup truck onto the loading bay. A young guy was driving a forklift, and I had never seen anyone drive a forklift like that. He was charging in and out at full speed, like a NASCAR driver, but boy, what a brilliant operator.

It was getting near closing time, so I gave this guy a whistle. He turned his machine on a dime and raced towards our load. Then, about ten metres from our shipment, he locked up the brakes and skidded to a stop.

He jumped out of his forklift and shouted, "I ain't loading that shit! That's rocket fuel and the shit Fred Goeske uses for drag racing." Fred then stepped forward, introduced himself, and we got it loaded.

I still had a few days to kill before leaving his place, so Fred put me to work, helping him. "Fearless Fred" was one of the most infamous blokes I had ever met. He would sell his mother if he got the right deal.

His daily activities were driving all over Los Angeles doing "unusual" jobs in a Chevy Vega wagon. I travelled with him whilst staying at his house, and our first job in the morning was to go and feed his elephant! Which was on a property on the outskirts of Santa Clarita. Fred said this was the area where the Dukes of Hazzard TV series was shot.

"Why do you have an elephant?" I asked.

"I have taken possession of her until a debt is paid," he responded.

I didn't ask any more questions after that. It would only go downhill from there very quickly. With Fred, it was better not to know.

After a full day of driving around Los Angeles, my first job after arriving home was to go to the back of his house and pass a high-pressure gas line to Fred. This line was plugged into three NASA titanium spheres he had mounted in the back of his Chevy Vega wagon. When he gave the word, I would fire up his compressor to charge these spheres. At the time, I thought *This was a bizarre thing to do, and why would you bother doing this when fuel wasn't that expensive in those days?* I finally decided to ask Fred why.

"Because it costs me nothing, I am driving 400 miles a day for free."

I had to learn more. Fred explained that his Chevy Vega wagon ran on compressed natural gas (CNG). This was unheard of in Australia in 1980.

"OK," I said, "But gas costs money."

"Not if the compressor is tapped into the gas line before the meter."

"OK, but what about the cost of the compressor and all of the parts to make this work?"

"It's all sponsored."

Now, I was on a bit of a roll with questions. I was also intrigued and asked, "What are those two guys machining in the shed?"

"They are making ignition breakers for the Detroit Mafia," he said calmly.

These were sold as breakdown kits throughout the USA and were being made in their hundreds!

After spending some brilliant time with Fred and learning how crazy he was, I had to get back to Perth with my new toy. I also had newfound knowledge to get my rocket bike working correctly. I also considered putting the go-kart rocket engine in my bike. But first I had to get this engine through customs in my hand luggage!

I arrived at Los Angeles airport with a suitcase and one piece of carry-on luggage. I was trying to walk as if the hand luggage bag was just an average weight. I approached customs with my rocket engine, trying not to attract attention. Luckily for me, the head of customs was an ex-Marine who had served in Vietnam with a load of crazy Aussies. He had a soft spot for them, so when I explained what I was carrying and intended to do with it, he just laughed and allowed me and the rocket engine onto the plane. You have to love the 1980s.

Once back in Perth, I was obsessed with getting this bike running and for it to be sanctioned by the Australian National Drag Racing Association, known as "ANDRA". I worked on the engine further but needed ANDRA's approval to run it at Australian drag racing events. So, I completed the necessary paperwork and applied for a licence for my rocket bike and the rocket go-kart.

Whilst waiting for these licences to be approved, I got permission to test the rocket go-kart privately at Ravenswood Raceway. I asked a few people at SECWA, where I worked, for some volunteers to help prepare and oversee the go-kart runs.

Wayne Bell, his friend Keith Lovatt and a few others put their hands up to help. Surprisingly enough, neither of them had rocket engine experience but thought it would be fun and were keen to learn. So, it was a baptism of fire, and quite literally, when some hydrogen peroxide was spilt and started dissolving bits of the track surface and some of their clothing. From that day on, Keith Lovatt became a great friend, and he and his wife, Jen, crewed and worked with me on other cars for the next 30 years.

As previously stated, in the years leading up to my building this rocket bike, there had been a few "incidents". People had been seriously hurt or killed in the USA whilst driving rocket-powered vehicles. It wasn't necessarily because they were rocket-powered, but because of their speed, and when things went wrong, they did so in a big way. Racing is racing, and risks exist in all forms of motorsport.

The governing drag racing body in the USA, the NHRA, deemed rocket cars too fast. They imposed strict speed limits on these incredible machines. Rocket cars were so much quicker than the conventional dragsters of the day. They showed them up, and the NHRA didn't like it.

A Top Fuel Dragster didn't hit 480 km/h (300 mph) over the quarter-mile until 1992. In the 1970s, rocket cars had run 640 km/h (400 mph) quarter-miles. The NHRA put speed limits on both rocket dragsters and rocket funny cars. Drivers were told they could not go under a 4.5-second elapsed time for the quarter-mile. These speed restrictions were almost impossible to comply with. Any breaches of these speeds or rules could result in a driver's suspension or loss of their licence. To even get close to complying with these speed limits, rocket car drivers would have to shut their engines off three-quarters of the way down the track. It was impossible to judge and easy to get wrong and lose your racing licence. I certainly think that's what the NHRA really wanted.

Drag racing is big business and all about sponsorship dollars. It thrives on selling stuff to car nuts, who want their cars to go faster. Selling oil, fuel, tyres, and race parts makes drag racing tick. These rocket guys didn't bring in sponsorship dollars. They used no motor parts, no oil, none of it. With the possible exception of Fred Goeske, no one was going to put one of these cars on the road (that story comes later). The NHRA couldn't see an "upside". They didn't like the safety risks and wanted these cars off their sanctioned tracks. These restrictions for rocket cars in the USA at drag racing events ended the rocket car era.

Unfortunately, where the USA leads, Australia tends to follow. I received a letter from the ANDRA Director Dennis Syrimis, a friend and fellow racer. Dennis laid out the ANDRA decision to decline my licence application to ride my rocket bike on Australian dragstrips. I appealed the decision and asked them to reconsider, but they wouldn't. I was bloody pissed and more than upset. I had put a lot of time, sweat and money into that bike. It was my future to earn a living at what I loved, and I was fuming. I manhandled the rocket bike onto my truck, took it to the tip and dumped it!

This refusal to sanction my rocket bike meant the rocket go-kart was also unable to run in Australia. After the demonstration run at Ravenswood Raceway, I sold the go-kart, which is still on display in the York Motor Museum in Western Australia. The 253 mph (407 km/h) it ran in the USA is still the fastest a go-kart has ever run over the quarter-mile.

Riding Krazy Horse, which I bought from Wally Pushkey. I fitted it with a Pro Stock V8 engine in the mid-1970s.

Testing my rocket-powered motorcycle - early 1980s.

More testing of the rocket motorcycle.

My rocket go-kart demo at Ravenswood Raceway – 1980.

The world record rocket go-kart is still on display at York Motor Museum, WA (0 – 253 mph in 5.97 seconds).

-7-

Trips, Travels and Tales in The USA

In my racing career, I have travelled to the USA, sometimes for work, sometimes for pleasure, but it was always an experience. In the 1980s and 1990s, I was constantly backwards and forwards between the USA and Australia, leading to some great stories and real adventures.

Meeting Ken Warby For The First Time

I was racing at Oran Park Raceway near Sydney and discovered that a hero of mine, Ken Warby, lived nearby. This first meeting was just after Ken had set the world water speed record at Blowerin Dam, NSW, in October 1978. Ken pushed this record to an incredible 511 km/h (317 mph) in the jet-powered boat he'd built in his shed. On the return run, his speed was clocked at 555 km/h (345 mph) when *Spirit of Australia* exited the measured mile.

I knocked on Ken's door, introduced myself, and congratulated him on his world record achievement. We became firm friends and worked and played together over the next few years. Ken was a very gifted and practical mechanic, in the same mould as Art Arfons. He had lifted the jet engine into his boat, *Spirit of Australia*, with a rope slung over the bow of a tree.

His achievement of breaking the world water speed record cannot be understated. This record must go down as one of the best Australian record-breaking feats ever, probably not Australian. The record he set in 1978 still stands today, with the last two people who attempted to break Ken's record sadly killed in their attempts. Water is very unforgiving, and if you get it wrong in a car, you might get another chance. There's no such luck on water. It's like hitting concrete! Ken eventually moved to the USA and retired there.

Recently, Ken's son David Warby has been trying to break his father's water speed world record with Ken's blessing. Ken admits he has held the record for far too long and has been helping David design and build a boat to beat his record over the last few years. We would love to see another Warby in the record books and wish David every success.

My good friend and land speed legend, Richard Noble, has recently also thrown his hat into the ring to break Ken's record. He is now developing a new craft. His project is Thrust WSH, so things are happening on the water record front, which is brilliant.

Lucky to Dodge a Bullet

After starting to work with Ken, he asked me to travel to the USA to oversee the jet dragsters he was having built by Romeo Palamides in Chicago. Romeo was a well-respected chassis and jet car builder. So, I flew from Perth via Sydney to Chicago in the USA. I took the opportunity to catch up with Ken in Sydney. I told Ken the rocket bike had been a precursor to my land speed record car. I also told him I was now interested in racing jet cars for a living and getting as much practical experience as possible.

Once I met with Ken, I flew on to Los Angeles and then to Chicago, where I stayed at the Rolling Hills Motel. Romeo Palamides explicitly told me to ask how much the fare was to the motel before I got into the taxi. It should be about $17, but often, the taxi drivers were good at taking unsuspecting tourists the long way around and charging them $50 for a $17 ride.

I arrived at the Rolling Hills Motel in South Chicago, which was quite a rough area. A big fat security guard was lying on the sofa half asleep, with a gun falling out of his holster. I was strictly instructed not to go outside; whatever I did, I was to stay in my room until the morning. Romeo was coming past at 8 a.m. to pick me up and take me to his workshop. So, I went to my room, which was pretty average, and sat on the bed and looked out the window. Over the road was a shopping mall; it was buzzing, and I couldn't believe it. It was Sunday afternoon, and I thought, *Jeez, don't these people go to church?*

The number of the motel I was staying at was in the thousands, and where I was being taken the next day was in the 33,000s of this street. I couldn't believe that there could be streets that long. Even though I was instructed not to go out, my inquisitive nature got the better of me. I decided to look and see what the big crowd over the road was.

I left my room and walked over the road; nothing was happening, just shoppers. Then I decided to walk on to see if I could find Romeo's workshop, which was further up the street. I started walking. I passed a few guys on the street, said "G'day", and carried on.

After walking a few kilometres, I was still a long way from the number I was looking for, so I decided to return to the motel. I didn't want to walk that far, and the jet lag was starting to catch up with me now. I had seen a few buses, so I decided to catch one, but none would stop. Eventually, I threw myself in front of one, which luckily did stop, and jumped on. The guy didn't understand me much, but I got him to stop at the motel and jumped off.

When Romeo picked me up the next day, he said, "How did you sleep?"

I told him I was tired, as I went for a bit of a wander down the road, and he was pretty pissed with me.

"I told you not to go out."

I said, "I had never seen a street that long and wanted to see a street number in the 33,000s."

I showed him how far I got as we drove to his workshop. He said, "You got there? I've had my shop 22 years, and I have never heard of a white guy walking that far and not ending up dead."

He told me I had gone through several gang territories that protect their areas with extreme gun violence.

"Did anyone hassle you?" Romeo asked.

"No, I spoke to a few guys on the way; they were fine."

He said, "You need to buy a bloody lottery ticket, my friend."

After overseeing the dragster builds, I left Chicago. I returned a few more times whilst Romeo was building these cars, but I learnt my lesson about venturing out. I had used up all my luck on the first trip.

Later, when these jet dragsters were completed and back in Australia, Ken invited me to join his team and drive them. So, we travelled to all the major dragstrips throughout Australia to race these epic machines. What a show we put on.

How Ross Became Rosco

In 1981, on one of my many other trips to the USA for Ken Warby, I ended up in Las Vegas for a few days. I was in a bar, having a drink, and I started chatting with a guy. He told me he was a professional gambler and very superstitious. So, naturally, I was interested in listening to what he had to say, as I have always been very superstitious about my racing.

When I race, I only wear black underwear, and as you will learn later, I crashed *Aussie Invader 2* on the 13th. I didn't want to run the car that day, but other factors overrode that decision. The 13th barrel marker on our land speed track is always labelled 73, not 13.

The gambler and I are chatting away, as strangers do, and we introduce ourselves properly. I don't recall his name now, but when I said I was Ross McGlashan, I could see him working out something in his head. Then, a worried look came across his face.

"You know that your name, Ross McGlashan, has 13 letters, and that's very unlucky; you need to change it straight away."

So, at 31, I started calling myself Rosco McGlashan. My wife, family, and some older friends still call me Ross, but almost everyone else knows me as Rosco.

The World's Fastest Street Legal Car

Around 1995, I was desperate to locate a hard-to-find fitting and was in California. So, I visited my favourite rocket part shops, Norton Sales Inc. and Joe Factor Sales. These are close to where "Fearless Fred" Goeske lives, so I decided to drop in and see him. I arrived at his house, and it was great to see him again after so many years. After our initial handshake and saying "G'day", Fred said, "I want to show you something."

We walked outside, past rows of shipping containers in his yard, and stopped at one container. He opens the metal door and, packed in the cluttered container, is a slightly dusty, red 1980 Plymouth Arrow pickup truck. It looked pretty stock, except for the skinny chromed wheels and specialist race tyres. I looked in the cab, and it was also pretty standard, but for a few extra controls and levers between the seats and a smart-looking roll cage.

Fred says, "The original engine is under the hood with an auto transmission." He then tells me the rear axle has freewheeling electric hubs and a complete rocket system in the pickup tray at the back. He then explains it uses two braking parachutes and a centrally mounted rocket engine, all hidden from view when the tailgate is up.

"You can drive it down the road; it's registered and street-legal," Fred informs me excitedly. I look at this little old red pickup truck that you wouldn't give a second glance on the road, but it would leave any modern-day supercar in its wake. It has a 3,500 lbs thrust hydrogen peroxide rocket engine, equivalent to several thousand horsepower, sitting in the back of it.

"How do you drive her?" I asked.

"You drive her just like a normal small pickup," Fred replies.

"I have been down to Van Nuys for a semi-legal street race but haven't been brave enough to run her down the Boulevard just yet." Fred then proceeds to demonstrate how it all works.

"To go racing, all I need to do is flick this switch, which operates the actuators that lower the tailgate. I then throw this switch, which transfers nitrogen pressure onto the fuel. Next, I turn this knob and select what percentage of power I want via a dome-loaded regulator. Then I throw this switch, and it purges the rocket engine. This switch puts the hubs into freewheel. I then line the car up, and we are ready to race. I pull this throttle lever, and this baby reaches 340 mph in just a few seconds. Rosco, you're looking at the world's fastest licenced street car!"

I am astounded and have no doubt, even without a demonstration, that everything Fred said would work exactly as he had described it. He was a bastard and a bloody legend.

Fred retired from racing after suffering a nasty crash in 1981. The parachute of his rocket car got caught around the rear wheel at over 275 mph (440 km/h), pulling the car hard to the right and straight over an embankment. The car was destroyed, and Fred was seriously injured.

After retiring from racing, he founded Design Deluxe Manufacturing. It specialises in the manufacturing of custom wheel adapters for aluminium wheels.

Fred died in October 2014 at the age of 76. I could fill a book on our adventures and the stories he told me; most would have gotten him a prison sentence, but he's gone now, so I feel the statute of limitations is off. He seemed to always be under surveillance by the police. I would see their cars parked up or go past his house whenever I was there. I always waved at them; they would duck down or look pissed at me.

Fred and several other pioneering rocket guys will sadly never be seen again. Their careers were cut short by motor racing red tape and politics. It meant many people never saw a rocket car race down the quarter-mile. It was certainly a spectacular event, and their demise is our loss.

-8-
My Land Speed Dream Becomes a Reality

The rest of the book refers to the five *Aussie Invader* cars. I think it will be helpful to list these cars and what they are to save confusion later on:

Aussie Invader or **Aussie Invader 1** – A jet-powered dragster that I helped build in Chicago and later purchased from Ken Warby. It was initially named *US Invader*.

Aussie Invader 2 - The first jet-powered land speed car with a Mirage ATAR engine. It started being built in 1988 but was severely damaged in 1994, soon after setting the Australian land speed record.

Aussie Invader 3 - The second jet-powered land speed car. It was an updated design of her sister with a shorter chassis than *Aussie Invader 2*. It had a slicker, more rounded body shape and a "hot-rodded" ATAR jet engine. It was built in just 18 months and ready to race in 1995.

Aussie Invader 4 - The second jet dragster, built to match race against *Aussie Invader 1*. It was built in 1996 and powered by a J34-36 Westinghouse turbojet.

Aussie Invader 5R - Our latest creation is still under construction and nearing completion. Powered by a 62,000 lbs of thrust bi-propellant rocket engine, hence the "R" in her title.

Please note: In the following chapters, quite a few records and speeds quoted are from the USA. I have listed those in miles per hour (mph) first where appropriate.

-ooO0oo-

When I started driving with Ken, we would travel all over Australia to race meetings. It would involve many hours of driving and truck stops. Every chance I got, I would pull out a drawing of my latest land speed car design and talk about it to Ken. After many hours of driving on this particular day, we ate at a rough roadhouse. Again, I pulled out my trusty land speed car design, and Ken finally cracked.

"If you're going to build a bloody land speed record car, just get on and do it; don't keep talking about it!"

"Ken, I don't have the money to build a car. How do I get going?"

"Start at the beginning, and work through the opportunities."

I took this advice onboard and soon began seriously looking at my land speed record ambitions and how I would achieve them. I started by buying the jet dragster *Aussie Invader* from Ken Warby. He was focused on his newly completed jet funny cars and jet truck. *Aussie Invader* later was referred to as "*Aussie Invader 1*" when we knew we would have other *Aussie Invader* cars.

My focus was on earning money through racing, which took me all over the country and trying to build my land speed car. This didn't sit well with Dianne. She wanted a husband solely focused on her and Tenneille, not my racing obsession. So, after a couple of years of me going off racing, we agreed to split up in 1983. We lived together for about a year whilst we sorted things out. We got on well, and it wasn't an issue. I bought Dianne and Tenneille another house for them to move into.

Just before Dianne and Tenneille moved out, I met Cheryl, who was to become my third wife in 1984. I dedicate a whole chapter to Cheryl, our meeting and life together later in this book.

I put together my own jet car show, driving *Aussie Invader* at race meetings around Australia. I had a small, dedicated team at this time, all volunteers. We certainly believed *Aussie Invader* could exceed 649 km/h (403 mph). This was the magic number I needed to beat to take Donald Campbell's Australian land speed record, set in 1964.

On two previous occasions, our jet dragster, *Aussie Invader*, exceeded 500 km/h (310 mph) on a short race track, setting a Tasmanian land speed record. This happened at a promotional exhibition for the Lions Club of Hobart. Later, we also reached a similar speed whilst shooting a UK car commercial for the Vauxhall Belmont SRi in March 1987.

I was always looking for new ways to promote my land speed record ambitions and generate interest and sponsorship. So, I jumped at the chance to do a car commercial for Vauxhall. The ad was a twist on the hare and the tortoise story, with the land speed car being very fast and running out of fuel quickly. Conveniently, the Vauxhall Belmont SRi had a large boot and dropped off several cans of jet fuel, and kept going while I was filling up.

Aussie Invader needed a complete makeover to look more like a classic, streamlined land speed car. A factory unit in Bayswater became the headquarters of the operation. I was away racing with Ken Warby on the "Thunda Down Under Tour", so Keith Lovatt and another mate remodelled the bodywork with fibreglass. They built a folding nose cone, front wheel covers, and wraparound windshield and repainted it black. It looked like something out of a Batman movie.

The venue for filming the Vauxhall commercial was Lake Deborah near our state's Goldfields. I had visited salt lakes all over Western Australia, searching for a venue for my record attempt, but none were suitable. However, this lake had an excellent hard salt surface and enough distance to make the commercial and possibly break the Australian land speed record.

Lake Deborah was hot, and the flies were in plague-like proportions. It was quite an uncomfortable experience. A preliminary inspection of the lake resulted in our ute becoming bogged. We "borrowed" a nearby tractor, which also became bogged, resulting in an offer of a night in the local jail. Some fast-talking and chequebook diplomacy saved us from that fate.

We took *Aussie Invader* to our local dragstrip and ran a flying quarter-mile to prove its performance. We achieved our first four-second pass at Ravenswood Raceway. However, we crashed on two separate occasions due to the limited braking area. We overshot the track when the parachutes failed. We were using Mirage cross-ply braking parachutes to stop the car. When used on a Mirage, these chutes were logged on a Time Expired Log, and once they reached a certain number of landings, they were thrown away.

My Land Speed Dream Becomes a Reality

The chutes we were using were still in service but designed for deployment at under 200 km/h (125 mph). Instead, we were deploying them at over two times that speed, with a massively shortened braking area, as opposed to an air force base runway. On our first full blast of the flying quarter-mile run, both chutes didn't unfold properly, so our car ran off the end of Ravenswood Raceway. It completely buried itself in a huge sand embankment at the end of the racetrack's braking area.

The car and I were buried in sand, and a tractor had to pull us out. It took some time, and my team and a TV crew had no idea if I was alive, injured or dead. Once we were out, I jumped out of the car and immediately asked, "How fast was that run?" I was unscathed, but *Aussie Invader* was not and in a pretty bad way. We had severe chassis damage, and the front axle had been ripped off. In addition, the engine had ingested a lot of sand.

Nevertheless, we were impressed with the speed results, which were close to 480 km/h (300 mph). We believed we could still exceed 530 km/h (330 mph) with a longer run-up and better ring slot chutes. We had to rebuild *Aussie Invader*, and we would return to Ravenswood to try again.

Whilst *Aussie Invader* was undergoing a rebuild after the crash. I remember ending up waiting on some parts I needed. So, I decided to go surfing this particular day and went to Trigg Beach, just north of Perth. I paddled out, and after catching a few waves, suddenly, I was in all sorts of trouble. I had a searing pain in my right foot, and the water was turning red. I had been bitten by a shark!

I paddled back to shore, where others had said they had spotted a shark in the water. Its teeth had done a great job on my foot, and I was bleeding quite a lot. The top of my foot was shredded, with a big skin flap hanging off. I didn't go to the hospital, but my foot was quite bad. My doctor, a mate, and Tae Kwon Do master stitched it up but thought my foot might not repair too well.

I was a regular at a local pub and had an important meeting that night. I limped into the pub on crutches, with my foot in a ball of bandage. The pub manager had already told all the regulars about my shark encounter, as he had seen a local TV news story about it earlier that evening.

I was lucky it was just a glancing bite, and the shark obviously hadn't liked the taste. Otherwise, it might have been a lot worse. My foot took quite a long time to heal, but it is perfectly OK now, with no lasting effects.

After *Aussie Invader* was rebuilt, I drove her again at Ravenswood, even with my sore but healing foot. This time, we were trying to exceed a target speed of 530 km/h. This distance, time and acceleration data would be helpful at our salt venue. Lake Lefroy near Kambalda in our Goldfields was our chosen venue. Unfortunately, it had only 12 kilometres of usable track length.

With our new Deist ring slot chutes, we headed back to our local dragstrip to perform more high-speed, short-distance runs. Our first two runs went well but were still under 480 km/h. We decided to increase the fuel flow into our afterburner and set our engine RPM to 108 percent. Our poor J34 Westinghouse jet engine was set on KILL (maximum power). When I passed the timing markers at the end of the track, all I heard was crack, crack. I only got a brief tug on the rear of our car, so I knew we were in trouble.

Once more, she speared her way into this massive sandbank. Again, I was towed out and wasn't hurt, but our poor car was pretty beaten up. Luckily, both times that this happened, we dug into the sand bank and did not take off over it. Things would have been a lot worse if that had been the case.

We conceded that our *Aussie Invader* jet dragster would not cut it as a land speed record breaker. It was time to consider building a bigger, more powerful car to break the Australian record. We needed a new vehicle design and dedicated track. We now had to think about what we would power our new *Aussie Invader 2* car with.

The critical part of building a land speed car is getting the right engine. I knew we needed something very powerful for *Aussie Invader 2*. Through my experience with jet engines in drag racing, I settled on the ATAR engine from a Mirage jet fighter. However, you can only build a jet-powered land speed car once you have an engine. So, wanting one of these engines was one thing. However, getting hold of one was a completely different ball game. The car's frame and system are custom-built around that engine, so we wanted to know if we could get one before the build could start.

-9-

Friends in High Places

In my quest to get hold of a Mirage jet fighter engine, I decided I needed to go straight to the top. However, I knew I would be cut off at every opportunity if I spoke to non-decision-makers. Luckily, I got hold of the name and phone number of someone who could help. This contact was very senior in the RAAF: Air Vice Marshall Neil Smith AM, MBE, BE(Aero), FRAeS.

The following chapter was written with considerable help from Neil Smith, who retired from the RAAF in 2001 but is now the Managing Director of the RAAF's Wings Magazine publication. A similar story to the one you are about to read appeared recently in one of the issues of Wings Magazine.

-ooOOoo-

It was 1986, and I knew I would get a frosty reception from Air Vice Marshall Neil Smith when his Personal Assistant introduced me. The PA says over the phone to the Air Vice Marshall.

"Mr McGlashan is on the line, and he would like to talk to you about getting hold of a Mirage engine and mounting it in a car!"

He would think I was a bloody nutter, but luckily for me, my name rang a distant bell. Another stroke of luck was that he was having a bad day and thought, *This conversation might offer some relief to my overflowing in-tray*, so he took my call.

I introduced myself, got down to business, and asked him if he could help me try and get one of these Mirage engines. He informed me that there was very little chance of me being able to find one of these engines, let alone buy it. They never came up at an auction, and if they did, the price would be huge, well out of my league.

We chatted and got along really well. I felt I sold the concept of what I was trying to do, and I think Neil realised I was deadly serious and would not take *No* for an answer. He said he would keep his ear to the ground and tell me if he heard of any being "retired" or sold.

Every month or so, I would call him up and pester him about these engines. He would always say the same thing. "Sorry, none available, and I cannot see how they would become so." These engines would have cost the taxpayer millions of dollars. Any that got pulled out of an aircraft would be used for spares to keep the current aircraft flying.

After about a year of constantly pestering, Neil called me one Friday afternoon to say four engines were coming up for auction. He said the engines had just been released and were being auctioned in Sydney tomorrow.

I asked him, "If I wanted to buy one of the engines, which one of the four would be the best to go after?"

"The one with the least number of runtime hours."

"Which one was that?"

Air Vice Marshall Neil Smith said he would enquire and call me back. He rang a bit later and said number two on the auction list would be the best for what we wanted.

These engines were still quite secretive items as far as the public was concerned. The RAAF and some people in Canberra felt it would be irresponsible for Defence Forces to sell these engines and parts at any price. The risk of "damage" I might do to myself was pretty high, and the RAAF's reputation might take a bashing if the worst happened. However, Neil persuaded them I could be trusted and was well aware of the risks.

There was also a precedent: I was already using a J34 jet engine from a Neptune P2V7 in my *Aussie Invader* jet dragster, and I'd become an expert on these. I was using it to delight the petrolheads and spectators attending drag racing venues across Australia.

I asked my wife Cheryl if she could book me a flight to Sydney that night on her credit card. I would go over and see if I could secure one of these engines and worry about paying for it later. So, that night, I caught the "redeye" from Perth to Sydney and arrived first thing in the morning.

It was the most exciting auction I have ever attended. There was some neat stuff there; if I had my way, I would have bid on nearly everything. Unfortunately, I didn't even have $100 to my name, but despite this, I was determined to come home somehow with one of these engines.

Luckily for me, the four engines were late entries and, therefore, the last items on the list. All the engines were listed with their auction ID numbers, so there wouldn't be any confusion over the number two engine I wanted. Unfortunately, it was a very hot day, and the auctioneer took about four hours to reach our first engine. All four were displayed with their transport container lids open.

The auctioneer was being pushed around on a wheeled platform. There was a lot of interest in these engines, with bidders climbing all over them. I was very discouraged to see all this interest, as I would be against several other interested parties. They all would have more money than me, as I had none!

Bidding started on the first engine and, from memory, went to $3,500 quite quickly but then stalled. Then the auctioneer announced, "The containers around these engines are worth more than $3,500. It's too hot and too late in the day; pass them in."

I saw the guy pushing the trolley the auctioneer was standing on, and he started pushing him towards his office. It took a few seconds for the penny to drop, and when it did, I yelled at the auctioneer.

"Mate, I got on a flight from Perth in the middle of the night to specifically bid on one of these engines. If you're not happy with the offer on your first one, you can't drop all four individual listings."

"Which one do you want to bid on?" he asked.

"Number two on the list."

"What is your bid?"

"$500, Sir."

"SOLD!"

"What about the next one?"

"$500", I responded again.

"SOLD! What about the next?"

"$500," for a third time.

"SOLD!"

"What about the first one?"

"$500."

"SOLD!"

Everyone present, including me, was gobsmacked. It was a fantastic moment, and I was in shock. I rang Cheryl and told her the exciting news: I had bought four ATAR Mirage jet engines. Initially, these cost millions of dollars each, for just $2,000! She was as surprised and excited as I was.

Then the reality struck Cheryl, "Where on earth are you going to find $2,000? I don't have it."

"I don't know," I replied, but I got working on it, made a few phone calls and pulled in a few favours, and somehow, the next day, I had the cash.

The next problem to solve was that these acquisitions were only "core" engines. We also needed to acquire the "optional extras", such as an afterburner, a fuel control unit, a starter, etc., to make the engine run. Ideally, we need a couple of each, but we were away if we could get just one engine running. So, I again asked Neil to help make these units usable for my land speed ambitions.

It transpired that No. 3 Squadron in the RAAF was already operating the F/A-18 Hornet, and No. 77 Squadron was re-quipping with them. This meant they were winding down Mirage operational fighters. The Defence Force was starting to dispose of the aircraft and spares, hence the disposal of four engines in the first place.

Neil suspected several repairable items would also be available, so he volunteered to enquire about it with a well-placed contact in the equipment world. He asked if I could buy the required items at "disposal" prices, and we did manage to get these items. The problem now was how to fit them and test-run an engine.

The engine shop at No. 481 Wing was still servicing Mirage engines. Still, with the number requiring maintenance declining, there was some spare workshop capacity. So, again, the RAAF came to the rescue and assembled and test-ran one of our engines at Williamtown, New South Wales.

The RAAF then found space on a Hercules aircraft going to Perth, so they waived me (and the engine) goodbye with their best wishes for our project. I owe Neil a massive big thank you for the way he helped secure these engines and started me on the road to my land speed record dream. It was 1986, and I was thirty-six years of age and beginning to realise my boyhood dream of breaking Donald Campbell's Australian land speed record.

I recall having a conversation with Neil sometime later after the auction. At the time, he thought this would be the last he would see or hear from me unless I achieved my goal or spectacularly failed and killed myself. How wrong he was!

-10-
Aussie Invader 2 Starts With Sound Advice

Now we had our Mirage ATAR jet engine. We started planning to construct our first land speed record car, *Aussie Invader 2*. We had zero financial backing or sponsors, but we started working on that immediately. We also started to assemble a crack volunteer team to build the car.

One of the things that always gives me an incredible thrill is when you achieve something very few have done. Twice as many humans have walked on the Moon than have driven a car at over 600 mph. I am proud to say I am one of the 600 mph club. That group reads like the Who's Who of land speed racing, and in that group are one or two names that may surprise you. One is of a lady, the late and brave Kitty O'Neil.

Kitty was a fearless pioneer of motorsport, a stunt woman, a diving champion and was born deaf. Kitty still holds the record for the fastest quarter-mile recorded in any vehicle, for any driver, man or woman. Kitty drove a rocket-powered dragster from 0 – 412 mph (0 - 663 km/h) in just 3.22 seconds in 1977.

A year earlier, Kitty had driven the *SMI Motivator*, which was an early version rocket car for the program to break the sound barrier (Project SOS – Speed of Sound). It was owned by Hal Needham and built by Bill Fredricks. In 1976, Kitty O'Neil drove the rocket-powered *SMI Motivator* to 512 mph (824 km/h). This was a new world record for a woman, beating Lee Breedlove's record of 308 mph. Kitty hit over 600 mph on one of her record runs and should be recognised as part of the 600 mph club.

If it had not been for sponsors stopping her from driving the *SMI Motivator* to its full potential, I believe Kitty O'Neil could and should have broken the world land speed record. Kitty was fearless and undoubtedly capable of mixing it with the guys.

Hal Needham was supposed to challenge for the record, but he was busy with his job as a film director, and this left Kitty to drive the *SMI Motivator*. Unfortunately, big business intervened. The toy companies that sponsored Hal Needham's attempt planned to make an action figure of him. These companies ensured that only he would race for the record, taking Kitty O'Neil out of the driver's seat.

Hal Needham later crashed the *SMI Motivator* at over 600 mph. This car program also went on to produce the *Budweiser Rocket* car. The *Budweiser Rocket* car was controversial in its day and still is. It was only built to break the sound barrier, even for a fraction of a second, not to break the official world land speed record.

The controversy surrounding the car and its fearless stuntman driver, Stan Barrett, is centred around how they measured its speed and judged it to have gone supersonic. The United States Air Force tracked it at the Edwards Air Force Base using radar, and on the day only showed it had gone 38 mph, that's right, 38 mph. They believed the radar had picked up a truck in the distance, not the *Budweiser Rocket* car. They then used the onboard accelerometer data to calculate its speed and, eight hours later, announced it had achieved 739.666 miles per hour (Mach 1.01).

I don't think it broke the sound barrier, and the evidence supports that. It went fast and almost certainly exceeded the then-current land speed record of 622 mph, but there was no sonic boom, unlike *Thrust SSC*.

Hal Needham was a celebrated stunt expert, director and NASCAR team owner. He inspired Brad Pitt's character Cliff Booth in the 2019 film by Quentin Tarantino, Once Upon a Time in Hollywood. Tarantino based Booth and Dalton's relationship (played by Leonardo DiCaprio) on the real-life friendship between stuntman Hal Needham and actor Burt Reynolds. The legendary duo worked and lived together at the same property for twelve years.

-ooo0oo-

I contacted Art Arfons when I started building *Aussie Invader 2*. He was a clever racer, often creating ground-breaking designs on shoestring budgets that outperformed many more "well-engineered" and far better-funded cars. I was drawn to him as he was just like me; we both raced on virtually zero budgets. I was confident he would offer the sound and sensible advice I needed, not expensive solutions I couldn't afford.

When designing *Aussie Invader 2*, I drew inspiration from several sources, especially Art's cars. I had studied his *Green Monster* car down to the last detail and knew all its measurements and data. So, I called him and asked Art, "How did you come to those dimensions for the *Green Monster*?"

I wanted to know why he had built it, 22 feet long with a rear track of 8 feet 6 inches wide. Of course, I expected a lengthy, logical answer supported by mathematical reasoning. Still, in true Arfons style, he said, "That's the size of my trailer."

That was a brilliant lesson and something I have tried to do ever since. Come up with a simple plan and make it work; don't keep looking for better or more complex solutions. They may be out there, but they will slow you down, and you will constantly change your mind and never finish anything.

I was constantly annoying Richard Noble with questions about his cars. As *Aussie Invader 2* progressed, I fired a lot more questions at Richard. Finally, he decided to put me in contact with his car design engineer, John Ackroyd, known as "Ackers". I spoke with Ackers at his home on the Isle of Wight in the UK. We hit it off from day one, and I was astounded that he would be interested in helping my team beat Richard's and his current record.

Ackers was known as the "Gypsy Engineer" and had an outstanding pedigree in engineering. He was definitely old school, as all his work was carried out with a slide rule and drawing board. The most technical piece of equipment he possessed was a fax machine, and boy, did that start running hot. I began to receive all sorts of calculations and hand-drawn component ideas. He had no mobile phone, computer, car or TV.

I have over a thousand of his faxes, and I still show them to other engineers who visit our workshop to show off his old-school engineering style. He worked with NASA, Richard Branson, Per Lindstrand, Craig Breedlove, and hundreds of others on their engineering adventures.

Ackers never asked to be paid, as he knew the answer would be, "We don't have any money." Ackers just loved the engineering and design of these cars and wanted to share his knowledge with anyone who would listen.

On several occasions, he hopped on a plane and flew from where he lived on the Isle of White in the UK to Perth to help with designs or advice. He would often tie it in with a holiday.

In later years, he had a travel companion, Meryl, who came with Ackers on several trips to Perth and stayed with us. Cheryl and I loved their company. Ackers had been married early in life, but that ended in divorce. Ackers once told me he used to get so absorbed in his work that he forgot he was married. So, when he returned home after several months away, not surprisingly, he found his wife gone!

One of his career highlights was the 2010 Delhi Commonwealth Games floating Helium structure he designed for Per Lindstrand's company. This contained the largest amount of helium ever used for a single project, with 22,000 cubic metres of this inert, light gas. Not only did Ackers design this structure, but he also made provision for recycling the gas after this event.

Ackers and I shared many trips around Australia and the USA. We met some incredible people together, and I will tell some of these stories later.

He didn't have a car but was ahead of his time. Ackers developed the first electric city car in 1973, called the Enfield 8000. It had a top speed of 78 km/h (49 mph) and was meant only for city driving, with a range of about 65 kilometres.

Sadly, John passed away in 2021 at the age of 83. RIP, Johnny Ackroyd; you were a bloody legend.

The finished design of *Aussie Invader 2* does bear a clear resemblance to Richard Noble's *Thrust 2*, with only subtle differences. The bodyline of the cockpit is lower, as I'm only a little guy, meaning I can sit much lower in the car. It has a single tail fin, whereas *Thrust 2* has twin tail fins. The jet engine's air intake was much squarer than Thrust's, and our car had a smaller frontal area, so we thought we had a great chance to beat Richard's record. *Aussie Invader 2's* bodyshell was a mixture of fibreglass and carbon fibre. Its construction was overseen by myself and master fabricator Lindsay Varcoe.

The solid aluminium wheels were similar to *Thrust's*, but that is not a surprise, as they were designed by Ackers, too. However, running on Lake Gairdner, this wheel design later proved an issue for us. The front wheel profiles were great for the Black Rock Desert, where *Thrust 2* ran, but they did not suit salt that was much harder and more slippery. In addition, the wheels tended to sit more on the surface and could not sink in and, therefore, didn't give us the sidewall grip we needed. This grip would help keep the free-spinning wheels in sync and allow them to all spin up together.

-11-
Construction of a Record Breaker

Construction of *Aussie Invader 2* started in 1988, and we set about creating a steel frame from chrome moly tubing. The frame was 8 metres long by 2.2 metres wide to house the ATAR jet engine, four wheels, and a small one-man-sized cockpit on the righthand side. It had two brake chutes at the rear, all enclosed in a slick fibreglass shell.

We purchased four lengths of chrome moly tube, 38 mm in diameter. This was all we could afford at the time. We proudly laid the tubes on the workshop floor and put a plastic garden chair, with the legs cut off, for the driver's seat and cockpit location. Next, we started to mock-up bits of the car, so we had a plan of what we would build and where everything would go.

We had told the media that we were starting construction of our land speed car. As a result, we had four TV stations interested in this story. They were all jockeying to produce a TV segment about the new iconic *Aussie Invader 2* land speed car being built in Perth.

They all came out to cover this exciting story and see this new car under construction. They turned up, only to find me sitting on my cut-down plastic garden chair amongst a few well-placed lengths of steel tubing and mocked-up bits of the car. To say they were not impressed was an understatement. Still, we got some excellent media coverage and a bit of ridicule. It didn't deter us from moving ahead and ignoring the doubters. We had always built vehicles this way. You have to have a visual picture of what you intend to create in your head, and then you can start filling in the gaps.

Cheryl and I had been busy recruiting a large number of supporters and expert volunteers, including many from the RAAF at Pearce Air Force Base. These included fitters and technicians, who worked with me to build my jet-powered drag racer. Most of these people became good friends of Cheryl and me and long-term members of the *Aussie Invader* team.

By owning our house, we were in a position to borrow money against it. I was always brought up to pay for things with cash and hated debt. Cheryl had worked closely with someone for a long time who showed her how to buy properties and make money. Cheryl convinced me that I needed an overdraft loan and a cheque book to build this land speed car.

At our workshop, Cheryl and I met with a group of investors to help raise more seed money to start the build process, but it was slow and tough going. The investors we attracted for the land speed project to get it underway only accounted for quite a small proportion of the money we would need. This was the first time we had built a land speed car. We didn't know what other costs we would have to get this car to the start line. The last time the record had been broken by Donald Campbell, the South Australian and Federal government had tipped in about the equivalent of $40 million in today's money in 1963-64. We had no such bloody luck.

We mortgaged our house, using the capital and the investors' and sponsors' money to start this project. Over time, we also bought several investment properties, with equity from one funding the next. Each property increased our assets, allowing us to borrow more money and buy the much-needed trucks, trailers and transporters for the race cars. One of the investment properties was a 12-acre property, great for storing larger vehicles.

It was a big job looking after the tenants, rentals and extra work maintaining the properties, but it was all worth it. The rental income helped us achieve our goal. Many people thought we were wealthy, but every cent we earned went into the car and the project. We often robbed Peter to pay Paul. I know no one knew that supporting all this spending was a mass of loans, mortgaged properties and debt.

Over the next eight years, we performed at drag racing, speedway exhibitions and motor shows. We created a show to demonstrate the power and versatility of the jet dragster, doing laps around an oval speedway track. I followed this with a car burn, where a road car was chained to the back of my jet dragster. I would then blow the car apart with the power of the jet dragster's afterburner. The crowd loved this, and it was an incredible sight, watching the thrust and heat of a jet engine completely destroy a car.

These appearances and shows were our main form of income and kept the bills paid and money coming into the project. Although the land speed record was my obsession, Cheryl threw herself into it, wanting to support and assist me in making my ambition come true. She became as passionate as I was, but the more money that came in, the more money went out. The more money we could borrow meant we could move the project forward quicker, nothing more.

There were no nice clothes, holidays, or meals out. It was all work to achieve the goal I had set for myself at age 12! We lived hand to mouth; it takes a remarkable woman to live like this. Cheryl is the best and most supportive wife you could ask for.

I have lived in the same house for over 40 years. It's in a northern Perth beachside suburb of Mullaloo. When I first bought this property, only a few houses were in the area, mainly perched on sand hills or beach sand blocks. We spent a lot of time travelling interstate with our *Aussie Invader 1* jet dragster. Around this time, I worked out of a tiny shed and workshop attached to our house.

Each new race season would see modifications performed to make *Aussie Invader 1* faster and more reliable. Before heading east, I would always have to do an engine start to check that there were no fuel or oil leaks. Then, we would check that my engine and chute controls were all adjusted correctly and fully operational. The trip over east was 4,000 kilometres, and a long way to go to find you had a problem and not get paid. The only way to test our car was to give her a two-minute blast in my driveway. The nearest alternative test site was an Air Force base 40 kilometres away. Firing her up there also entailed lots of time-consuming legalities to perform a short two-minute test.

I would park my ute at the end of the driveway, facing the back of my dragster. I'd place a giant deflector board over the windscreen to deflect the blast from the jet engine upwards and out over the road and away from the neighbour's house. I would then beat on the doors of the closest houses to me and tell them it's that time of the year again. Are you OK with some noise? It's just for two minutes.

These people were great, all loving what we were doing, and gave us their blessing. I would fire up the car with a crew guy checking the underside for any evidence of leaks. We always got away with one yearly test and no leaks.

One day, one of our lovely ladies from around the corner bought me some chocolates and a best wishes card. She then told me that every year, when I beat on her door to say I was going to run our jet for two minutes, she would go into a hot sweat. She told me she had two long wooden poles in her garden that were used to support her bedroom and lounge windows. She stood in the hallway between the two rooms with a long stick in each hand supporting the glass. When I fired up the jet dragster, these windows would bow inwards considerably. I apologised and decided it might be a good time to find a new test site.

The following year, I decided to visit a big beach car park only a kilometre north of our house. This whole area was basically vacant land waiting for development and perfect for testing our jet dragster. So, we unloaded our jet car, fired her up and went through our test procedures. The car checked out fine, and there were only a handful of spectators. The following year, we set up in the exact location again, but since our last visit, many more houses had been built, and many more people lived there.

Again, we fired up our car, and all hell broke loose, with people understandably coming to look to see what all the noise was about. We couldn't get out of the bloody place quickly enough. As we were loading up to leave, the cops arrived, and boy, were they pissed with me. Someone reported a helicopter crashed at the marina, and I was about to be arrested for being a public nuisance.

My help came from our bubbly friend Sue, who had a rather large chest. She arrived in skimpy shorts and a small see-through top. "Has he been a naughty boy again?" she asked the two cops. The cops forgot about me and switched their full attention to Sue.

I signalled my guys to keep loading up the car and fire up our truck. In between all this excitement, the cops got my name and address, but I found the right moment to disappear. Driving off in my truck and looking back, I could see Sue mesmerising these cops with her fun attitude and oversized chest. This wasn't the last time Sue's chest came to the rescue!

Aussie Invader 2 was evolving, and we had offers to build her in several workshops around Perth. We accepted these kind offers, as we didn't have enough room in our home workshop. However, every time we got underway and settled into one of these workshops, there would be some drama with the premises.

Either the business owner would sell, need to rent out or wanted the space back urgently. Moving a large, partly constructed car wasn't a cheap exercise, and the costs of constantly moving her were killing us. So, I said to my lovely Cheryl, "We need to build a huge workshop next to our house," and did some drawings of what I wanted.

Aussie Invader 2 was still under construction, and with nowhere else to build it, the car was back at our house. Unfortunately, half of it was hanging out of the workshop, draped in a tarp. It wasn't ideal, and I hated it.

Cheryl was experienced in real estate and knew what I wanted to build, and she said, "You will never get that approved. It's way too big."

"OK, I'll contact our local shire office and talk to their building inspector," I said.

I was hoping to make a friend who might assist me in getting this structure approved, but no such luck. The inspector I spoke with wasn't prepared to help.

I persevered and asked him if he might be good enough to come by and look before I wasted everyone's time submitting plans. "I'll come by Thursday night at 6 p.m. I can give you five minutes, but that's all," he replied. Boy, was I deflated. Then I thought, *Our friend Sue is the answer.* I had learned that the inspector was a bit of a ladies' man and was a keen diver.

I arranged for our friend Sue to come to our house and arrive early on the night of our building inspector's visit. I borrowed some diving equipment and spread the diving bottles and other gear around our front door. Then, I positioned our dining table in full view of the front door when it was opened. At six o'clock sharp, the doorbell rang, and there stood our inspector.

"Hello, mate. Pleased to meet you. Do you have time for a quick drink?" I said.

"No, I told you I could only give you five minutes."

He then looked at the dining table and saw the two girls, one with her breasts looking bigger than ever and my wife, Cheryl. There was also a big bottle of champagne on the table. He stopped and said, "Perhaps I have time for one quick drink." He finally got up to check out what I wanted to do with my shed at around 11 p.m.

Everything he mentioned that we couldn't comply with, he countered with, "Ah, forget I said that."

We got our big workshop approved very quickly. Thank you, Mr Inspector and our friend Sue, for your help again.

ROSCO THE FASTEST AUSSIE ON EARTH

-ooOOoo-

While building *Aussie Invader 2*, I often went away on one of my many paid drag racing appearances on Australia's east coast. I was driving the truck with the dragster back across the country to Perth and got a message from Cheryl. A French company wanted to film me racing my jet-powered dragster, *Aussie Invader 1*.

OK, great, I thought, but they wanted me to race my jet dragster down a main public street! The town they were talking about was Boulder, a sister town to Kalgoorlie in WA's gold mining heartland. I was intrigued and could swing past Boulder on my way home. It wasn't that far out of my way. I hoped it would be great exposure for what we were trying to achieve with *Aussie Invader 2*, so I agreed to meet them in the town and talk.

Once I got there and spoke to the film director, I realised he was serious, but what he wanted was almost impossible. He wanted me to race my jet dragster down a public street on a Sunday morning at very high speed. If I remember rightly, I used the expression, "As long as my arse points to the ground, it won't happen. We needed the Police, Main Roads and the Shire's approval and the mayor's permission to do this. It's Sunday morning; it just won't work."

Luckily for the French film crew, I knew the mayor and the police chief personally. After a discussion on safety, and to my surprise, they agreed this event could take place. This all came together in about an hour. With both of these people doing what is sadly rare in today's society, they were able to make a decision.

I lined up our jet dragster, *Aussie Invader 1*, alongside the Grand Hotel on Brockman Street, with her pointing southbound. Every available cop or person with authority stood guard on all the alleys and side streets leading onto Brockman Street. We started *Aussie Invader 1*, and I wound her up to 108 percent, performing several burner pops (shooting flames out of the afterburner) on the way to maximum rpm. The noise echoing down the street was incredibly loud. If anyone was going to church that morning, they would have thought the world was ending and prayed extra hard.

A suicidal French cameraman positioned himself in the middle of the intersection. I lit the afterburner and blasted down the street, past where he was, deploying the chutes at the end of the run. Our racer ended up a long way down Brockman Street, stopping at a T-junction. Everyone, including me, could not believe what had happened on a public road.

Someone said, "You were close to that cameraman."

I replied, "I knew he was there but didn't see him."

He happened to be lying in the middle of the intersection. Then the producer said it was great but asked if we could do it all again, as he wasn't sure he got the right shot.

I will never forget the horror on the faces of everyone involved when we started preparing for a second run. This will never happen again in this country; I can assure you of that.

I blasted off on the second run, and a cop with a speed gun outside the police station clocked me at 420 km/h (260 mph) down Brockman Street. I would have lost my licence for that one, but I probably set a record for the highest speed on a public road in Australia. For kids reading this, racing is for racetracks, so please do not try to beat that record.

To this day, I have never seen any footage of this incredible event and do not know what happened to it or even if it still exists. What a pity. It certainly would have been entertaining to watch. I did discover some photographic evidence of this taking place on a trip to Kalgoorlie in 2014, but that story comes later.

-ooo0oo-

Back to *Aussie Invader 2*, the building program had hit a significant hurdle. Around this time, the stock market collapsed, and several investors pulled out of their promised investments in our car due to financial losses. So, Cheryl and I were left "holding the baby" once again. We refinanced our house to keep things moving forward. Still, bad news turned into good when we met a West Australian financial advisor and entrepreneur, Paul Terry. Paul loved what we were doing and invested in *Aussie Invader 2*. He believed in us and that we would set the record. Paul was an inspiration.

Paul had built a luxury hotel and motor museum named The Esplanade Hotel in Albany, WA, to house his seventy-rare car collection. The idea was *Aussie Invader 2* would be owned outright by Paul once we had set the record. He would then house *Aussie Invader 2* in his museum with the rest of his cars for all his guests to see.

Paul travelled from Albany, WA, to Sydney and all over Australia, advising his clients on upcoming recommendations or changes to their financial portfolios. My wife Cheryl and I spent time with Paul and his lovely wife, Joan, at their Albany Hotel. We were making arrangements for our record-setting car to be the main feature at their newly completed Esplanade Hotel and car museum.

Sadly, Paul was killed only two days after our last visit, and he never got to see *Aussie Invader 2* run. He was involved in a helicopter accident in 1993 in Hawaii, just before we ran the car for the first time at Lake Gairdner. His death was a massive loss for WA, his friends and his family. We had met him through *Aussie Invader 2*, but he was more than that. He was a good friend.

It had taken ten years to complete *Aussie Invader 2*, from my original concept to getting it ready to run. This included designing and manufacturing our solid aluminium wheels, which had never been proven on salt. Wheels with tyres were just not an option at the speeds we wanted, and no one made them these days. Art Arfons had used tyres and was constantly experiencing punctures and tyre failures. We didn't want to share that experience.

Our legendary design engineer Ackers had arranged for six hand-forged aerospace-grade aluminium blocks to be produced in the UK. John Deere had produced and sponsored nearly all machining jobs needed to complete our car. The wheel machining and testing were our last significant hurdles, and we were anxious to get our hands on these.

In the interim, I contacted a worldwide shipping agent to transport these to Perth. The head of this company told me he supported our project and would air freight our wheels from the UK to Perth for the same cost as sea freight. This appeared as a shot in the arm until our forgings landed in Perth. The air freight bill was more than the cost of constructing our car!

We couldn't get our hands on our aluminium blocks to commence their machining work, and the lawyers had to get involved. Finally, two months later, the issue was resolved on the courthouse steps, with this company agreeing that they would honour their sea shipping cost to us. This issue cost us months of valuable time and unnecessary stress. We finally had our wheels made by these brilliant John Deere engineers and machinists.

In the past, I dealt with Air Vice Marshall Neil Smith quite a lot. He had helped me get the four ATAR Mirage jet engines in 1986. Well, what a small world. Six years later, Neil arrived as the newly appointed Operational Commander at WA's Pearce RAAF Air Force base in 1992.

On the initial tour of his new base, he was somewhat surprised to find a vehicle that closely resembled my drawings from six years earlier in one of the hangars.

When we met years later, he laughingly said, "I guess I shouldn't have been surprised that I wasn't the only person to fall under your powers of persuasion."

We needed a place to test the car when the build was complete. Thanks again must go to Neil, as we commenced test runs (on pneumatic tyres) on the Pearce Air Force base's runway after flying finished on Friday afternoons. The car ran straight and true on the tarmac and reached speeds of 300 km/h (185 mph) on our limited runway space. That was about the take-off speed for the Mirage jet fighter whose engine powered our car.

Construction of a Record Breaker

Aussie Invader 2 was ready for the record attempt, but the location was an issue. Several salt lakes in WA were considered, but none could provide the track length required for the runs we were going to undertake. Lake Lefroy was the exception, but torrential rain had left the surface soft and muddy. We needed at least 22 serviceable kilometres of rock-hard salt, most of which was for slowing down and a run-off area in case the chutes failed.

So, our quest to find a suitable track made us look further afield. Eventually, Lake Gairdner in South Australia was our preferred selection. This was a vast, dry Salt Lake north of the Eyre Peninsular and about mid-way between Port Augusta and Ceduna.

Glen Davis had previously investigated this site. He was determined to set a world wheel-driven record with his incredible car, Spirit of Woomera, powered by twin V12 Rolls Royce Merlin engines with turbochargers.

Glen had gained an audience with the South Australian Tourism Department. They had offered to cover the surveying costs to whoever was going to establish their record first at this venue. As it happened, we were ready to run first. So, the South Australian Government contacted a leading Adelaide surveying company, Coffee & Co., to perform this work for us.

Perth's Channel 7 arranged a flight with Glen to do an aerial recce of this massive salt lake. We talked with the Andrews family, who leased the Mount Ive Station. They had the only access to Lake Gairdner, which ran alongside their sheep station. We negotiated a deal to use the salt lake, their homestead and ex-Maralinga radioactive huts for our crew's accommodation. I don't think we had to worry about carrying torches at night, as our team would now be glowing in the dark.

Our 36,000 hp Mirage ATAR jet engine is ready to go into Aussie Invader 2's chassis.

Aussie Invader 2's chassis moved out of the workshop.

Construction of a Record Breaker

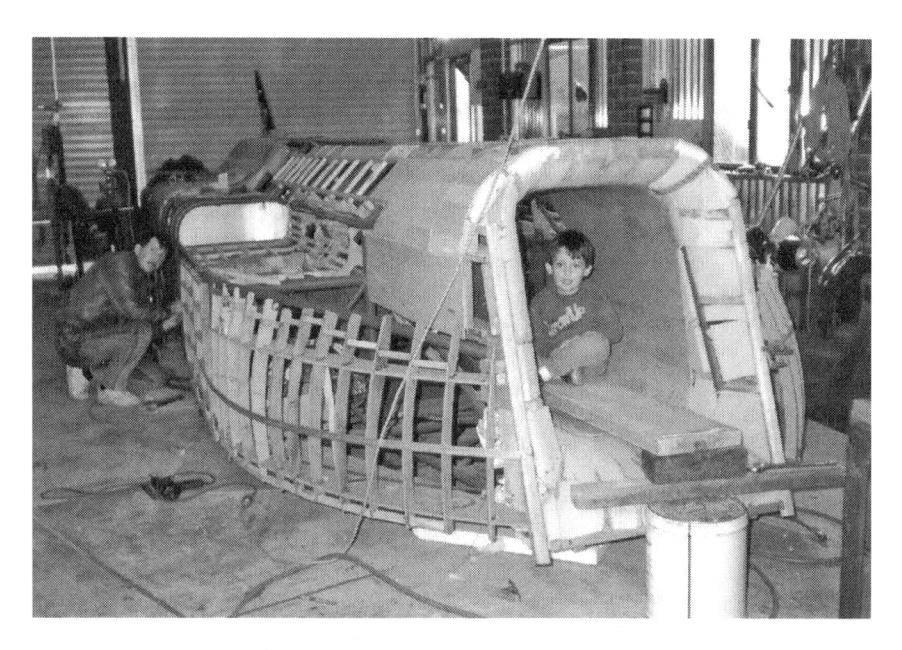

Starting to fabricate Aussie Invader 2's body.

After months of hard work, the body of Aussie Invader 2 emerges from its mould.

Aussie Invader 2 is starting to look more like a land speed car.

Testing of the car and systems at Pearce RAAF base in Perth.

Construction of a Record Breaker

The press is invited to film the testing of Aussie Invader 2.

Final testing of Aussie Invader 2 at Pearce RAAF base.

Thank you, John Deere, Western Australia, for our 6 hand-forged aerospace-grade Aluminum wheels.

Thanks to some of the great people who helped us get to the start line.

-12-

Early Trips, Travels and Tales in Australia

I have travelled across Australia more times than I would care to remember. My day job for most of my life was to appear at motor and drag racing events from one side of the country to the other. I was competing, putting on a show or making personal appearances with one or some of my many cars. It led to some great stories and adventures across Australia; here are a few.

The Prime Minister We Nearly Didn't Have!

My first test drive in *Aussie Invader 1* was at Canberra's Capital Raceway in the early 1980s. This first run was fast, bloody fast. Ken Warby commented, "That run was probably a new speed record for Canberra's Capital Raceway."

We had to run it down the dragstrip in the opposite direction to allow more braking area, as the track wasn't built for the speeds we were going. We achieved this by opening a gate that led onto Canberra's Air Force base, which doubled as a civilian airstrip, often bringing politicians to Australia's Parliament.

As I slowed down after this fast run, the airport security guys drove across my path with their lights flashing, trying to pull me up quickly. The security guys later said, "If you had travelled another hundred metres, you would have collided with an incoming jet." On that jet was a government minister called John Howard. John later became one of the best Prime Ministers Australia has ever seen. I might have denied Australia that great leader had my braking chutes failed.

Many years later, when he was Prime Minister, I received a letter from John Howard congratulating me on my Australian land speed record. He also wished me well on my attempt at the world record. I hold that letter in high regard, displayed prominently on my living room wall.

Big Rig and a Brush With The Law

In 1983, I was invited to join Ken Warby for an Australia drag racing tour with three jet-powered vehicles. Ken had shipped two brand new Jet Funny cars and a mind-blowing jet truck powered by a J79 General Electric turbofan from the USA. This truck produced 16,000 lbs of thrust and had a target speed of 320 km/h (200 mph) over the quarter-mile drag strip.

The composite-bodied Funny Cars resembled the latest model road vehicles of their day. Ken was driving a Mustang, and I was driving a Datsun 260Z. Both cars had J85 General Electric single-shaft turbojets with about 5,000 lbs of thrust. The truck had arrived in Australia before it had ever been down a race track. It had not even been started or tested. The jet truck needed setting up and testing before we could race her in Australia.

Ken planned that he and I could perform together in these cars throughout Australia. We would match-race each other in the cars whilst we waited for the arrival of Craig Arfons from Florida. Craig was the son of Walt Arfons and nephew of Art

Arfons. He was coming over to prepare the truck's jet engine for racing. So, Ken and I travelled from state to state in the toughest-looking truck and trailer combo ever seen.

Our transporter truck was a Cab-over Louisville, which was at least six inches wider than any trucks on our roads and left-hand drive. The trailer was very long, with living quarters for six at the front.

Perspex windows ran down the side and displayed the jet truck. The two Funny Cars sat on top of each other at the very rear of the trailer. It's tough enough to drive big rigs across Australia, but it's a bloody nightmare when your truck is very wide and left-hand drive.

We started our tour by unloading the complete rig off a ship in Melbourne Harbour. The unloading should have happened on a Friday, but it didn't. So, Ken arranged to unload it on Saturday, which would normally be impossible. But, being the fastest man on water in the world, Ken somehow persuaded the customs guys to unload it.

We headed off to Willowbank Raceway in Queensland for our first race. The meeting went off perfectly, and the cars performed well. Our next stop was Melbourne's Calder Park Raceway, but I said to Ken before we got on the road.

"Ring Craig Arfons. You must get a date when he is flying in, Ken." So he rang Craig and was given a day when Craig would leave Florida.

We raced at Calder Park, then headed back to Sydney's Eastern Creek. I asked Ken again, "When is Craig coming over? Ring him and forget about what time it is in Florida. We need him to commit; don't worry if you get him out of bed."

Again, Ken received another promise for another departure date and time. We had to head west on a 4,000-kilometre drive to my home state, WA and its famous Ravenswood Raceway.

Travelling across our Nullarbor Plain was horrific. Our truck was too wide for the narrow roads, and passing oncoming road trains, was putting lives in danger. For most of this trip west, I was riding shotgun. It was horrifying to look down at the road's centreline and see it running under my arse. I constantly told Ken to move over, but there was no road or shoulder to move over to. Boy, I gained some grey hairs on that crossing.

We arrived unscathed, somehow back into Western Australia and were approaching a small town called Merredin, about 300 kilometres from Perth. I knew Merredin well. It was the town I wouldn't stop in when I left school at 12 because it was full of cops. Ken had his Slim Dusty music playing and wearing his favourite cowboy hat. We were both happy to be nearly reaching the end of our big trip.

I said, "Ken, this town is notorious for traffic cops. Turn the music down, watch your speed and don't even think about stopping here." So we drove quietly through town, heading west. I thought *We have made it*, and I leaned forward in my right-hand passenger seat and looked in the mirror. "Ken, pull over. We've got bacon hanging out of our arse." A cop car came around us with lights flashing.

He put his hat on and came to my door, usually the driver's side. I should have mentioned that this truck wasn't only left-hand drive but also very tall, so the cop couldn't see in the cab and could hardly see me.

The cop said, "Pass me your driver's licence."

"Sorry, sir, I don't have one," I replied.

"Right, step out of the truck, please." The cop had his book out and could smell blood.

"So, you don't have a licence to drive this then, and what do you call these?" he asked, pointing at the truck's number plates.

"They are number plates, sir."

"I can see that, but they are not from Australia."

"No sir, the truck is registered in Ohio, but we have a permit to drive it in every state."

"Not without a driver's licence, you don't."

"Why did you stop us? We weren't speeding?" I asked.

"You left your flasher on", the cop replied.

"Turn your bloody flasher off," I yelled back to Ken, which he did.

"We will leave this rig here, and you must accompany me to the station." The cop said.

"Why I'm not driving; he is," pointing at Ken, who was grinning like a Cheshire cat.

Ken got out and gave the cop his licence and the cook's tour of the truck, trailer, and jet cars. Ken was then given a $150 fine for leaving his flasher on, but the laughs we had made the fine almost worthwhile.

200 MPH Jet Truck Fix

After our brush with the law, we arrived at Ravenswood, raced there, and again the cars performed well. We then packed up to head back to Melbourne for our first meeting, with the two Funny Cars and the truck attempting to run 320 km/h.

I told Ken to ring Craig again, "If he's not on a plane within 24 hours, he's just blowing smoke up our arse, and he won't be coming."

We headed east again, being super careful getting through Merredin.

We arrived in Melbourne, staying at the Keilor Motor Inn, close to the racetrack. Ken rang Craig, surprise, surprise he couldn't make it! I immediately picked up the phone and rang Jack, a pilot mate who had built a jet-car many years previously. Jack flew nearly every night out of Essendon Airport to Tasmania.

I asked Jack, "Mate, can you get us onto Essendon Airport today to do some engine ground runs with our jet truck?

We need a concrete surface to fire the truck up on, as bitumen will melt and get blown away."

Jack took my number and promised to call back within twenty minutes.

Twenty minutes later, he called, "Sorry mate, we can't get you onto Essendon, but you have a date with the crew at Tullamarine Airport."

I wrote down the entry gate number and who had authorised our entry. We arrived with the jet truck at Tullamarine Airport. We quickly set her up on a side runway in front of the Australian Airlines Hangar.

We pumped our jet A1 fuel into the four 200-litre race truck tanks and prepared for a start.

I told Ken, "All we need to do is find out what exhaust gas temperature (EGT) we have. Go for a start, hold her at 80 percent engine revs, and note the temperature."

We fired this beast up, and ground crews suddenly came out of their workshops to see what was happening.

Ken, being Ken, pulled every bloody lever in the truck, including scheduling the afterburner, which was massively over-fuelled and put out an 80-metre unlit smoke plume.

I yelled to Ken, "SHUT HER DOWN," which he did.

"What was the EGT?" I asked.

"I forgot to look once the revs picked up," he responded.

Now we have to do the whole deal again, refuel and set engine rpm at 80 percent.

This time, we got a reading of just 420 degrees, which was way too cold. We shut the engine off, and I removed the afterburner command ring and took it into the Australian Airlines Hangar. I asked if there was a resident welder around. I met their welding specialist and asked him to chop a hundred millimetres out of this ring and place some good tack welds to join it back together.

Whilst in this hangar, I asked if they had a fuel dump.

"Yes, we have about fifty jet fuel barrels around the side. How many do you want?"

"Heaps," I replied.

These guys delivered six as a starting point. We fired the truck up again, and the temperature stabilised at 560 degrees. I knew we wanted it around 650 degrees, so I returned to the welding shop for another haircut on our command ring. This time, a further 40 mm was removed, and we again went for a start. Our temperature had settled at 670 degrees, and we were rapidly running out of time.

I told Ken, "Now we have our engine temp where we want it; let's go for afterburner." We fired up again and set the revs at 60 percent, and I signalled to Ken to select the afterburner and streak it. He did, but all we got was this massive fuel flume again and a slight rumble in the tailpipe, with the burner trying to light. I removed a control mechanism that throws the afterburner fuel control feed and shortened its stroke.

Our next test was getting exciting. The afterburner was leaner and starting to light off, but not quite right. Once again, I shortened the amount of stroke the afterburner control could have. We went for a start and a selected afterburner ignition test through the rev range of 40 percent to 105 percent. Once Ken lit the burner at full rpm, he could not stop the truck on the concrete. It launched forward towards one of Tullamarine's main runways and stopped about 100 metres short of it and an incoming aircraft.

Amazingly, the incoming flight was carrying my new teammate, Tom Brown from Detroit, Ken's wife and her dad. They were all looking out of the aircraft windows, amazed to see the jet truck below them on Melbourne's main airport runway. Once Tom was cleared through customs, he told the airport security he needed to go out onto the runway, not out the airport's front door. So, Tom, Ken and I had a reunion on the airport runway and raced that night. Tom and myself in the funny cars and Ken driving the truck like he had done it forever. That night, Ken ran close to 320 km/h in this incredible jet truck—bloody fun times.

Sadly, Craig Arfons was killed in July 1989 whilst attempting to beat Ken's world water speed record at Lake Jackson in Florida. Craig was young, just 39 years of age. RIP Craig.

Breakdown Leads to Meeting a Legend

On another trip with Ken Warby, we were leaving Perth to race in Adelaide, taking turns driving. We were in our infamous Cab-over Louisville, left-hand drive, over-width truck. We towed a purpose-built trailer that carried the two jet-powered race cars, one sitting above the other. The trailer had a tri-axle single-wheel configuration, and the wheels were an eight-bolt Dodge/Chrysler pattern.

We had travelled non-stop across the country and were approaching Port Augusta in South Australia. We had travelled about 2,300 kilometres from Perth and were making good time. We planned to arrive in Adelaide at about midnight on Friday. We were racing on Saturday night at Adelaide's International Raceway.

A truck passed us on the outskirts of town and called us on the CB radio, telling us we had a loose wheel. We pulled over the first chance we got and discovered that four of the eight studs on that wheel had broken. Amazingly, we had only checked our lug nuts about 300 kilometres before. We tightened up the existing nuts and limped into Port Augusta. I immediately started grabbing all the tools we needed and got to work on removing the wheel with the broken studs. I told Ken that if we remove the other leading wheel, we can punch two studs out of that drum and have a 6-stud arrangement on both of our left-side trailer wheels.

Doing this would take a couple of hours, but we can still make it to Adelaide in plenty of time. Ken didn't like this idea, and I did appreciate that these race cars were his babies. I told Ken that Adelaide is only 300 kilometres away. If we do the stud swap idea, we can check them for tightness every 100 kilometres. If we stopped here, we could be asking for trouble, as it was a rough area.

Ken was adamant that we would find studs and nuts in town and do our repairs in the morning. When the local Chrysler dealer opened, we were there with a sample of the nuts and studs we urgently needed. The young guy on the counter claimed he had never seen anything like these parts. He asked us what sort of truck they were off, and we didn't know. He looked through his parts boxes for some time, returned with nothing, and said, "I can't help you, I'm afraid."

I had a friend who owned a huge wrecking yard on the western side of town, and we had passed it coming in. I rang my mate Leon Carpenter, who owned this yard, and described our lug nut setup. He suggested we come on out and look at what was in his yard. We agreed, and he came down to pick us up. We looked at several of his light truck axles, but nothing matched. Leon made several calls and thought he had a lead on these parts.

The location was around 50 kilometres away, and I was stressing about the time now. Then, as we were about to take off, Leon said to a mate in his yard.

"Bob, do you want to come for a ride?"

Bob jumped in, and we set off on our journey. We were introduced to Bob properly just as we were getting into town.

Bob asked, "What are you chasing exactly?"

"Six of these suckers," I said and showed him the sample stud and nut. He straight away said the part name and quoted the part number.

"They will have these in the Chrysler Dealership downtown."

"No, that was our first stop this morning,"

I thought, *This Bob was a wise guy, quoting part numbers; what bullshit.*

Again, Bob said, "They will definitely have these."

Leon turned around and took us to the dealership. We all walked into the same counter and saw the guy we had dealt with a few hours previously.

Bob went up to the parts guy and said, "Get us six-wheel studs and six-wheel nuts," and quoted the part numbers from memory.

The young parts guy raced off and surfaced about two minutes later with our parts. We all drove back to where our rig was stranded, and I said, "Bob, I am amazed. How on earth did you know those part numbers?"

Leon stepped in before Bob could answer and said, "This is Mr Chrysler; he is the guy who designed and jointly built the Australian Chrysler Valiant Charger."

We had met the legendary Bob (Robert) Hubbach, Chrysler's Senior Design Corp Manager. A guy who designed the Valiant Charger using parts from other model Chryslers, tacking them all together. Chrysler USA said, "OK, let's build it." I believe this car was the biggest seller of its day.

Bob later went on to help design the Dodge Viper, the Dodge Copperhead and Chrysler Atlantic concept car, based on a 1930s Bugatti Atlantique. The Atlantic was an absolute stunner, but sadly, this car never went into production. The prototype resides in the Chrysler Museum in Auburn Hills, Michigan.

We got our truck going and made the racetrack in time, but we never forgot our experience with Leon and his mate Bob.

Sadly, Leon was murdered by a couple of drug-crazed arseholes a couple of years later. What a waste.

Learning More About My Hero

I didn't get to meet Donald Campbell CBE, but he was the first person I was obsessed with beating in my land speed quest. He was my motivation to build and drive fast cars. I left school at 12 to fulfil that dream after a run-in with the headmaster about parking my car in his shaded spot.

Donald came to Australia in 1963-64 to break the land and water speed records. He is still the only man to have broken both records in the same year. Donald broke the land speed record at Lake Eyre, a large dry salt lake in South Australia. He also set the world water speed record on the last day of 1964 at Lake Dumbleyung in Western Australia.

Donald was the son of a famous father, Sir Malcolm Campbell MBE. Sir Malcolm held many speed records on land and water and died of natural causes at 63. He was one of the few racers in those days not to be killed whilst attempting speed records.

Unfortunately, Donald died attempting to up his own water speed record in 1967 on Coniston Water in the UK.

In the 1990s, I got to meet a man by the name of Evan Green. Evan was a great racer in his own right and a rally champion. He is known as a gentleman racer, with a remarkable act of sportsmanship that cost him a chance of winning the 1968 London-Sydney Marathon.

Evan stopped to tow Scotsman Andrew Cowan out of trouble in the Flinders Ranges. Cowan was fifth at the time and went on to win the event. But, unfortunately, this act of sportsmanship put Evan Green out of race contention.

Evan was the strategist, publicist, and keyman for Donald Campbell's land speed record attempt at Lake Eyre in 1964. This meeting with Evan Green occurred when he joined us at Lake Gairdner on one of our record attempts.

He told a few great stories about Donald's exploits and why breaking the record took him so long. Yes, there was a lot of bad weather, but Evan told us several times that they had prepared the car for him to run, only to find his Donga (living quarters) empty. Donald had caught a plane the night before to drink and socialise with the rich and famous in Adelaide.

The other great story told by Evan Green was about the South Australian and Federal Governments' financial help to Donald Campbell. They had spent the equivalent of $40 million in today's money, bringing him to Australia to break these records. The cost of infrastructure and preparing the tracks and equipment was enormous, given the remote locations for these record attempts and the two years it took him to set these records.

I told Evan, "I can't even get our government to spend the cost of a postage stamp to respond to our requests for help, let alone them constructively assist us."

I am still amazed about Donald Campbell and the support that he got. Of course, I appreciate that it was in a different time and era, but boy, was that some help and cash injection.

Big Tom The Wrecker

Big Tom was born in Glasgow, Scotland, a thickset man nearly 2 metres tall, with fiery red hair and beard and an even more fiery temper. Tom had the broadest Scottish accent I have ever heard. He was a great mate and was with me on many of my life's adventures. Tom worked as a panel beater and paint sprayer, and he was a bloody hard worker and an even harder fighter.

It took me a long time to understand what he was saying, as most of his talk was swearing in Glaswegian slang. Tom could never go anywhere without starting a fight, and after the dust had settled, I would ask.

"What on earth was that all about?"

Mostly, he would answer, "I dunno laddie, they said something to me, but I dinney catch it."

Tom rang me one morning, very excited, and after repeating himself several times, announcing, "There is a wrecking yard for rent in Bayswater. I've just seen it in the paper, laddie. So, get your arse in gear, and we'll go and take a wee look."

I went to Tom's house and shoehorned him into my ute, which was a tough job because his right knee joint was very bad from playing football. He had to sit sideways across my bench seat but never complained. He just battled on. We responded to this ad and met the owner and licence holder at his yard. We did a deal to rent it for two years, with the idea of Tom managing it and me being part-time, working between race meetings.

We excitedly moved into our new premises, but there was a minor issue: there were absolutely zero cars to wreck and be able to sell parts from. I recalled an old mate in Brisbane who purchased Australia's first car-crushing machine, and he made a fortune. Let's call him Ron. Ron would drive the streets of Brisbane, searching for abandoned cars. If the tyres were flat and covered in leaves, he would then radio his tow truck operator, and the wreck was a small block of steel quicker than you could say "Jack Robinson." The Brisbane shire loved him, and many discrete calls came from them to Ron because, as far as they were concerned, he was doing the city a big favour by cleaning up these wrecks.

My idea was to do the same. We visited many flats, housing units, airport dump sites, and panel shops. All had vehicles where the owners had disappeared or abandoned them. We paid a very nominal price for these cars to the people who wanted them cleaned up. Within a month, we had a yard full of vehicles, mainly old or unpopular models. However, we had a plan, and it was working. From there, we could sell some parts and then afford to update to later model stock.

Two months later, we acquired a truck with a massive flatbed tray and our own tow truck. Tom was an absolute classic minding the store. When we started having later model stock, many young guys would come into the shop, which was open all weekend. Tom would bark at these tough guys, asking what they were chasing. Then, immediately give them a price for the parts they wanted. He would follow through by getting them to put their cash on the counter to prove they had the money and weren't wasting his time.

Tom was doing a lot of walking around, playing havoc with his knee; he was starting to develop a very bad limp. I was still driving him to and from work. As a joke, I kept teasing him, saying that bloody Aussies have bad knees, but they keep going, not limping around like a gimp.

Finally, Tom went to the hospital, and the surgeons completely removed his right knee joint, fusing the bones together and making it straight. To this day, I have never heard of anyone else having this procedure. He came back to work about a week after his operation on crutches. He never complained for a minute. He brought the remnants of his mangled knee in a big glass jar, and boy was it a sight. It had some severe calcium balls and bone fragments in his trophy jar.

Tom returned to work almost immediately and said, "Well, laddie, are we gonna sit around like two stale bottles of piss or get a fish supper?" He had a way with words, did Tom.

All the young guys who came into the yard would be amazed at how he was sitting. He could sit with his right leg straight out without a chair or anything to support it. When people asked me why he sat like that, I told them he was a habitual show-off and wanted to challenge anyone who thought they could hold their leg out longer than him.

A few weeks later, I purchased a 4-door VE Valiant VIP V8 automatic from a new contact who owned a repossession yard. I was excited to get Tom into a car of his own finally. I picked up this vehicle and drove it back to our yard. She was beautiful. I pulled into the front yard of our business and summonsed the gimp, as Tom now referred to himself.

"I've bought you a car, mate; come and have a sit in it." I opened the driver's door, and Tom shuffled around on his crutches and sat his arse behind the wheel. He got his left leg in OK, but his straight right leg hit the end of the door, about at knee level. I told him, "I will make some mods. You get back to work." I made some brackets and moved the driver's bucket seat back. Once again, we tried to get Tom into this car, but his leg was still hitting the door at about shin level. Again, I extended these brackets further, but still no success. Finally, I grabbed the driver's bucket seat, stormed into the office, slung the seat on the ground and told Tom to sell it. I told him, "Now come on out and see if you can sit in this car, and if you still can't, I'm going to burn it!"

Tom came out for his fourth attempt. He slid his body diagonally through the driver's door and across to the far side rear seat, and we succeeded. Finally, Tom could swivel his body into position sitting on the back seat. His feet could reach the pedals, and his right foot could still function and control the throttle.

This was one of the funniest sights I had seen in years. Tom drove his car from the back seat, with me in the front passenger seat. We got very funny looks pulling up at the lights. People would casually look across to see who was driving the car. But, of course, they would see no driver, only me in the front passenger seat.

Sadly, the wrecking business ended abruptly when the police discovered we had a metre-high stack of old licence plates. The licence plates should've been returned along with the proper paperwork stating the owner, vehicle make, model, VIN, etc. The police weren't pleased, and our licence was cancelled, forcing us to shut up shop.

Ken Warby in one of his jet cars with me on his team.

L - R Tom Brown, me and Ken Warby with two of Ken's jet cars and a jet truck. Aussie Invader 1 in disguise, ready for a Vauxhall car commercial.

Early Trips, Travels and Tales in Australia

Ready for racing with Ken Warby's jet-racing spectacular.

-13-

The First Record Attempt

With *Aussie Invader 2* completed, the next challenge was funding the attempt, which could only come from finding more sponsors. The logistics of getting *Aussie Invader 2* and its support team to such a remote location was significant. There was no infrastructure for at least 160 kilometres, and we needed to operate there for up to three weeks.

I don't think anyone can contemplate this, and when I say nothing, I mean absolutely nothing. We had to take everything, including toilet blocks, cooking facilities, tents, water and food to feed a large team. We also had to take everything for the car and engine, including a workshop with tools, fuel and spares.

I was keen to share the event with all the *Aussie Invader* people who had helped get us this far: crew, wives, and sponsors. About seventy-odd people. This group included our *Aussie Invader* land speed team, RAAF support, a Channel 7 film crew, surveyors, and Confederation of Australian Motor Sport (CAMS) timing officials. A large group of people in a very remote location was highly challenging.

The large team arrived at Mount Ive Station at Lake Gairdner in South Australia. We had travelled over 160 kilometres of rough dirt road and driven 2,200 kilometres from Perth with a mass of borrowed and sponsored equipment. Cheryl and I knew only about two-thirds of the people there; many didn't know me. The team's essential crew were all experts in their fields, giving their time for free and taking leave from their jobs.

Finally, on the 3rd of December 1993, we arrived at the Lake, exhausted from the long and arduous trip. The choking red dust covered the convoy, with *Aussie Invader 2* having taken a pounding for the last 160 kilometres on its trailer. The good thing was that this car was built tough and would take far worse treatment than that over the next few weeks. We collapsed into outbuildings recovered from the old atomic test site at Maralinga to the North.

The December date reflected the local knowledge of sunny and dry weather conditions over the last twenty years. However, we woke to the sound of rain, the first December rain in twenty-two years. Most of the lake bed was awash, and the track surveyors predicted weeks for the water to recede. I said, hopefully, it would clear in a couple of days, and miraculously, I was proved right. The wind got up and blew the surface water away to some of the more remote reaches of the Lake, and we were back in action! With the water gone, the jet car moved onto the salt flats. It was housed in a large tent hangar/workshop. The sun was fierce, and we needed the shade desperately.

We also had the blessing of the traditional Aboriginal landowners and looked around at this magical place. All you could see was salt in every direction, and you could even witness the curvature of the Earth. It was a miraculous sight.

We were now ready for the big event. *Aussie Invader 2* was rolled from its transporter onto Lake Gairdner. The car was set up for racing based on the salt conditions at Bonneville in the USA. It proved to be an issue, as Lake Gairdner's surface was much harder than we thought it would be. Our problems were only beginning, with many more obstacles and setbacks ahead.

The First Record Attempt

Before we left Perth, we needed to get the CAMS timing officials' clearance to be permitted to race, and their WA chief technical guy got the job. Unfortunately for us, this was the same guy who had told the world we would never get our car to the salt. We were not sure why he took this stance, but he seemed to not want us to succeed, which was disappointing. We had enough hurdles to overcome to get this record, so we didn't need an official whose job it was to confirm us in the record books, making it even more difficult.

He had inspected our car before it left and picked out a few issues he thought might be problematic in a serious crash. We gladly obliged and modified the car as requested, and our thoughts and focus were now on ensuring the car was running properly and breaking the Australian land speed record.

We met up with CAMS guys at the lake who were very racecar savvy with years of experience in many facets of motorsport. They mentioned that they had received a communication from the WA CAMS technical chief who had got us to modify our car. He had just sent through a defect concern about the construction of our windscreen, its materials and structural strength. His concern was this could fail in a bird strike situation.

This issue had never been discussed at our initial technical inspection. It created a major problem for us, being 2,200 kilometres from home and 300 kilometres from the nearest town. We could only assume he was trying to make it hard for us to race and felt pretty pissed about it.

I wasn't the only person upset. Many people in my team had worked for years to get this car built and ready to tackle the records at Lake Gairdner. However, there was a collective determination to overcome this setback. We put our heads together to see if we could devise a test to satisfy the CAMS officials at this late stage with what we had available.

Luckily for us, one of the team members had brought a high-powered crossbow with him. We had a second canopy and cockpit screen in our many spares, so team members Don Bremner, Keith Lovatt and Dan Boseley soon established a test that the onsite CAMS guys approved.

We would fire crossbow bolts at the car's windscreen at close range. These bolts had a projectile speed of about 600 feet per second (185 metres per second). Should the screen shatter or crack, we would be in big trouble. Nevertheless, we removed the windshield, set it up in a safe location, and videoed our tests.

The first three bolts ricocheted off the 12 mm thick Mulford Plastics screen. All the people present, including the CAMS officials and us, were very impressed. We then decided to set the windscreen in a vertical position and fire a bolt directly at it. The tip of the arrowhead penetrated the 12 mm thick Mulford Plastics windscreen by a mere 5 mm, and it didn't crack or shatter.

At 600 feet per second, a crossbow bolt travels at well over 400 mph (640 km/h), with this sharp projectile barely penetrating our windscreen. This satisfied the CAMS officials that it was safe for a bird strike at 600 mph (960 km/h), and our engineering guru, John "Ackers" Ackroyd, also confirmed it. So, we were now set and ready to race.

We never saw it tested with a bird strike but were confident it was fit for purpose when we hit a timing stand at over 800 km/h, but that story comes later!

Most people don't realise that on a perfectly flat surface on the earth, anything over four kilometres away starts to

The First Record Attempt

disappear into the horizon due to the earth's curvature. I found this out later when I began to drive the car. All my high-speed driving had been at dragstrips, so it was never a problem. However, later on, when I was driving the car at high speeds on the salt flats, I would get out of the car and think to myself, *My neck feels stiff*. I couldn't for the life of me work out why.

After most runs, the team and I would review the cameras' footage inside and outside the car. The internal footage of my cockpit kept showing me trying to lift myself out of the seat as I was driving. I was pressing my head against the top of the canopy because you could only see about four kilometres ahead due to the Earth's curvature. But, of course, you always want to see as far ahead as possible at very quick speeds.

All you have are marker barrels to reference your distance against the vast whiteness of the salt. I should have had an unobstructed view right to the end of the track, but I could only see about four or five barrels gradually lowering into the horizon. My natural reaction was to try and increase my visual distance by lifting myself out of the seat. This is because you would have to react very early to avoid any object in your way or correct your steering if going off course. At these speeds, a kilometre was travelled in just a few seconds. Once I realised what was causing my stiff neck, I managed to keep my arse glued to the seat.

We also had spotters around the track to warn of potential dangers. Tracks were always checked before a run, but spotters couldn't see everything. Animals had the perfect right to wander around, and we were in their environment. Hitting an animal at these speeds was game over for everyone.

We held a meeting at the base camp to work out our plan of attack. At the crew meeting, we planned that I should only go about 160 - 240 km/h (100 – 150 mph) for my first test pass. I was to ease myself into driving the car and checking that all was well. I set out northbound, putting on the afterburner for a short blast, and I thought, *Right 240 km/h, here we come!* Well, that plan soon went out of the window, and my enthusiasm got the better of me. The car felt great, and I took the car to nearly 500 km/h, much to my amazement and the crew's disapproval. They certainly let me know their feelings when I returned. My response to them was, "Why start at the bottom when you can start at the top!"

However, in subsequent runs, the wheels started to cause all sorts of issues with the steering. We would get one good run in, only to find the return run was a disaster. It was just getting too dangerous to run the car at these speeds and not be able to steer properly. If we ran off course, we could hit a marker barrel, cameras or timing equipment. If that had happened, we would have destroyed the car and almost certainly ingested debris into the engine. In addition, I might not have come out of it unscathed.

One of the subsequent runs was unbelievable. The timers had said we had hit a peak speed of 900 km/h (560 mph). That speed was over 250 km/h more than the current Australian record, set by Donald Campbell. But, we couldn't back it up on the return run and write ourselves into the history books. Putting two runs together in opposite directions within an hour, as required by the FIA rules, was proving to be a big issue. We also needed to check the car over, refuel and repack chutes before setting off again.

We nursed speeds higher and higher and travelled at close to record speeds. However, I was mindful that losing steering at this point could prove fatal. One erratic steering wheel movement could send the car into a spin. We discovered the problem was with the front wheels, unlike the rear wheels, which had a "V" shaped profile. Instead, the front wheels had a convex profile, similar to Richard Noble's current *Thrust 2* land speed car.

The wheels were machined from solid aerospace-grade aluminium, and the car slid all over the place with no rubber tyres for grip. These wheels would have been ideal for running on a hard desert-baked surface, but the front wheels' flatter profile appeared unsuitable for Lake Gairdner's hard salt.

We had a spare rear wheel and decided to put it on the front to see if things improved, and they did. It was still not right or very safe, with different profiles on each front wheel, but it had shown us where the problem lay. We thought we could nurse *Aussie Invader 2* to get us past Donald Campbell's 649 km/h record. But, it certainly wasn't safe enough to attempt the 1,019 km/h (633 mph) world record of Richard Noble and *Thrust 2*.

Sadly, the media had invited the State Manager of Ampol, one of our main sponsors and a group from Channel 7 Television. It was a significant inconvenience as they believed the Australian record was about to be broken. We were only in the early stages of testing, and with the problems we were having, we were nowhere near ready to challenge for the record.

On the next run, I slowed the car down to about 400 km/h (250 mph), and the cockpit started filling with fumes and smoke. Even with my breathing mask and oxygen, it was almost impossible to get my breath. I was choking, and the fumes were stinging my eyes. I couldn't see where I was going. I slowed the car down to about 300 km/h and punched the canopy open with my right hand. I held the canopy up whilst steering with my left to get some fresh air into the cockpit so that I could breathe. I wasn't sure what had caused the smoke and was very worried about a fire in the front of the car. It turned out that excess grease on the front wheel bearings had caused the problem. The team worked to fix the issue for the next few hours, but it was another delay we couldn't afford.

Then, just as we were ready to run again, another issue arose: the wind was starting to increase. *Aussie Invader 2's* design limited it to running in a maximum 8 km/h crosswind. Over that, the car could be blown off course. At the speeds we were travelling, even a tiny amount of drift sidewards would mean the car would deviate a long way off its correct line. If that happened, we could again hit equipment or miss breaking the timing beam, making the run void.

I was becoming frustrated and impatient with all the delays and problems. We were now losing the ideal weather conditions we had experienced to run in. The wind was gusting up to about 15 km/h, but I felt it was more head-on than a crosswind. Despite their warnings, I overruled the team and decided to give it another try. The team were concerned I might not return if I attempted this run.

We started the run, but I was proved wrong immediately, and the team was right, as I lost the car off the start line and had to abort the run. The wind blowing us off course was getting stronger, and today was the 13th of December! I am a superstitious man when it comes to racing and would never usually race on the 13th. Still, despite this, we continued even with the crosswind as time was running out.

Due to all the issues with wheel design and trying to compensate with workarounds, the front wheel bearing had been severely overworked. On the next run, one of the front wheel bearings decided to let go at almost 600 km/h (375 mph). It caused one of the front wheels to lock up and the car to slide sideways, heading straight for the cameras and crew. The only thing I could do was pull the chutes, and hopefully, this would "tug" the back of the car and straighten her up. Thank God it did.

That night, the crew and I worked feverishly to change the wheel bearings and swap another rear wheel to the front. However, all our work was in vain, as overnight, there was an electrical storm, and we woke to the worst news possible. A bush fire was burning one side of the Lake, started by lightning, and the whole Lake was awash. We had no choice but to pack up quickly and go home.

A massive weather low was heading in from the south. Although it usually took two hours to pack the car onto the transporter, we did it in an hour. The car's wheels had just been locked in place on the transporter when 160 km/h winds hit the Lake. A 5-tonne truck, fully loaded with tooling and accessories, was pushed 30 metres, even with the handbrake on. Remember, this was December. It shouldn't rain, let alone get the massive storm we experienced!

Looking back on our first visit and attempt at Lake Gairdner in 1993, we were naive, not knowing what to expect. It was understandable, though, as no one had raced there. Also, our money was limited, but with the sponsor's support and Ampol being a major one, we learned a lot to help with our second visit.

As soon as we arrived home in late December of 1993, we planned our return as quickly as possible, hoping to return around March of the following year. The long-range weather forecasts looked promising.

We took much of what we learned from our first venture to Lake Gairdner to plan our next visit. We modified the car slightly during these three months and reprofiled the front wheels. The next time, we would have a complete village to transport back to the Lake, with every piece of equipment sponsored. The village included a proper kitchen, toilet and wash block, generator sets, etc. All of which was set up and tested at Pearce Air Force base.

We had to borrow more money to return to the Lake in three months. Our properties had increased in value, so we could leverage our funds and raise the necessary capital. We were accumulating a lot of debt that we needed to repay. All of this added to both Cheryl's and my stress levels. We relied on Scotch and coke, sometimes as early as 10 a.m., to get us through, which wasn't good. It was certainly not the answer, but it did help us deal with the many people and pressures we were experiencing.

The First Record Attempt

Arriving at Lake Gairdner for the first time in December 1993.

Photoshoot with Aussie Invader 2 before we go racing.

ROSCO THE FASTEST AUSSIE ON EARTH

We were constantly cleaning Aussie Invader 2 as the salt was very corrosive.

A flooded Lake Gairdner - running this car was a constant battle against the elements.

The First Record Attempt

The car is prepared for a record run. Everything is checked and rechecked.

Ready to attack the Australian record.

Cheryl and Bryce hitch a ride as the car is pushed to the start line (above).

The team retrieves the car after a run (right).

The First Record Attempt

Team workshop on the salt with hours spent preparing the car (above).

Everyone played their part to try and break the record.

We still have the windscreen we tested with a crossbow bolt.

-14-

Return to The Lake

In March 1994, we returned to Lake Gairdner for a second time. Managing the logistics for the first visit and a team of about seventy people was a massive nightmare. It had fallen on Team Manager Pete Taylor and Cheryl for the first attempt on the lake, but it had been a big headache. For the second attempt, we wanted a dedicated Project Manager. However, we decided we would have to manage the second attempt ourselves again. We tried to recruit a Project Manager, but they wanted a lot of money that we just didn't have.

We had acquired a monstrous forklift, and two crew guys and I took all the equipment on the back of three massive trucks. It was a very eventful trip, with the trucks being over length, over width and very tall. We pulled a few overhead powerlines down before leaving the city. We were lucky not to be arrested on our way to South Australia!

GKR Transport was delivering the crew village that we tested at Pearce Air Force Base. They were coming to Lake Gairdner from the other direction, and we would meet them there. Hopefully, we would arrive two days before them so we could set up and unload everything as soon as they arrived.

We turned onto the dirt track leading to Lake Gairdner, only to find that a significant storm had flooded the road and was closed for road trains. We managed to pull some strings and eventually got our trucks through, but this had set us back a couple of days. So, we arrived at about the same time as the GKR Transport trucks, which certainly wasn't ideal. We hastily unloaded our forklift and then unpacked the units from the GKR trucks. We did this as quickly as possible, so the GKR drivers could make it back along the dirt road to Iron Knob before it flooded again. Then, we set up the village, hoping to get the perfect weather window.

Cheryl and I had brought our young son Bryce again. He was easy to look after because he was constantly experiencing new things and became part of the crew, and he loved it. His childhood was full of fun, and he learned many new skills along the way. At 6, Bryce learned to drive his own car across the vast expanse of Lake Gairdner, a Mini Moke. He worked alongside all the teams, was a great team member, and was happy living the dream. Cheryl and I were so proud of how he handled anything thrown his way in such a remote location.

We all lived at the side of the lake in team areas: Land Speed Team, Channel 7 Media Team, RAAF - Fire, Rescue & Medic Team and Cook, Surveyors and Timing Officials' Team. We decided to have regular team leader meetings to stop everyone from doing their own thing. Coordination was the key to getting the car runs happening consistently and well organised. The good thing was we had a lot of RAAF people who were either currently serving or retired, and they knew the drill. One person not in the right place at the right time could mean a record run was void.

It worked well, and the camaraderie was good between everyone. Still, there were times when the pressure and homesickness got to people. It is hard to explain to someone who has never been in a remote location with no escape. You are on your own, under a lot of pressure, even strong people crack, and Cheryl had many a big guy come to her very upset. We were all there to support each other with a common goal of getting this record.

There were little disputes among the team members, but that's human nature, and they all got sorted. Remember, everyone here was a volunteer, giving up work and pay and sometimes taking a whole year's holiday to make these attempts happen. If you had a family crisis at home, you couldn't just leave! There were 160 kilometres of very rough dirt track road before you got to anything that resembled a more driveable surface.

We had to leave a few team members back in Perth for the second attempt, which was sad, but this time, we were a leaner, more essential, people-only crew. We learnt a lot from the first trip. Non-crew members were a distraction and an overhead we could ill afford.

As we arrived, prevailing winds had blown surface water from some 50 kilometres away straight up the lake and over our track. The water cut our race track size down to about 13 kilometres, which was frustrating and not ideal, but we thought we could work with it. We had no choice, and we just had to make it work.

On one of the first runs, we clocked 707 km/h (440 mph), far exceeding Donald Campbell's record of 649 km/h set in 1964. The car behaved better with the new profiled wheels, so we thought things were looking up. All we had to do was back it up with a similar speed in the opposite direction, and the Australian record was in the bag.

We set off on the return run within the hour, hoping and praying nothing went wrong this time. The run looked great, and I exited the measured mile, knowing the salt was in poor condition about three kilometres ahead of me. But that shouldn't have been a problem, and I should've been able to stop in plenty of time. I deployed the chutes, and both failed! Now, I was in trouble, knowing I wouldn't be able to stop before hitting the soft, water-logged part of the track. I hit it at about 500 km/h and immediately knew the car was severely damaged. Saltwater was everywhere, I was soaked, and the inside of the cockpit was a bloody mess. Still, I felt pleased that I had backed up the previous run. I knew it was fast, and we would almost certainly have the Australian record we had chased all these years.

The recovery crew found me sitting on top of the car, surrounded by water. The good thing was that although water was everywhere, it wasn't deep enough to have affected the engine. We towed the car back to camp and learned from Pete Taylor and the CAMS timing guys that the 10-kilometre timer hadn't tripped. It meant we hadn't recorded a time on the return run, so once again, we had the record snatched from our grasp!

A large portion of the floor had been ripped away by hitting the water at such high speed. I remarked, "We would have probably set a world water speed record as well." There was nothing to do but make light of the situation we found ourselves in. It was worrying that we seemed to be back where we left off, the last time, battling the "Spirit of the Lake."

Channel 7 flew an RAAF member and me in their helicopter to the RAAF Air Force base in Adelaide to get parts to build a new floor. We got six large sheets of 4 mm thick aluminium, and within a week, the car was repaired, set up and running well.

On the 27th of March 1994, at 5:45 p.m., we managed a great first run of 814 km/h (506 mph) northbound. The issue for us was that only one chute had deployed. It meant we were nearly four kilometres further down the track than we wanted.

We had to turn the car around and tow it back to the return start line within the critical hour. We had to repack the chutes, refuel and check Aussie Invader 2 over before we could go again. The team were magnificent and did it with time to spare. I blasted down the track with full afterburner against the setting sun, which was magical.

Once I stopped, the rest of the crew ran over to me, and we heard what we had wanted to hear over the two-way radios for so long. The southbound run had been slightly slower, but the two-way average speed over the measured mile was 802.6 km/h (500 mph). This was a new Australian record! There was a full moon and a beautiful sunset, and we couldn't have asked for a better setting.

We had a big celebration on the lake that night. The chefs and RAAF team members helped put on a massive party, which was fantastic. We were also honoured to have Air Vice Marshall Neil Smith there. He had flown over from Perth and arrived just in time to witness the record. Neil being here was perfect after all the help he had given us to get the car to the start line.

The next day after the celebrations, I was ready to tackle the next record, the world record of Richard Noble and *Thrust 2*. The car was running well, and even though we had a reduced track length, what we had available was in perfect condition. We pushed the car faster and faster on that water-shortened track, but there was nowhere to stop. On one of our subsequent runs, I hit a top speed of 956 km/h (nearly 600 mph) and stopped just 500 metres from a water-logged patch of the soft salt lake. Faster runs were out of the question; we couldn't stop in time.

Lake Gairdner is a magical place. The problem for us was we were experiencing the dark magic of its nature. It seemed the "Spirit of the Lake" had decided we had outstayed our welcome this time. It didn't want us to take the outright record and made the Australian record bloody tough. *Aussie Invader 2* should have easily smashed the old Australian record, but it had taken two years and two visits. We had been made to work very hard for every run and every kilometre per hour we had achieved.

With no chance of the lake drying out within a week and commitments by crew members back home, who were all volunteers, we decided to pack up. Our funds and provisions were also running very low. So, that was it. We travelled home after achieving one of our goals and planning how to get to the next one. We needed to regroup, recharge and re-energise our spirits and finances.

When we got home from Lake Gairdner, *Aussie Invader 2* was stripped, cleaned thoroughly, and checked for salt damage. Salt is so corrosive, left for too long, salt would permanently corrode parts of the car.

Planning for our next trip started almost immediately. The logistics of taking a crew of 17 back to Lake Gairdner with associated equipment rested with Cheryl, who by now had this down to a fine art.

A larger tail fin was fitted to give better directional stability for the faster runs we needed to get that elusive world record.

Return to The Lake

Back on Lake Gairdner, it's just a magical place.

Waiting for the support crew after hitting water at 500 km/h.

The floor is ripped from the car. Pete Taylor and I inspected the damage. It takes a few days to repair.

Ready for another run at the Australian record.

Bad news: the 10-kilometre timer didn't trip, so no record run was recorded!

Leaving the start line trying to back up an excellent first run.

The crew celebrate. Finally, the Australian record is ours!

New Australian record on the 27th March 1994.

Media interviews are part of the job.

It is the perfect setting with a full moon and sunset to welcome in the new Australian record of 802.6 km/h (500 mph).

-15-

Inches From Disaster

In February 1995, we returned to the lake for the third time. It had been almost a year since I had sat in the car. I was about to battle the "Spirit of the Lake" again. However, we couldn't believe it! Just two weeks before we were due to leave for Lake Gairdner, it rained there. The salt was wet, too wet really to run the car, but with sponsorship dollars drying up after this attempt, we couldn't delay it further.

On the first morning of running the car, I don't recall why, but I was singing to myself in the cockpit as I was being towed out to the start line. Team Manager Pete Taylor said it wasn't a song he had heard before and didn't sound like me singing.

Cheryl had also remarked to Pete that there was a peculiar feeling that morning, and Pete agreed something wasn't right. Pete even considered asking me to call off the runs that day, but he knew I would never agree. Then, more strange things started to happen. It was an early start, 4 a.m., and we were ready to run just as the sun rose. Jet engines make more power when the air is denser, so the colder, the better, and sunrise is ideal. Pete also reported that several radios would not communicate with each other. "I could hear people, but they couldn't hear me," he said.

He returned to camp to test the radios and swap them over; strangely, they started to work fine. So, we put it down to a glitch and got on with trying to set a new world land speed record.

We wanted to clock 900 km/h (560 mph) on the first run. I headed down the track, and as I increased my speed to over 500 km/h, the car started to tramline, and I aborted the run. The salt was too soft due to all the rain in the previous weeks. The surface was breaking up and not providing any steering stability; this happened every run. I knew it was going to be a tough day at the office!

Added to the issues we were experiencing, the computer which records the car's performance failed to operate correctly. Instead of showing the current date of the 8th February 1995, it reset itself to 00:00 1st January 1990. Then, on our return run, the unexplained continued, and *Aussie Invader 2* refused to start! We had to call the crew back to help us and check the car, and eventually, we got the engine started.

We always prepared several tracks to race on, so we swapped to another track to try and stop the tramlining issue. Unfortunately, the car veered sharply to the left on the next run. I knew the car was out of control and could do nothing to avoid one of the marker cones.

This cone was sucked straight into the engine and killed it. The only good thing to happen on that run was I realised the car was out of control and quickly cut the power and popped the brake chutes. Engine damage was minimal and confined to the inlet guide vanes in the compressor. Although bad, it was a repair we could carry out at the lake.

The collision with the plastic marker cone meant we had three days to repair the engine and determine why the car was back to not steering straight again. The salt wasn't great, but the steering shouldn't have been that bad. We found that the veering to the left was caused by the afterburner nozzle being 3 mm out of shape. During the repairs to the compressor, the nozzle was re-adjusted, and the next run went as planned.

On top of this, the weather was changing again, with bad weather heading our way. The *Aussie Invader* crew and I were under tremendous pressure to produce a result. We needed the car to perform at speeds we knew it could. Unfortunately, it seemed like one step forward, two back, with resources, patience, and money running very low.

After these runs, I knew the salt was making the car unpredictable. I realised that the car wasn't going to steer straight, and if I was going to set records, I just had to try and manage *Aussie Invader 2's* handling the best I could. I was asked if I might be over-correcting the steering when these issues arose. Perhaps I was; it was hard to say, but I don't think anyone could have driven it any differently, as, at times, it just had a mind of its own.

A different wheel design would have helped, knowing what we did now about the salt surface, but we didn't have that luxury. We certainly didn't have time or finances to design another set of wheels, and we had already reprofiled these once. These wheels cost $20,000 each, and we would need six of them, including the spares.

Over the last two years, the *Aussie Invader* crew had experienced a rollercoaster of highs and lows, but there was one final sting in the tale. The next northbound run went well, exceeding 800 km/h (500 mph). I felt confident, and the car was set for a much faster return run, but it wouldn't bloody start again. The time lost getting it started meant the mandatory hour for a return run had expired.

The southbound run started well, with the car running straight for the first three kilometres. Then, once again, it veered to the left, only gradually but sufficiently to put *Aussie Invader 2* on a collision course with one of the timing markers. I was accelerating at over 800 km/h just as the car hit the 20 mm thick upright of the solid steel timing stand. The timing transmitter's battery and infrared sensor were sucked into the engine, wiping out the compressor. The steel pole ripped into the fibreglass shell, causing severe damage. The multi-million-dollar engine was now effectively a pile of scrap metal.

Luckily, the debris had missed the driver's cockpit, and I walked away unscathed. It was amazing how well the fibreglass body had held up. The 20 mm solid steel support that held the timing device off the ground was bent in a perfect shape that followed the contours of the car's body, incredible.

Driving a car at very high-speed at Lake Gairdner is not excessively dangerous in most circumstances. Speed itself is not the issue. Most people reading this would have flown in a passenger aircraft at over 600 mph; it's very safe. What buggers you up at high speed is if you stop or change direction very quickly, that's not good. Your body's mass wants to keep travelling in its original direction. So, if the car stops, you don't!

Luckily, the timing marker was small, and although it damaged the engine, the debris missed me. It hit the left-hand side of the car, and I was driving, sitting on the right-hand side. One of the biggest fears with driving this type of vehicle is if something breaks when going very fast and you lose control. Things can get very ugly very quickly.

If there was an upside to this incident, it was thanks to our "hot and bothered" auctioneer a few years earlier. Because then, we had purchased three more core engines we could now take our pick from, but they were back in Perth. This fix was a workshop job, so the team packed up, and we returned home.

After returning home, Cheryl, myself and Bryce needed a break, and we were spent. These land speed attempts tested everyone to the extreme. We went away for nine months, racing *Aussie Invader 1* and attending motor shows all over Australia again. We went to Brisbane, Melbourne, Adelaide and Perth. Land speed records were not in our immediate thoughts or on our calendars. The shows and appearances were good money earners for us and helped us to recover some of our depleted finances. We were also trying to repay some of the enormous debts we had incurred on the previous attempts and setting the Australian land speed record.

When we got home, Cheryl said, "I think that's it. We cannot keep doing this." I knew it was hard coming home after having an incredible nine months away. Returning home, looking at a broken car, and then realising the work needed to get back to the lake was just too much for her.

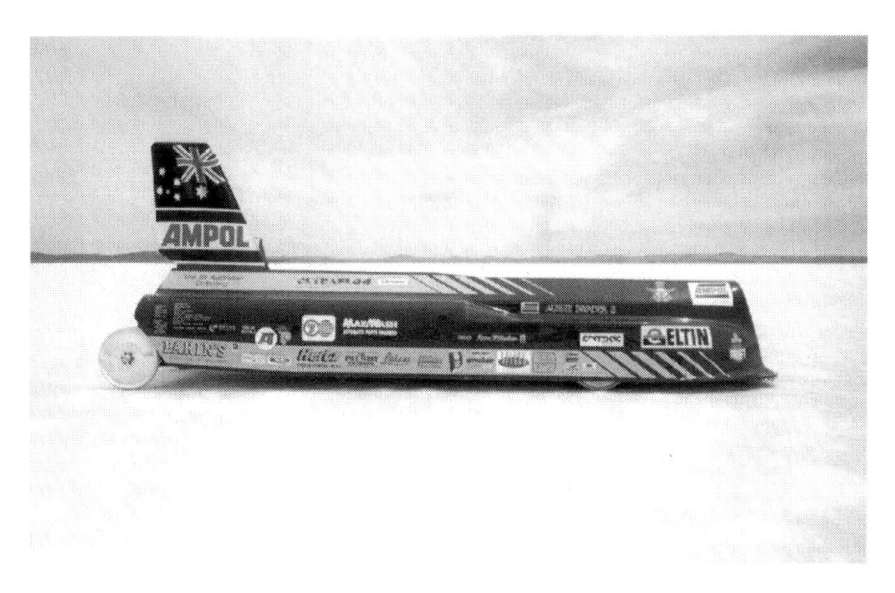

Back on the salt in February 1995, for our third visit with Aussie Invader 2. This time, we are going for the outright record.

A larger tail fin was fitted to help with directional stability.

Inches From Disaster

We return with a very skilled and essential personnel-only crew. Going after that elusive world land speed record.

Pete Taylor and I discussing the last run and track issues.

The team checks the afterburner.

We ran off course due to the soft salt surface, taking many hours to recover the car.

Inches From Disaster

The car constantly needs maintenance and repairs.

Disaster strikes as I hit a timing stand at 800 km/h due to the soft salt.

Aussie Invader 2's body and jet engine are destroyed.

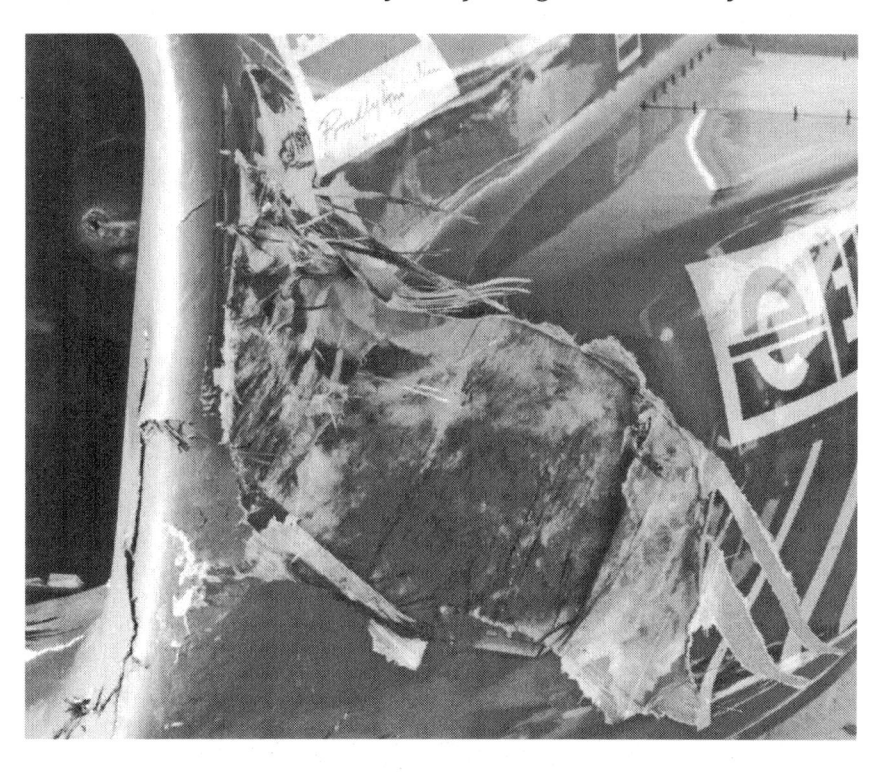

-16-
Aussie Invader 3 – So Near, but So Far

Once the dust had settled, Cheryl and I returned to everyday life and felt more optimistic. Valuable data had been gained from the three previous record attempts. The telemetry, which sent operational data from the car to our computer, revealed that *Aussie Invader 2* created 11-tonnes of downforce over the front wheels at 800 km/h. This was far too much and needed to be rectified. However, with all the damage and hard life *Aussie Invader 2* had been through, we decided it would be easier to build a new car than try and repair and modify this one.

Significant modifications to the tubular steel frame were performed, reducing some 600 mm from the front and making it lighter. We also planned on making the body more rounded, with fewer flat surfaces, which would help with the excessive downforce.

A new one-piece body was built out of fibreglass with a Kevlar carbon fibre-reinforced cockpit. Master fibreglass expert Lindsay Varcoe oversaw it, and *Aussie Invader 3* was born.

It took thousands of volunteer hours to create *Aussie Invader 3*. It had a more powerful "hot-rodded" Mirage ATAR jet engine and a sleeker shape to help with straight-line stability. Top this off with a fantastic paint job featuring the red car draped in a great big Aussie flag. This car was something special and certainly looked the part. It was stunning and ready to race in just eighteen months. We were going to return to the Lake one more time to try and get the elusive world land speed record.

-ooOoo-

Just as *Aussie Invader 3* was being finished, there was land speed action on the other side of the world. In the USA, the Black Rock Desert, Nevada, hosted Craig Breedlove in *Spirit of America - Sonic Arrow*. Unfortunately, he crashed his car at over 650 mph (1,050 km/h) in October 1996 and was luckily uninjured. This accident meant Craig was out for over a year whilst he made repairs to his car. Craig returned to the Black Rock Desert with his car but could never match that speed again.

Craig Breedlove was the first man to reach 400, 500 and 600 mph in land speed cars he designed and built himself. Craig was always my hero as a kid, and I followed his adventures and admired his heroism. I caught up with Craig in his workshop in Rio Vista, California, soon after we had set our Australian land speed record in 1994 with *Aussie Invader 2*. I saw his incredible *Spirit of America - Sonic Arrow* car, powered by a General Electric J79 turbojet engine. This car was a fantastic piece of engineering, and we shared many ideas about how to go very fast.

Most land speed record teams had considered using carbon fibre filament wound wheels for some time. The mass of the solid aluminium wheels was one of the biggest engineering obstacles to try and overcome when breaking a land speed record. Craig took the bull by the horns and developed a carbon filament wound tyre onto an aluminium wheel centre. Sadly, the considerable effort undergone by his team saw these wheels delaminate at high speed. Craig was a pioneer and always willing to try new things, and that's why he was a champion.

The *Aussie Invader* team planned to return to Lake Gairdner in South Australia in February 1997. That was as soon as the salt conditions were right, which was a dry, hard track and no rain forecast. The car would then be shipped to Lake Gairdner, and a slimmed-down crew would fly to meet the car on arrival. Timing officials would be on standby, and if we reached the target speed of 1,000 km/h (600 mph), the officials would fly out for a world record attempt. We were confident of *Aussie Invader 3* being able to hit that speed and more.

The weather at Lake Gairdner was terrible; it just rained, and it rained, month after month. As a result, the lake was never suitable to run on. So, we watched Andy Green and *Thrust SSC* break the current record in September 1997 and up it again a month later.

This new record was a massive 1,227 km/h (763 mph). It was the first official supersonic run, achieving Mach 1.02, with the sonic boom heard across the Black Rock Desert. At the time, we applauded *Thrust SSC* and driver Andy Green. He was the best.

The record Andy set in *Thrust SSC* effectively made *Aussie Invader 3* redundant. We believed we could beat Richard Noble's 1,019 km/h, but we were kidding ourselves if we thought we could better Andy's 1,227 km/h.

Like all land speed cars, *Thrust SSC* had great points and faults. Art Arfons summed it up beautifully when he said this about *Thrust SSC*, "It wasn't a pretty car, but the faster it went, the prettier it got."

Thrust SSC was designed with its rear wheels steerable and off-set, which was quite revolutionary but proved very problematic. The leading rear wheel would destroy the Black Rock Desert Playa, leaving the trailing rear wheel with minimal ground contact. This effectively meant the car was only running on three wheels, one of which was off-centre.

Andy later told me this would cause the car to turn sharply to the left at high speed. To correct it, Andy would have to put the car on full right lock, throttling the engine on and off to keep it going straight. I believe only Andy could have driven *Thrust SSC* to make it perform the way it did and set that record. His fearless approach and jet fighter pilot experience allowed him to manage that colossal 10-tonne beast with its two massive jet engines. No one else would have understood how to overcome that issue and probably been brave enough to push through it.

-ooOOoo-

We got one outing with *Aussie Invader 3*, four years after her completion in 1996. We returned to Lake Gairdner on 23rd March 2000 for the fourth and final time. This time, I had a co-driver, an Australian lady called Paula Elstrek from Melbourne. Paula wanted to break the world land speed record for women. In exchange for a drive in *Aussie Invader 3*, she had promised to bring an agreed amount of sponsorship dollars into the project through her connections in racing. So, we signed contracts for her to do just that and to help promote the *Aussie Invader* project and the record attempts.

I spent a lot of time training Paula in my jet dragster, *Aussie Invader 1*. I helped her obtain her jet car licence, something she needed before she could go anywhere near *Aussie Invader 3*. Paula had raised a deposit amount to book her seat in the car, and for me to help her get the jet dragster licence, she needed to drive *Aussie Invader 3*. We needed those promised big sponsorship dollars from Paula and her backers for her to go after a record.

Paula had raced dragsters and other cars. Still, nothing would compare with the power she would experience with *Aussie Invader 3*. Remember, this car had the power of two complete grids of a Formula One race, some forty F1 cars. You can't get into a car like that and drive it without serious training and safety expertise. I wasn't going to see my team's hard work, blood, sweat and tears destroyed by someone else, especially someone who hadn't fulfilled their promised obligations.

As a passionate Aussie, I had wanted to put Paula in the driving seat of our land-based missile and Australia on the map with a new female world record. To do that, Paula needed to exceed the mark set by the legendary Kitty O'Neil of 512 mph (824 km/h) in the *SMI Motivator* in 1976. I also wanted to improve my Australian record of 802 km/h. Poor salt conditions and bad weather had hampered our previous attempts in *Aussie Invader 2*. The team and I felt the Australian record was unfinished business.

I also believed that the current Australian record of 802 km/h wasn't a true reflection of *Aussie Invader 2's* potential. We had run nearly 180 km/h (110 mph) faster than that record on single runs. But we couldn't back it up for the record books. *Aussie Invader 3* was sleeker, more powerful and running well, so we thought we could set a new Australian record. The big issue for us was we only had a very short time to achieve it due to a lack of funds.

Our arrival at Lake Gairdner was nearly three years after Andy Green had pushed the world record to an unbelievable 1,227 km/h in October 1997. *Thrust SSC* had two jet engines, so if we could exceed Richard Noble's 1983 record of 1,019 km/h for the measured mile, we would have been the fastest single-engine car. Although there was no category for this, it gave us something to aim for. It had been estimated that Craig Breedlove had reached over 1,050 km/h in *Spirit of America - Sonic Arrow* when he crashed in 1996. However, that speed wasn't official, so it didn't count as a record.

We arrived at Lake Gairdner with a skeleton crew, as the big sponsorship dollars from Paula's backers had yet to materialise, which was a disappointment. I needed to test *Aussie Invader 3* first, so I climbed into the car for the first drive, wanting to see how she performed. I had to test it out, ensuring everything worked fine and the car behaved. Remember, no one had driven *Aussie Invader 3* yet. I certainly didn't want a less experienced driver taking it out first, and there be something seriously wrong or challenging with it. We went through our check procedure; all was OK, and we started her up. Hearing that familiar and mighty roar, we hadn't heard for so long was brilliant.

I managed a few runs on the first day, a slower run to get the feel of her again, and once I was happy, then full speed runs with afterburner. On one run, we hit a peak speed of 1,027 km/h (638 mph). This was faster than Richard Noble's old record, but once again, we couldn't back it up. If we had been able to take an entire team, who knows what we would have been able to achieve, but it wasn't to be.

The next day, it was Paula's turn to drive. I was still upset that we had not seen the big promised dollars from her over the preceding months. However, we were here now, and if she was motivated and good to her word, this exposure might be the catalyst for her to fulfil her agreement.

After all the briefings and training, we decided she should run the car over just four kilometres to give her a feel for it on salt, with no afterburner. Like me before, on previous trips, she found it like driving on a wet road with slicks.

We decided to put her straight back in the car for another run. This time, we used a longer track and full power with the afterburner. Paula hit a peak speed of 575 km/h (358 mph) at the end of the measured mile, the fastest speed recorded by a woman on four wheels in Australia.

Paula commented on the second run, "Until 300 km/h, it's quite calm and peaceful, but once the afterburner kicks in, all hell breaks loose. Nothing prepares you for the vibration and noise, with the car getting quicker and quicker."

We were on borrowed time. We only had funds for those few days to run the car. We hoped this would give Paula the feel and the inspiration to want to drive it again and challenge for the record. But, if Paula was serious and wanted to go after the women's world record set by Kitty O'Neil, she needed to find those elusive sponsorship dollars for us to return.

We packed up and went home, hoping to hear good news from Paula soon. But, unfortunately, we never did see those big sponsorship dollars. This was disappointing and a big slap in the face for my team and me. It taught me a massive lesson: no one will ever drive one of my cars again unless they pay the full price up front!

It was an anticlimax for us, and *Aussie Invader 3* was retired. It never raced again. It wasn't even started after that. I felt happy that we had proved that the car we originally built to break Richard Noble's record had exceeded the record speed he set. Given time and more runs, we could have pushed *Aussie Invader 3* further. We were sad and frustrated that the Australian mark remained at 802 km/h. It was a case of so near, but so far.

At the end of this chapter, we have some fantastic pictures of *Aussie Invader 3* and Lake Gairdner on this visit, taken by Adelaide photographer Richard Humphrys. Richard kindly let us print several of his incredible photos.

Looking back at all our land speed attempts in both *Aussie Invader cars*, our aluminium wheels were our undoing and not suited for the hard salt of Lake Gairdner.

After reading Richard Noble's 2020 book *Take Risk!*, I learnt that Richard had experienced exactly the same grip issues in *Thrust 2* when he tested it at Bonneville in 1981. Richard found the car was uncontrollable on the salt, as it kept going sidewards and sharply veering off course. This unnerved the very experienced USA timing officials, especially when, on one run, *Thrust 2* headed for their timing stand.

If we had been running at the Black Rock Desert, where Richard set his 1983 record, we would have had a seriously good chance of bettering his record mark. A desert mud lake allows the aluminium wheels to slightly sink into the surface, giving them the sidewall grip they desperately need.

Our *Aussie Invader 2* car had similar power to *Thrust 2*, but I am a lot shorter than Richard, so we could lower the car's roof. This gave it the aerodynamic advantage of a smaller frontal area. *Aussie Invader 3* had even more power and a very slick shape. However, a world record wasn't to be, and we had to accept the outcome.

We felt that *Aussie Invader 3* was one of the prettiest land speed cars ever to grace any salt flat. It went into storage, and many years later, we sold it to the Gosford Motor Museum. Unfortunately, the Gosford Motor Museum was forced to close only three years after opening. So, *Aussie Invader 3* was sold at auction again.

We would have loved to have kept *Aussie Invader 3* in WA and approached the Government about buying it at the time. It was the fastest car in Australia and part of Western Australia's motor racing history. Even before the sale to Gosford Motor Museum, we were approached to put *Aussie Invader 3* into the newly expanded Motor Museum of WA at Whiteman Park. The museum had the space, and they desperately wanted it, but we heard nothing back from the Government; there's a surprise.

Governments these days feel their hands tied because if it's not a social issue, they would be criticised for "wasting" taxpayers' money. Projects like ours inspire the next generation to achieve. Governments must start looking to build for the future, not just try to build a lead for the next election.

If we had been able to donate *Aussie Invader 3* to The Motor Museum of WA, we would have gladly done so, but we weren't. When we eventually sold it in 2016, we were desperate for money to repay some of our debts and move our *Aussie Invader 5R* project forward.

Fitting the "hot-rodded" ATAR jet engine into Aussie Invader 3.

Aussie Invader 3 is being prepared to run at Lake Gairdner.

Aussie Invader 3 – So Near, but So Far

Aussie Invader 3 in March 2000. It's one of the prettiest land speed cars ever to grace the salt.

ROSCO THE FASTEST AUSSIE ON EARTH

The calm before the storm.

Aussie Invader 3 sits perfectly on Lake Gairdner's hard salt.

Aussie Invader 3 – So Near, but So Far

Getting a push to the start line.

Aussie Invader 3 achieved a peak speed of 1,027 km/h (638 mph) on its first and only visit to Lake Gairdner in 2000.

Ready to break some records in Aussie Invader 3.

Even a flooded Lake Gairdner is beautiful.

-17-

The Dynamic Duo

I had raced our *Aussie Invader 1* jet dragster from coast to coast in Australia for over twenty years. I had raced her many times in New Zealand at Meremere and performed numerous special displays there. *Aussie Invader 1* was a versatile car well suited for charity outings, football clubs, country field days and even television commercials.

Drag racing was a very amateur sport in Perth in those early days. Cheryl and I wanted to increase the profile of *Aussie Invader 1* so we could attract attention to our land speed ambitions. Cheryl designed uniforms in colours to match the car for the pit crew. I went about raising our profile with sponsors and got them more involved with us. We became a big family; it was fun and really exciting.

We produced posters and had T-shirts printed that we sold at the race meetings. This type of promotional marketing was widespread in the USA but had yet to filter through to Australia. This merchandise helped promote *Aussie Invader,* raising funds and our profile towards the ultimate goal of breaking the land speed record.

Our team's race day routine was well organised and was perfected over the years; we all had our specialist jobs. I was the driver and would talk to the crowd, signing autographs on posters and generating public support for our land speed ambitions.

Cheryl was the Team Manager, Merchandise Officer, and mum to young Bryce, who was involved on race day. Keith Lovatt was Crew Chief, Mechanic and Parachute Packer. Jenny (Jen) Lovatt drove the ute with the battery pack for starting the car and retrieved it from the end of the quarter-mile after each run. I met Keith when I wanted volunteers to test the rocket-powered go-kart, and he and his wife, Jen, became the best husband-and-wife crew team ever.

Many other volunteers helped out on the start line and in the pits; it was great fun, and we all enjoyed it. Keith and Jen were to become part of the *Aussie Invader* land speed team, so it was great practice for what was to come later, and we loved their friendship.

Racing is risky; one night, we learned just how dangerous it could be. It wasn't unusual for Jen to have a passenger in the support ute to see the car start and some of the fire show before going to the end of the track to help with car recovery. For those unfamiliar with jet dragsters, the fire show was me on the start line, sending out a mass of flames and noise from the jet engine's afterburner, which the crowd loved.

On this particular night, Bryce, about four, wanted to be in the ute with Jen. So, after I started *Aussie Invader 1*, Jen drove to the end of the track, where she was to wait for me to go past and stop. Then, she would help recover and tow the jet car back to the pits,

As I crossed the finish line, the parachutes failed to open, and I had only brakes to stop the car. Those certainly weren't going to pull me up in time before I hit the end of the track, having crossed the line at about 450 km/h (280 mph).

The Dynamic Duo

At Ravenswood, the runoff area was in darkness and had a fence at the end. Jen's ute was faster than the fire trucks, and she arrived on the scene first. She could see the car had gone through the fence and was very concerned for me, and having Bryce in the car was an added complication. Jen had to tell Bryce to stay in the ute and trust that he would while she went to check on me and the car. When she got to me and the mangled wreckage of *Aussie Invader 1*, I was standing next to it and greeted her with, "How are you going, Sweetheart?"

After that, we just looked at each other and smiled. It was a hazard of the job and happened quite a few times. Once, it happened in New Zealand, and I ended up in a field with cows staring at me.

Race day always finished with an *Aussie Invader* Team barbeque in the pits. Cheryl and I saw it as a great chance to thank the sponsors and crew for a job well done. Often, at these barbeques, we would have an underwear inspection. I was very superstitious and always raced in black underwear, which also extended to the team. So, if something went wrong, there would be an impromptu team inspection to see who wasn't wearing black underwear and, therefore, was responsible for the bad luck. We often got a surprised look from non-team members when the underwear inspections took place; it could happen anywhere.

Our team became well known and was held in high regard by the promoters to draw a crowd. The promoters of Ravenswood Raceway in Perth contacted me. They asked if I would be prepared to race against some American jet car teams based in Arizona. These teams were coming to Australia, with their cars and were going on a tour of our great country. My team was asked to be the support and logistics guys to make this tour successful. Our crew members Keith and Jen Lovatt had full-time jobs, so it was tough for them to fit in a six-week state-by-state tour.

They soon came back to me asking for the race dates.

"Yes, let's do it," they said.

That's when I told them they would have to drive the American jet dragster transporter. It will probably be a 20,000-kilometre drive, hopping from track to track and zigzagging across the country.

"No problem; when do we leave?" they answered.

The tour involved two USA teams; the first was Doug Brown and his jet car, Wildfire. Then Joe Brown, with his Arizona Outlaw Team.

They arrived in Perth with their 1957 Chevy-bodied jet-powered funny car. Joe had his own Crew Chief, Mike Druse.

We all got together, checked out their car and did some bench racing over a couple of beers. We shared a lot of laughs and realised these guys were fair dinkum and experienced jet-car drivers. We raced side by side at Ravenswood, with *Aussie Invader 1* winning on the night.

After the first race meeting in Perth, we travelled to Willowbank in Queensland. I took *Aussie Invader 1*, and Keith and his son Matt took Joe's car in two separate Pantech trucks in convoy.

I reminded our American friends that Western Australia is over three times bigger than Texas. It was also a non-stop eighteen-hour drive to our border with South Australia and a fifty-hour drive to Brisbane. "You best fly over, and we'll see you there," I said to these guys.

At the first race, at Willowbank, Joe's car wouldn't start. After I had made my pass, Keith asked the track marshal if he could have a couple of minutes to help Joe get his car started. Keith decided it was important for both cars to run as it was exhibition racing, so both drivers got paid. The problem appeared to be their starter battery pack, so Keith used our battery to get Joe's car started.

On return to the pits, Joe emptied his wallet into Keith's hands, a total of about $30. Joe said that never would have happened on a race track in the USA. Teams didn't help each other over there. Over here, we were all mates putting on a show for the crowd.

One of the issues I had with this tour was that I said I would appear at the Brisbane Motor Show with our *Aussie Invader 3* land speed car. This show was in the middle of our Australia vs. the USA jet car tour. Once we raced at Willowbank, we had a week before our next drag racing meeting at Melbourne's Calder Park. So, I flew home and drove back to Brisbane with my wife Cheryl and son Bryce in another transporter. I left them once *Aussie Invader 3* was set up and organised. So I could go racing without being missed too much.

Our next meeting was in Sydney at Eastern Creek Raceway. We completed this meeting, and I had to fly back to Brisbane for the Motor Show. Joe and Mike decided they wanted to see a bit of our beautiful country. So, they drove a hire car up to Brisbane to have a better look.

I still laugh today when I tell this story. Joe and Mike told me their story of arriving in Brisbane after a very eventful trip. Every time they stopped for fuel or tucker, they would ask, "How far is it to Brisbane?" It was always the same reply, "It's just down the road. Keep going that way. You're nearly there."

Racing against Joe Brown had established just how good it was to have a matched pair of jet cars race against each other. These were great guys, and we talked about Joe driving one of my jet dragsters, which wasn't even built yet. We could tour Australia and New Zealand with a matched racing outfit. We could shoe-horn both cars into one big Pantech truck. "Let's go for it," was his reply.

Aussie Invader 4 was to be powered by a J34 Westinghouse jet engine with a purpose-built afterburner, originally fitted to the Lockheed Neptune as a jet-assisted take-off (JATO) engine. *Aussie Invader 4* had 5,000 lbs of thrust, equivalent to 6,500 horsepower and was capable of 0 - 450 km/h (0 – 280 mph) in about five seconds.

We got started on our build, having Greg Byrnes, a Perth-based race car builder, prep all the chrome-moly chassis tubing. Our inspirational team member Steve "Suggie" Sugden tig welded and stress-relieved the completed chassis. Keith Lovatt oversaw the build, and *Aussie Invader 4* was completed in 1996, in under a year.

We now had our "Dynamic Duo" set of cars to race against each other. I'd been drag racing *Aussie Invader 1* for over twenty years, and we entertained and delighted crowds across Australia and New Zealand. We could put on a show and double the excitement with *Aussie Invader 1* and *Aussie Invader 4* going head-to-head at events.

USA driver Joe Brown drove *Aussie Invader 4*. We appeared at several Australian tracks and visited New Zealand with both cars. Keith, Jen and I flew to New Zealand, with Joe Brown flying in from the USA. The Kiwis do things in a much more relaxed way. Several track staff met us at the airport and showed us to the airport tavern while we waited for our luggage.

The race track reminded us of the good old days at Ravenswood, except the runoff at the end of the quarter-mile went uphill into a cow paddock with actual cows. Again, it was a great family atmosphere, with people watching from their cars along the track and on picnic blankets in the paddock.

The fans made us feel very welcome; the kids even made posters to support both drivers. In addition, the local kids took Joe and me down to the creek during one race meeting to catch eels.

The track staff were great people, and we met the head security officer, Neville. He was in charge of track security, and his main job was to search all the cars as they came into the raceway and confiscate any alcohol he found. It was stored safely in his caravan until after the race meeting, when he shared it with track staff and honoured guests like us.

Nev was a very accomplished partygoer and would upend a two-litre Coke bottle and cut out the base. Then, he would drink some of the Coke and pour in the rum. Holding the bottle upside down, goblet style, he swayed and wobbled all night but never spilt a drop.

We had three weeks in New Zealand and toured the North Island with Joe and his crew between meetings. The Highway Patrol Police stopped Joe for speeding in the rental car. He showed them his US driver's licence and told them he used to be a policeman. They shook their heads, worried about all the paperwork and let him go without a ticket.

We had a great time in New Zealand, and leaving was sad. Our welcoming committee were also our send-off committee, and they made sure we visited the airport tavern on our way out again.

After the successful tour, Joe Brown returned to the USA, and we continued thrilling the crowds around Australia with the jet dragsters. *Aussie Invader 4* was a great addition to our show. We invited other guest drivers to drive her over the next few years as we traversed our beautiful country.

Going along in the background was my world land speed ambitions, so thoughts turned once again to a new car to break that elusive world record I had wanted for so long.

The Dynamic Duo

Aussie Invader 1 in its early days.

Putting on a show for the spectators.

Aussie Invader 1 in disguise for a Vauxhall car ad in 1987.

Completely destroying a vehicle with Aussie Invader 1's afterburner. The crowds always loved it.

The Dynamic Duo

The jet drag racing team. Keith and Jen Lovatt (L) Cheryl and I (R). A young Bryce is in the driver's seat.

Aussie Invader 1 in a later colour scheme 2002.

Joe Brown (USA) in Aussie Invader 4 racing in New Zealand.

Aussie Invader 4 was completed in 1996.

The Dynamic Duo - Aussie Invader 1 & 4 racing each other in New Zealand.

-18-
False Starts for Aussie Invader 5

I had said before that these land speed record attempts were not just one man's quest to be the fastest but a team effort to bring the world land speed record to Australia. I cannot deny I wanted my name in the record books as "The fastest man on Earth," but it is always a team effort. Without a team behind me, all trying to achieve a goal for Australia, it wouldn't happen.

So, the first thing to do was to find out if the team were behind me. Once the team said "Yes," I started researching new car designs, engine configurations, and possible sponsor support. *Aussie Invader 5* would be years in the planning, let alone the building.

Just as our thoughts turned towards building *Aussie Invader 5*, we were privileged to have Richard Noble join us for a barbeque at my home. Richard Noble is a Scottish entrepreneur who set a world land speed record "For Britain and for the hell of it" in 1983. Richard took the record from the Americans, set in October 1970 in *The Blue Flame*, with his 1,019 km/h run in his jet-powered *Thrust 2* car.

Richard has been an absolute godsend to our lifelong endeavours in chasing a world land speed record for Australia. After he and his team set the record in 1997, I pestered him on many technical issues with the design and data he gained from his experience at the Black Rock Desert.

At this barbeque, I still remember being told everything Richard does is designed to make dollars towards the success of his projects. If you ask him for an autograph, it will cost you. If one of his friends wants a free T-shirt, it won't happen. If you want to sit in the car, it's a donation.

Richard is a dynamic and motivated adventurer. I enjoy being in his company, and he is a larger-than-life character. When we met, he and I spent a lot of time discussing land speed design, which was brilliant for me, as I was just about to embark on our new car build.

It made my team laugh when, at our barbeque, I managed to talk him into handing over his coat free of charge. Then I got his T-shirt and beautiful wristwatch before leaving my house. I hoped to score his *Thrust 2* underpants, but I had to leave him with something to wear!

To show you what a gentleman Richard is, he called me before the official announcement of the *Bloodhound SSC* project on 23rd October 2008. He knew we were about to start construction of our new car and personally told me about their plans to build a 1,000 mph car, so I wasn't shocked. He's a good, honest friend and a lovely, genuine guy.

-ooOoo-

Earning a living at drag racing took a big chunk of my life and me away from my land speed ambitions. The opportunity arose whilst I was performing at Canberra's Summernats in 2002 to sell both *Aussie Invader 1* and *Aussie Invader 4*. Cheryl and I had to consider this offer seriously. The sale included our truck, transporter, spare engines, and everything you would need to go racing.

Until now, we had been running jet dragsters at shows and generating some income from this. However, it had become clear that I needed to be full-time to get this elusive world record. This would mean giving up driving the jet dragsters and travelling all over the country.

Our minds were made up when there was a massive increase in personal and public liability insurance costs. We had to have this to operate, but I was only occasionally racing the jet dragsters because of my land speed quest. So, with all the costs, it wasn't a great income earner, and this insurance was a massive overhead. Also, selling both dragsters would give us a cash injection to start *Aussie Invader 5*, so Cheryl and I decided we had to do it.

Selling the dragsters was a big wrench for us, as we'd had fantastic times travelling around the country and entertaining the crowds. I would now go full-time on building *Aussie Invader 5*, which meant Cheryl would be left to be the main wage earner.

We sold both cars to a prominent Gold Coast Racer, Graham Slapp, in 2002. *Aussie Invader 4* surprisingly now resides back in Perth, owned by well-renowned racer Ian Wood. Our beloved *Aussie Invader 1* now lives in Brazil, and we hope she is being well looked after and pleasing the crowds there.

Cheryl was a qualified real estate agent, which could generate a good income for us. I also took my real estate license to help at weekends with home opens, viewings and appointments when needed. Day to day, I was going to be working on the land speed car and trying to get things happening.

Kidnapped by The Russian Mafia

Now we had some clear direction and support, my thoughts turned to what *Aussie Invader 5* would look like. One of the first ideas and designs I'd worked on for a while was to build a twin-engine turbofan jet car similar to *Thrust SSC*. Andy Green proved the concept worked, and we could learn from their design and avoid some of the issues they had encountered. It happens with all land speed cars; you only discover design flaws when you push them to the extreme.

For this concept, we needed the most powerful military jet engines available. I discovered during my research that there was a Russian engine that produced 34,000 lbs of thrust with afterburner. These engines were fitted to a Russian *MIG-31*, so these were on our Christmas list. I had to get to Russia and somehow bring back two of these very powerful engines. There were only three minor setbacks, and I'd be on my way.

Firstly, I didn't have a visa to enter Russia. Secondly, I couldn't find a Russian-speaking engineer in my home state of Western Australia. Thirdly, we still would not have enough money to purchase these engines, even if I could find them. The Russian-speaking engineer would be critical to understand and use these engines, as modifications would be required to reconfigure these to operate on full power at ground level.

I approached a sponsor, Tom Mower, who supported our previous Aussie Invader 2 and Aussie Invader 3 adventures. Tom was the owner of Neways, a network marketing company in Utah, USA. Tom mentioned that he had a good contact in Moscow, Prof. Sergey Chernyshev, who was very senior in TsAGI, Russia's equivalent of NASA. Tom had found a Utah University place for Sergey's son. I was given his contact details, and a visa appointment was arranged with some of Sergey's Russian contacts. This was the first obstacle out of the way.

The next job was to find the airfare to Moscow and some accommodation dollars. I spoke with several airlines and met with the Australian Emirates boss. Thankfully, he was most supportive and sponsored a return business class ticket to Moscow. Other loyal sponsors chipped in some dollars to cover my other expenses. However, my lack of serious funds, should I find these engines, was still a significant problem. The second and third issues were still outstanding, but I had to wing it, as I had always done.

Undaunted, I left Perth and arrived twenty-one hours later at Moscow's Domodedovo Airport. I was amazed as the aircraft taxied us on a grand tour through a series of runways. We passed hundreds of aircraft with names on them I had never seen before. Some aircraft had engines off, and people were repairing them on piles of snow. We finally came to a stop at our designated disembarking area.

Before we had a chance to stand up, a group of machine-gun-toting soldiers entered the back door of the aircraft and raced in line to the front. They were all shouting and looking pretty pissed off. Then, they turned around and walked back out the rear door. God knows what that was all about. Perhaps that should have been a warning of what was to come.

I checked into the Radisson Hotel in Moscow, got a good night's sleep and met with Sergey at 10 a.m. the following day. His interpreter arranged a visit to an army base about 50 kilometres away with a driver assigned to me. I arrived at a massive hangar after passing a severe security interrogation. Without an interpreter, it was what I had feared: very tough going.

Conversing with these people was almost impossible. Finally, after working with a team of six army guys for a while, I discovered they had two D30F6 engines. I was shown two huge wooden crates stored high up on racks. I tried to communicate for some time that I needed these crates on the ground. I wanted them opened, which finally happened, and it was a sight to behold. There they were, these beautiful engines still in service and just stored in wooden crates.

Being from Australia, where we are not famous for tipping, I had missed all the signs that these guys knew what I wanted. They were waiting on money to motivate them to get these crates down. This was my first mistake, but certainly not my last on this trip.

It was time to start talking about purchasing these engines. This group's most senior-looking guy was their main negotiator. I was surprised that he was interested in US dollars, but that made it easier for me to understand the price. Before we even discussed purchasing the engines, I had been told the price would be for both. I was also warned that these engines would have to be shipped from Moscow to the UK. They would be confiscated if they passed through any other country. I thought to myself, *It was all becoming too hard.* Even if I could purchase these engines and have them back in Australia, no one would be able to make them race-ready.

I decided it wasn't going to happen. So, I said goodbye to these guys and can still recall the looks of bewilderment on their faces. I am sure they must have thought I was a really wealthy

Australian coming with bundles of cash to buy these two engines.

I headed back to my hotel. It was 3 p.m., and it was pitch black and freezing. There was a train station next door, so I decided to go and take a look, and wow, there were some sad faces there. Along a fenceline, there must have been 50 dogs. They were all lying huddled up on the ground in the snow.

The next day, I agreed to do a promotional story in the morning for one of the sponsors who had helped me get to Moscow. Neways had business interests in Russia, and I did it as a thank-you for them. The afternoon was free, so I decided I must see Red Square. The hotel concierge got me a taxi and told me that on the way back, only use one of the recommended taxi companies. It should cost me about $20 US from Red Square to the hotel.

I arrived at the Kremlin Wall, walked the cobbled path to Saint Basil's Cathedral and tried to speak with several guards at the Kremlin. I then decided to head back to the hotel as it was snowing very hard. At the end of Red Square was a car with its engine running. The snow was making it hard to see, and I had no way of knowing how to identify a genuine taxi. There were no lights on the top of the car, and God knows what the licence plates said. I opened the passenger door of this car to see a big guy in a fur coat in the driver's seat.

"Are you a taxi?" I said and repeated it several times.

"In, in," he just kept saying.

"$20 to Radisson Hotel?"

He was the only car that looked like a taxi. I jumped in the passenger's seat, and he took off like a land speed record car and screamed into his mobile phone. I now suspected I might be in trouble. Luckily, he headed down the main freeway my hotel was on, so I knew we were going in the right direction. The driver was still going very fast as we approached my hotel. I said, "Slow down. We were getting close." He ignored my instruction and blasted past. I realised that I had to act quickly and surveyed my situation. He was a big guy, and did he have a gun or a knife?

The law states in Moscow that visitors must carry their passports at all times. I had a few dollars in mine tucked into my full-length fur coat. The coat was lent to me by a friend in Perth, which obviously I needed in Moscow, but would now make me bigger and slower.

I was in a small car, probably a Lada. I glanced into the rear seat area, and there were no door handles! I had already checked my front passenger handle, and it was disconnected. I looked out the window and saw a pipeline running alongside the road, suspended just above it.

A bus had pulled up on the right-hand side of the road, allowing passengers to get off. At the same time, a bus on the inside lane blocked our vehicle. The driver was still screaming into his phone and aggressively moved out, trying to force the bus to let him in. Our car hit the bus, losing a wing mirror. I seized the moment, punched out my passenger window, and somehow got through that tiny space like I had a fire up my arse. I used my feet to push off the driver, who was trying to grab me and had now stopped the car.

I quickly dived under the pipeline I had seen at the side of the road and found a piece of steel bar for a weapon. I waited, half expecting him to come after me. I was going to give it to him, big time. I didn't see him, but I heard his car fire up, and it took off.

It was a busy freeway, and I walked back possibly two kilometres to my hotel. I was still carrying my steel bar, half expecting another visit from this guy and perhaps his mates.

Back at the hotel, the doorman who had arranged my original taxi was still there. He spoke good English, and I gave him my piece of steel.

"You might want to keep this for other tourists who want to venture out." I politely said to him.

I didn't dare leave my hotel room again and left Moscow the following day, promising myself I would never return. This land speed racing business gets me into some real scrapes.

After a year of work to design and plan a car around these engines, it was back to the drawing board.

Steve Fossett and I Join Forces

Later, in 2002, Steve Fossett was about to attempt a solo around-the-world hot air balloon record. He was leaving from a small country town east of Perth called Northam in Western Australia. Steve was an American billionaire who had made his fortune in the Chicago commodity markets. He had retired from business and was a record-setting machine that firmly established his name in history books, with over 100 world records.

He demonstrated a vast amount of physical and mental toughness in all facets of his extreme life and adventures. His accomplishments would be as thick as an old telephone book, with his record-breaking across a mass of sports and disciplines. These record feats included gliding, hot air ballooning, sailing, mountain climbing, cross-country skiing and motor racing. He even swam the bloody English Channel and competed in the 1,100-mile Alaskan Sled-Dog Race!

I had spoken with Steve several years before and called him when he arrived in Northam. He remembered talking with me when I was in California.

I told Steve, "We are out to set a world record, and I know my idea will excite you. Can we talk?"

"Yes, love to. Can you meet me in Northam?" He asked.

"Yes, I can," I said.

I thought he said, "Bring your passport," but I wasn't sure if I had heard that correctly.

I arrived in Northam at the Shamrock Hotel, where he was staying. We shook hands, and both sat down for a drink. We talked about his upcoming solo circumnavigation, and I marvelled at this man's bravery and confidence. Solo around the world in a bloody balloon, and they call me nuts. I mentioned that I had an idea that would offer both of us a world land speed record.

"Sounds interesting. Did you bring your passport?" Steve asked.

"No, I didn't, and why would I need a passport?"

"The wind is up for the next two or three days, so my crew, you and I are flying to Bali until the winds subside. So, that will give us some time to hear what you have planned."

"Sorry mate, I am flying out of Perth in the morning and can't join you. However, if I outline my idea, you might give it some thought, and we can reconnect once you land safely back in Oz."

"Shoot," Steve said.

"My team and I want to build a car that can reach 1,600 km/h. I have been chasing the world land speed record all my life, and we have designed, built, and raced some of the world's fastest and prettiest vehicles. Nearly all of these were conceived and built in my home shed. The car I am speaking of will be built by my team in Perth, and it can be tested in Australia and painted in Australian livery.

The current world land speed record is 1,227 km/h. To claim a new record, we need to exceed the old one by just one percent, which is my drive and my time at the record. This attempt can be staged in the USA, preferably in the Black Rock Desert. I have a year to achieve this record from when the car is race-prepped. Regardless of whether I establish a new record in that twelve-month window, the car is then surrendered to your crew. You repaint her in your livery and add some cosmetic changes to make the car look exclusively American. Should I set a new record on my first outing, the deal between us will be that the new record is kept just above the existing record threshold. What do you reckon, Steve?"

Steve asked, "What is my commitment?"

"All you need to do is excite your friends at Bud Light and Chicago Securities that you are going after setting a world land speed record. Then, you have to bring in the initial seed capital for us to start building the car."

"OK, I'll get back to you as soon as possible."

Then Steve went out and achieved the world's first solo balloon record, travelling over 33,000 kilometres to circumnavigate the world!

Steve travelled back to the USA, and we started a series of discussions on how this idea could work. I sent Steve drawings of a concept car that was to be powered by a single liquid rocket engine with the details and engineering calculations attached. I also sent designs for Aussie and USA suggested liveries, performance, and aero predictions.

This was one hell of a project, and poor Ackers and myself were being stretched to the limit, waiting for the go-ahead from Steve. Over a year later, we still didn't know where Steve and his sponsors were with this project, but we needed to get started if this idea was going to happen.

I came home one evening after a tough day, and Steve rang me. He went over some of his concerns. What if I was to take the car to her maximum velocity, and it left him in the cold? Steve said, "I'm probably getting too old for this land speed business."

I still regret this and should not have taken his call with how I felt at the time. But I couldn't help myself. He was stalling me and had been for a while.

I told him, "Your life has been about setting records; age is just another number and another record to be broken. You're a bloody big girl's blouse!" Obviously, Steve didn't like my comment, which saw the end of Steve and me working together.

Later, in 2006, Steve purchased the Craig Breedlove car, *Spirit of America - Sonic Arrow*. This was almost certainly because our meeting and discussions had heightened his interest. It could have also been to get back at my comment and beat me to the record. The money he paid wouldn't have made him blink. Craig still owes me a big drink for that deal, as I am sure Steve wouldn't have even thought about buying his car without my critique of his masculinity.

Steve was twice the size of Craig, and I thought, *How on the bloody earth can he squeeze into that tiny cockpit.* I had seen the car first-hand when Craig and I met in California. Steve sent the car to Reno, Nevada, to have work by a leading aerodynamicist. I later met this aerodynamicist and his wife in Reno and looked at the modified Breedlove car. In my opinion, they had compounded the aero problem this car already had.

They had mounted a box structure on the top of the body and extended the back axle track out wider. That was almost certainly to try and stop the wheels lifting that had caused Craig's crash in 1996. Steve had also purchased the truck, transporter and spare engine as part of the deal from Craig.

They tried to test the car at El Mirage in California, driving from Nevada, and were denied entry into the state. The car's wider rear track had made side boxes necessary for the transport trailer. It made the trailer over-width, and it wasn't allowed to travel on Californian roads.

Unfortunately, Steve never even got to sit in the car with the engine fired up, as quite soon after that, he disappeared. Steve was visiting Barron Hilton's Ranch south of Reno and took a flight in one of Barron's light aircraft on 3rd September 2007. He vanished with no flight plan recorded and only half a bottle of drinking water. He never returned to his wife, Peggy, who was also staying at Barron's Ranch.

For a long time, his fans did Google searches to find him. They hiked in the remote areas of Nevada and along the California border, trying to locate the plane wreck. The US government mounted the most extensive civilian search in American history to find Steve, but still no sign of him.

Roll forward to early October 2008. A hiker discovered Steve and his plane's wreckage at Ansel Adams Wilderness in California, which I believe was one of his favourite spots. Apparently, the winds in that area are notorious and a probable cause of the crash. The official outcome of the crash was "The pilot's inadvertent encounter with downdrafts that exceeded the climb capability of the aircraft." Steve was a great bloke and, at 63, taken far too early.

At least another year had passed exploring this option with Steve, and it was back to the drawing board again.

Homeland Security Makes Life Difficult

In 2003, we were still looking at building our land speed car using two twin turbofan jet engines. This combination would offer considerable thrust in a car with a relatively small frontal area. In addition, it would be reasonably light and have a very slick shape.

Visiting several Air Force bases around Australia, I set my sights on using two GE F404 engines as fitted to the Hornet Fighter aircraft. This aircraft's engines use titanium and other lightweight exotic materials in their manufacture. Sadly, I couldn't get my hands on any engines in Australia or New Zealand.

However, I found two in Denver, Colorado and started a line of communication with an aircraft salvage company there. Several weeks later, we were advised that ITAR, a Division of Homeland Security, had banned the sale of these classified engines from leaving United States soil. Since 9/11, jets, rockets and all sorts of technology were deemed off-limits for export and purchase from the USA.

This brush with Homeland Security certainly wasn't my last conversation with them!

Early in the build of *Aussie Invader 5R*, around 2013, I acquired some rocket parts from eBay, entirely redundant for most people. Still, Homeland Security again called me to ensure I wasn't planning on firing rockets towards the USA. I explained the reason for our interest in rocket parts and our land speed car construction, which seemed to satisfy them. It's good to know Big Brother is alive and well.

Once again, our efforts had gone nowhere in trying to purchase these jet engines. We were burning the midnight oil to generate interest and make things happen. But unfortunately, all we were doing was going backwards, and time was slipping by. So, we needed a rethink, and our thoughts turned to what we would now power *Aussie Invader 5* with.

Hybrid Rocket Development with SpaceDev

In late 2004, I was in awe of Burt Rutan's Spaceship One's suborbital flight, which won the Scaled Composites $10m Ansari X Prize. So, I enquired through Scaled Composites and learned that the hybrid rocket used in their craft was credited to SpaceDev in Poway, San Diego. I followed this up and was given the name of the CEO, Jim Benson.

I called Jim from Perth and asked him about the possibility of SpaceDev building us and sponsoring two 15,000 lb thrust hybrid rocket engines. Jim was fascinated with the idea of a supersonic car using engines they would develop and asked me to fly over to California.

I contacted our guru engineer Ackers and asked if he had any air miles left. If so, was he available to join Jim and me in Poway, USA?

"Yes" and "Yes" was his answer.

We had a friend, Vernon Rich, who was happy to drive from Phoenix, Arizona, to Los Angeles to join us.

I always smile when I recount the story Ackers told me when he flew out of Heathrow Airport to meet me on this trip to the USA. Ackers was great friends with Richard Branson and bumped into him at the airport.

"Ackers, old mate, where are you off to?" Asked Richard.

"San Diego."

"What are you doing over there?"

"We are building two big hybrid rockets for a land speed record car to be driven by a crazy Aussie."

"Shit, who's paying for that?"

"You are!" replied Ackers.

Richard quickly slipped away as he felt it would cost him a lot of money to hang around.

Air travel was easy for Ackers. He would jump on a plane with an old airways bag. A spare T-shirt, socks, jocks, and a big notepad and pencil would be in it. Then, when he arrived at his destination and found the weather too cold, he would find the nearest thrift shop and walk out sporting a second-hand coat and some long trousers. Then, when flying out, he would dump his newly found wardrobe and worry about the weather on arrival at his next port of call. He was a master at this travel game.

We stayed at Jim's mansion and spent two weeks learning about hybrid rocket engines. We all shook hands with Jim, and he promised to commence work on developing these massive hybrids.

Our car would use two of these mounted, one on top of the other. You cannot mount them side by side because if one works more efficiently or shuts off early, it will cause the car to veer sharply off course. We knew these engines would have a few logistical and performance issues. This stemmed from them being very long and heavy when loaded with the HTPB (rubber fuel payload).

They would also make more thrust on their first run, but their performance would diminish the longer they ran. It's not ideal for a car application, as the longer they burn, the more power we need to overcome a massive aero drag as we get faster. Firing these engines into space would work great. The higher altitude they achieve, the less power they make, but an ever-reducing aero drag in the thinner atmosphere compensates for this.

Our "chauffeur", Vernon, wanted to show us his machine shop in Deer Valley, Arizona. Still, before heading out there, we were invited to meet a mate of his, Darryl Greenamyer. In 1977, Darryl set the world Airspeed Record by flying an F-104 Starfighter. He modified it to obtain 1,590 km/h (988 mph) at sea level, a record that I believe still stands today. It was great to have met the man and viewed some of the amazing aircraft he was building. It also brought into focus the huge task we were undertaking.

We were trying to build a car to run faster than that record and obtain a speed at ground level that no aircraft had ever achieved! I must be mad. It was much easier to go supersonic in a plane, where there was no ground effect shock-wave or rolling resistance from the wheels.

We arrived at Deer Valley with Vernon, and as we drove through the entrance to this airport, Vernon asked, "Do you know what this place is famous for?"

Both Ackers and I responded, "No."

"This is where America trained some of the 9/11 terrorists who bombed the Twin Towers," Vernon told us. Obviously, they didn't know their intentions at the time, but that was eye-opening. It was later reported that suspicions were aroused as these trainee pilots didn't want to learn how to land an aircraft!

As it turned out, Vernon wanted to build our *Aussie Invader 5* car for us and was keen to show us his workshop to convince us he could do it. But, as keen as he was, and Ackers agreeing that he was one of the best fabricators he had met, we knew his shop wouldn't be big enough. On top of that, we could build this twin-engine hybrid rocket car back in Perth cheaper by using my longtime loyal volunteer team, product sponsors, and home workshop.

Vernon would not take no for an answer, and as a sweetener to us letting him build our car, he would give us our own transport aircraft. This aircraft was a Fairchild C123 Provider. Not only did it have enough room to take a lengthy payload, our rocket-powered land speed car, but it also came with a history!

This aircraft had a starring role in the movie CON AIR and was bought by Alaska's All West Freight Company after the filming. We met with the All West Freight crew, and they said this plane was used to transport very long pipes into the Alaskan oilfields. They also confirmed that if we were friends with Vernon, and he wanted us to have it, the aircraft would be ours when they had transported all of their oil pipes.

Vernon then told us that this crew loads the pipes during the day and flies out very early in the morning. They take off with the tail door open, and the overlength oil pipes virtually scrape on the tarmac. They were fantastic guys and great fun to be around.

Sadly, a few years later, we learned all three guys were killed in 2010 in the same plane when it was on a mission to deliver a large generator. Unfortunately, the aircraft had stalled and crashed into the south-facing slope of Mount Healy in Denali National Park in Alaska.

We drove back to San Diego and checked on the progress of our BIG engines. SpaceDev was on the job experimenting with fuel grain combinations.

Jim showed us with pride a winning ticket he found in a cereal packet from his childhood. It claimed he had won a trip into space, and here he was, building his own "winning ticket" to take that ride. It shows what happens when you light the fuse to a child's imagination.

I got a call from Jim a couple of months later. He told me that because of the diameter of our rocket casings, they could not develop a suitable fuel grain for the proposed rockets.

The bigger the diameter of the rocket casing, the less integrity of the grain to stay intact. In rocket terms, it would "chug". This means the solid fuel that is attached to the inner wall of the rocket casing would delaminate, almost certainly blocking the exhaust nozzle and exploding.

Jim Passed away in 2008 from a brain tumour at just 63 years of age. He was a visionary and is sadly missed by our team and SpaceDev, who did some fantastic development work for us. Thanks, Jim and SpaceDev.

So, another year goes by, and we are back to square one. The only positive is that we now know we have to power *Aussie Invader 5* with rocket propulsion. So, *Aussie Invader 5* becomes *Aussie Invader 5R* (R=Rocket). All the other *Aussie Invader* cars were jet-powered.

Whilst all this research was going into building a supersonic car, my team and family were busy with motor shows and appearances across the country. Yes, we had sold the jet dragsters but not the land speed car. Initially, this was with *Aussie Invader 2*, our first land speed car, in which we set the Australian Land Speed Record. Later, we displayed our *Aussie Invader 3* car, which reached a peak speed of 1,027 km/h (638 mph).

I Get an Offer I Can't Refuse

One evening in early 2007, I received a call from a guy called Alex Copson, who was calling from Washington, DC. He introduced himself as the company President of F1 MAX-X. He said he was developing a mega race facility in Las Vegas. Furthermore, he understood that we had retired our *Aussie Invader 3* and were soon to start the construction of a new, much faster rocket-powered *Aussie Invader 5R*.

We discussed this for some time. Finally, Alex asked me if I would consider being a part of this team and if I would be prepared to move my team and family to Las Vegas and join him. Wow, that was quite an offer and certainly out of the blue. He explained that other race teams were coming on board. MotoGP's Kenny Roberts, Sr. and Team Roberts had already joined forces with Alex's new F1 MAX-X Auto Spectacular.

This offer certainly grabbed my attention, but I had a hundred questions, the main one being, how would this all work? His concept was to add two new floors to the MGM's Treasure Island and Mirage Casinos shared multi-storey car park. The new lower floor was going to be the team workshop with many motor racing codes building cars there. These include Formula One, MotoGP, NASCAR, Drag Racing, Rally Cars and Land Speed. In addition, there would be a mega lift to carry trucks and equipment to this workshop level.

The top level was for spectators, who would pay an entry fee to enter via a personnel lift to the top floor viewing area. They would be able to view the teams working on their race machines below. A team spokesperson for each code would always be present, and they would answer questions from interested fans.

Finally, all the approvals, plans and construction were ready to start. The big hook for the patrons was that a new F250 Ford Pickup would be raffled to a lucky ticket holder once a week. These Ford F250s would be painted in the F1 MAX-X livery and delivered to the winner's doorstep throughout the USA.

"OK, that's a great concept, but where are all these F250s coming from?" I asked.

"I have travelled across the USA and had meetings with leading Ford stakeholders in eight states. As a result, they're about to sign an agreement to supply a large number of F250s for our Auto Extravaganza." Alex replied.

There was a massive over-supply of these vehicles, and Alex had pounced on this idea. However, I needed to know a lot more about this, so I had to meet with Alex Copson in person, which would mean jumping on a plane to the USA. I also used this opportunity to meet with several rocket engine development companies based there. We were starting in California and finishing our visit in South Carolina.

I contacted a rocket development company owned by Gary Hudson in Mojave. Our first stop was to witness a test firing of his engine. He lived in Sacramento, so we arranged to meet at his test site. On that day, I met his team in the morning, and a test firing was scheduled for the afternoon.

Sadly, as another company's test firing was about to happen, there was an explosion in their test area. A propellant transfer accident occurred, killing three employees and injuring three more. It was devastating, and I'd been only chatting to one of the guys who had died just a few hours before—what a terrible loss for their families and friends. The whole of Mojave's Space Port was in shock and lockdown.

All operations shut down for several days while investigations happened. Support was offered to the employees' families who were killed and injured.

Once the facility was operating again, we witnessed the test rocket firing, which was magnificent. Some adjustments were made to the pintle injector, as it wasn't playing fair (a pintle injector atomises the propellants in a rocket engine). I only wish

I had the chance to study that injector more closely. The rocket nozzle we will use in our car is the same design. Sadly, I wasn't permitted to get anywhere near any rocket engines. Secrecy protocols protect the whole of Mojave. The transfer of even design ideas verbally had to be withheld, as the wrath of God would descend on both parties, with a possible lawsuit following.

I knew that driving cross country and trying to meet a lot of people and rocket companies would be a drain. So, I asked one of my best mates, Ray Baumann, a professional stunt driver, if he would join me. He would do most of the driving while I researched the next meeting or slept in the back.

Ray Baumann is one of my local heroes. A professional stunt driver, backyard battler and an all-around top bloke. Ray wanted badly to set a world car jump record, and after many heart-stopping attempts, he finally succeeded. Unfortunately, in achieving this milestone, he broke his back twice, legs and arms and endured extreme pain, but always refused pain medication.

Watching him perform many of his stunts was horrifying and hard to watch, but he was fearless.

After his record jump of over 72 metres, Ray decided to build the world's biggest motorcycle. This motorcycle is powered by a Detroit Diesel engine with dump truck tyres and weighs 13 tonnes. This monster bike had no "trainer wheels". Instead, it solely balanced on the width of its tyres. Ray's backside is about three metres in the air, and he charges at defenceless motor vehicles and flattens them. A bloody incredible sight to witness.

Boy, I still have nightmares about this trip with Ray driving. The number of times I would doze off and then be woken by the sound of a screaming engine was many. We both knew that when the peak hour ends in California, the vehicle speeds pick up, and the cops are happy to see the traffic clear. So, 100 mph down Highway 405 was commonplace, mainly because the guy in front was going that speed, and the other guy up your clacker was doing the same, and you had to keep up.

We had lots of laughs travelling West to East across the USA and visited all of the rocket engine folk I had arranged to meet. But, sadly, we came away with the impression that there was no support to design a rocket for our project, as these companies were all space-focused.

Both Ray and I met up with Alex Copson in Washington, DC. We enjoyed a night on the town with him and his Lawyer, George, who worked in Rudy Giuliani's DC Law Firm.

We talked for hours about the millions that had already been spent in bringing this F1 MAX-X concept to life, and the next day, we met for lunch. At that lunch, a contract that offered me $1 million a year to be a part of the team was given to me to sign. I couldn't sign it quickly enough. I also understood that this whole business revolved around the new BIG boss of Ford in Detroit, having to sign off on it.

We headed west towards Los Angeles to catch our flight home and could only guess how many hours that trip would take. Both of us regularly travelled across Australia, and a non-stop drive in a truck could be done in around 44 hours. We thought we would have a faster run west in the USA than in Australia. We headed off from DC, arcing through Pennsylvania, then onto a ring road around Oklahoma City.

We stopped for fuel just off this ring road in the early morning and were shocked to find that we had a toll gate blocking our entry onto the ring road. We checked our change situation and found the required toll fee. Much to our shock, another toll gate was around eight kilometres further down the road. Again, we searched for more coins and somehow found the toll money again. You guessed it, another eight kilometres and another one. Sadly, this time, we were out of change. All I could offer the coin bin was a half-eaten hamburger. Boy, that got the alarm bells ringing and the cameras flashing as we hastily left the scene. We flashed across the country so fast we had time to spare.

"Would you like to meet a guy who owns his own town?" I asked Ray. We decided we had time to stop and say G'day to Don Laughlin, whose town is Laughlin in Nevada and sits on the bank of the Colorado River.

We spent a couple of hours with Don, checked out his car museum, drank lots of coffee, and then headed toward Los Angeles airport and our 18-hour flight back to Perth.

We arrived back home, and guess what happened next? The Global Financial Crisis hit overnight in the USA and, a bit later, worldwide. Alex couldn't push the "go" button, and the F1 MAX-X Auto Spectacular dream fell in a heap.

At least another year had been lost with the discussions and negotiations with Alex Copson. We again found ourselves back at that old drawing board.

I Watched a North American Eagle Fly

On one of my many trips to the USA to discuss with Alex Copson about F1 MAX-X, I found myself in Gerlach, Nevada, around June 2007. I'd been invited out there by Ed Shadle to watch the progress of our friends and rivals, *North American Eagle*. They were testing their jet-powered car. I offered some design ideas to Ed and the *North American Eagle* team to overcome a problem with their car's over-flexing body.

The *North American Eagle* team were fantastic backyard battlers like ourselves, an all-volunteer team with no big financial backers but a tremendous amount of dedication.

At this time, the USA had not held the mile land speed record for over 40 years. The last time was when our good mate Dick Keller and his *The Blue Flame* rocket car, with Gary Gabelich driving, set the mile record at 1,001 km/h (622 mph). However, *The Blue Flame* kilometre record of 1,015 km/h (630 mph) was not broken until *Thrust SCC* smashed it in 1997.

Dick Keller has always offered us countless hours of support to get our *Aussie Invader 5R* to the start line. We are indebted to him for his help and are hopeful he will join us on our big day. Dick has written an excellent book on his extraordinary rocket ventures called Speedquest: *Inside The Blue Flame*. It's a great read by an amazing man.

A Reunion and a Gift From an Indian Chief

In October 2007, still working on *Aussie Invader 5R* ideas, I found myself back in the USA with Ackers joining me. I was in Arizona, and Ackers had just landed in California. We spoke on the phone, and I was reminded of *Thrust SSC*'s 10th anniversary, setting a new world land speed record of 1,227 km/h (763 mph). There was a big celebration taking place at Bruno's Bar in Gerlach, Nevada.

"Can you join us?" asked Ackers.

"Who's going?"

"A large group of *Thrust SSC* team will be there, and it should be a real blast," he said.

"I'm on my way."

Gerlach is a tiny town at the south end of the Black Rock Desert, with Winnemucca Lake at its northern end. This site holds great memories and history for our British friends and rivals.

Richard Noble, John Ackroyd and the *Thrust 2* team deserve serious credit for the hurdles they jumped through to make this happen. They put this unbelievable site on the land speed record map.

That evening, Ackers and I caught up with most of the *Thrust SSC* crew, the legendary Craig Breedlove and his mate Captain Ed Ballinger, a highly respected fighter pilot and rocket car drag racer in the seventies. Many fantastic stories and experiences were talked about over several beers and a load of laughs.

One of the men joining us that night was a long-time supporter of the Black Rock land speed team, and he loved the British. He was a Paiute Indian Chief, locally known as Ken, and he was a teacher at a local Indian school. He and I spoke extensively about Australia, its indigenous culture, Ken's love for Nevada's Pyramid Lake area, its sad history, and its native people.

I was asked to do a talk for the gathered group of land speed guys and talk about my team's achievements and future ambitions. My talk was well received, and it was back to the festivities.

Ken approached me, said he had a special gift for me, and made me promise not to leave until he returned. I immediately thought *I didn't want to take something valuable from him*. Getting this gift back into Australia could also be an issue through our strict customs and quarantine folk.

About an hour later, Ken arrived back at the pub sporting a tribal ceremonial bearskin coat that still had the bear's head fur as a hood. Everyone in the bar was fascinated to see this tribal ceremonial coat. Ken proudly placed it around my shoulders and fitted the hood over my head.

I was astounded, as were most of the *Thrust SSC* crew. Ken told me this bearskin took four Indian squaws about six weeks to chew all the fat from this skin. Then, it was blessed by four local Indian Chiefs, and Ken was one of them. I felt terrible accepting this gift because it was so special to him, and why me? He had some good friends from the *Thrust SSC* team that he had known for some time. However, he wanted me to have it, so I couldn't refuse.

I also wondered how I would get this back home. I did have a history of getting all my rocket and jet engine parts I collected worldwide through customs. I am pleased to report this unique gift made it back to my home safely in Perth.

I look forward to one day catching up with Ken and presenting him with a similar style Australian gift. What a great night, with so many land speed legends and team members together at once. Great memories.

-ooOoo-

My friend Ed Shadle, the leader of the *North American Eagle* team, died in December 2018 at the age of 77. As a result, the lovely Jessi Combs took up the North American team's driving responsibilities. Sadly, Jessi was killed driving *North American Eagle* in the Alvord Desert in Oregon in 2019, trying to beat Kitty O'Neil's female world land speed record.

Jessi was a popular TV personality and appeared in many shows, including Myth Busters, Overhaulin' and Xtreme 4x4. Unfortunately, I never got to meet Jessi, but by all accounts, she was a fantastic lady and will be sadly missed.

Later, data equipment recovered from the crashed car proved that Jessi had exceeded Kitty O'Neil's speed of 512 mph. As a result, Jessi was credited with a new female world record.

I needed a stiff drink after my Russian Kidnapping!

Bruno's Country Club and Motel in Gerlach, Nevada.

Craig Breedlove, me and Ed Shadle. On a visit to see the North American Eagle run in 2007.

False Starts for Aussie Invader 5

Looking over the North American Eagle 2007.

Dust storm during test runs of North American Eagle 2007.

John "Ackers" Ackroyd with me in Gerlach, Nevada. Ackers signing his book "Jet Blast".

-19-
Later Trips, Travels and Tales in Australia

In my racing career, I have travelled extensively across Australia, visiting every state and territory many times. These travels have led me to meet many incredible people and visit many beautiful places. There is always a story to tell, and here are just a few.

It Never Rains, But It Pours

Between the first three record attempts at Lake Gairdner from 1993 to 1995, we appeared all over the country with the jet dragster and *Aussie Invader 2*. Frequently, we were asked to appear in Melbourne, Brisbane, Adelaide and Perth for motor shows, plus lots of country trade shows. These shows were paying good money and kept the wolf from the door.

One of my most memorable shows and appearances was in June 1994 at a country town in the Hunter Valley, New South Wales, called Singleton. Ampol, one of our sponsors, invited us to attend, and they wanted us to bring our land speed car.

Aussie Invader 2 had an amazing disposition. Wherever she went, it bloody RAINED! I warned the Ampol bosses about this, and they laughed, saying, "Bring it on." At one point, we considered renaming *Aussie Invader 2* "The Rainmaker" because it rained whenever we took her to Lake Gairdner.

My wife Cheryl, son Bryce and I loaded up and headed east for the nearly 4,000-kilometre drive to Singleton. Once there, I was asked to talk about setting the Australian land speed record. I appeared at the local Civic Centre that night to do my presentation. I spoke about the trials and tribulations in achieving this record for Australia. I opened my talk by saying what a phenomenon our *Aussie Invader 2* was, and everywhere we go, it rains.

One of the locals shouted, "If it rains here this week, we'll make you our new mayor." I said, "Well, that's a great offer, but I would rather make love to this lovely woman in the front row." This remark caused a big laugh, and this lovely girl took it in her stride with a smile.

Though there was no sign of rain on the radar, we were walking around in four inches of water the following day! Everyone was smiling and shaking my hand. I had many offers to ship *Aussie Invader 2* to remote drought-stricken areas of Australia to perform the same trick. However, I rejected the offer of accepting the mayor's job, and the lovely girl I mentioned in my talk was nowhere to be seen.

Rally Australia Perth

Perth in WA hosted the Rally Australia from 1988 - 2006. We have made several appearances at Perth's Rally Australia over the years. Some of these were static, some we fired our land speed car up, and there were later ones where I drove the jet dragster, *Aussie Invader 1*, around a track.

In 1994, the promoters wanted the new *Aussie Invader 2* land speed car. So, they came to our workshop to look at our record-breaker. Their idea was to chain her down on the top of a mound created over a large concrete pipe that acted as a tunnel and bridge for the rally car circuit. This circuit was going to be in a massive park in central Perth.

I explained that this car was extremely noisy and would create havoc, panicking the public and creating a massive dust storm. It could also blow out a lot of windows in our city's CBD.

I mentioned that we have access to our local Pearce Military Air Force Base. When we test-fire our car there, the locals still complain about the noise and are used to military jets taking off!

The organisers were still keen for this to go ahead. However, I insisted that our *Aussie Invader 1* jet dragster was better suited to this event. "I can do laps of the track and a high-speed run along Riverside Drive", I said. Riverside Drive, the main road adjoining this park, was shut during this event, and the public would see much more this way. However, the organisers still wanted *Aussie Invader 2*, our Mirage Fighter jet-powered car.

The closer the day came to performing this display, which was to be over two separate nights, the more nervous the promoters became. Finally, they asked if we could increase our public liability insurance from $2 million to $5 million the night before our first appearance.

We wanted to set concrete blocks into the ground and chain our car to them. The organisers wanted us to tie chains to two large excavators spread behind the car, hopefully away from the jet blast. We were not happy campers about this.

It was time to fire up our car on Friday, the first night, around 7 p.m. I was seated in our car, looking west at the crowd on my right-hand side. With the OK signal from my crew chief, I pressed the start button. This fires up a small APU-style jet starter, which screams into life. Already, I noticed people ducking for cover, even before the main engine had fired. I watched the rev counter climb and cracked the main engine throttle, and our pride and joy roared into life, with dust and papers flying everywhere. The place looked like a scene from the movie Apocalypse Now.

Plenty of stories came out of this appearance and display, with damaged windows, people losing their hearing, and dust blanketing the city. My favourite was our great mate Gary Miocevitch, who was a legendary Australian drag racer and promoter. He had just arrived home to his house in Winthrop, a southern suburb of Perth about 20 kilometres away. Gary told me he got home late from work, put his key in his front door lock, and stopped, as all he could hear was an enormous jet noise. He said he listened to it for a few seconds, then decided it must be a noisy aircraft at Jandakot Airport, about 10 kilometres from his home. The next second, he heard our afterburner light, and he believed he could feel the shockwave from our engine at his front door. He said, "Bloody McGlashan, he's at it again."

The following year, we were invited back to Rally Australia, but what a surprise, they didn't want the land speed car. Instead, they asked me to bring our *Aussie Invader 1* jet dragster. This was great. I loved driving this car and could put it anywhere, around speedway tracks, salt lakes, and air shows. I even had her on a barge on the river once.

Again, we performed a two-night display starting with a high speed 320 km/h run down our Riverside Drive. I stopped the car, by using two brake chutes, jettisoned them and turned onto the rally track, where I did a complete circuit. I put the car sideways to get through a tight concrete pipe tunnel and hit the afterburner as I went through, blasting the drinks out of the hands of the VIPs in their viewing area. Finally, I went over the top of the bridge and finished up in our allocated pit area just as I ran out of fuel. We again performed the same display the following night and received a lot of accolades from the pleased public about our show.

His Holiness The Dalai Lama

The last appearance at Rally Australia in Perth was in 1996. We set up *Aussie Invader 3* in a marquee at their Langley Park venue. This appearance promoted our project and next run at setting a world land speed record. We had just completed setting up our car at Rally Australia. We were busy talking to patrons and fans when I received a call from Joan Terry.

Joan and her husband Paul were one of *Aussie Invader 2's* early sponsors. Paul was a brilliant financial advisor and entrepreneur. He sadly passed away in 1993 when he was killed in a helicopter crash in Hawaii. He was a brilliant man and a massive loss to our state and country.

Joan lived in an apartment overlooking Langley Park. She said she had some international visitors keen to look at our car. So, I told Joan to come over and arranged at the gate to get her and her special guest's visitor entry passes. A short time later, Joan appeared with three guys in orange robes. I was caught a bit off-guard, but I knew Joan was heavily committed to charitable works and helping people abroad. Joan often travelled to Tibet to teach English in schools after her husband Paul had sadly died.

Joan introduced me to her guests, announcing, "This is His Holiness the Dalai Lama," and then introduced his two associates. At that time, I didn't know who or what the Dalai Lama stood for. Only later did I learn what a great honour it was to have met this man personally and the outstanding international work he does worldwide. His Holiness, the Dalai Lama and his associates were the friendliest, nicest people you could wish to meet.

To my surprise, he and his party were keen to sit in *Aussie Invader 3*. Once they were in there, it was hard to get them out. There was lots of laughter, pretend jet noises and shaking of the steering wheel. At this point, Perth probably was the centre of The Universe, where the spiritual and physical worlds met. I only wished I had managed to get a picture of it. I believe Joan may have taken one, and perhaps it will show up one day. I was very honoured to be a part of this extraordinary meeting.

A Brush with Movie Fame

Over the years, I have been on a few TV shows, commercials, and documentaries with my various vehicles. *Aussie Invader 1* has appeared on both the Ray Martin and Steve Vizard Shows in Sydney.

There's one story that might have changed my life, and it featured a beautiful girl, a goat, a Lamborghini and a rising movie star! It sounds like a plot to some seedy porn film, but I assure you it wasn't.

In July 2000, I was driving to Newcastle, NSW, after appearing at the Townsville Dragway doing some exhibition passes in our *Aussie Invader 1* jet dragster. The phone rang, and

I couldn't hear very well due to the noise in my truck. My hearing is also bad, as I have spent far too long around drag racing and jet cars.

I thought I heard the name *Manu Bennett*, and he asked if we could catch up, and he mentioned a movie. I said I had to do a speedway show in Newcastle the next night and needed to haul arse to get there. I had a long drive ahead of me, and I needed plenty of time to charge my jet engine's starter pack.

I said, "I can't hear you very well, mate. Can you call again in the morning?" I wondered if I had heard right and thought, *A movie that sounds interesting*. Hopefully, he would call back.

I arrived at the gates of Newcastle Speedway at around midnight. The caretaker wasn't going to be there. I had been told where to find the gate key and power to start my charging duties.

I was told there were some heavy-duty 15-amp power sockets at the front of the canteen. So, I parked my rig in that area, in the allotted parking bay and immediately started to prep my charging pack. I was shattered after my big drive and was looking forward to putting my batteries on charge and hitting my trailer bed.

I walked the lead out to the front of the canteen with a flashlight in one hand. There wasn't a power socket in sight. I thought *Perhaps the caretaker meant the rear of the canteen*, so I proceeded to go around the back. I opened a gate and walked into a grassed compound. As soon as I did, a bloody goat charged me and bolted through the open gate and into the night. I found the power points, plugged my lead into one of the sockets and commenced the long charging sequence.

I was shattered and just wanted to lie down and go to sleep. Then I thought *That the bloody goat might disappear from the speedway area.* It worried me and played on my mind, so I decided I had to go and catch it. Boy, what an experience. I chased that bloody animal for about an hour, finally cornering it and grabbing it by the horns. At that time, I didn't know who had whom. I finally wrestled this beast to the ground and lay on top of it, completely drained of strength. I was lying there trying to figure out how to tie this goat's legs together. That way, I could drag it back to its compound.

I was so exhausted that I never heard the track manager and his wife arrive home. They were standing behind me, probably wondering what on earth is this bloke doing. I could read their minds and quickly responded. "I'm not having sex with the goat. He escaped. Honestly, he did!" I returned to my truck bed, still wondering if they believed my explanation.

Manu rang me again the following morning and talked about doing a movie script he wanted to present to one of his producer friends. He asked if we could catch up when I'm passing through Sydney.

I said to Manu, "I would love to, but we will have to shoot for a later date. I'm doing this show in Newcastle, then finding a quiet spot to sleep for a few hours. I want to pass through the city at night as there are 125 sets of lights from Northside to Liverpool. At 2 a.m. I can make about 80 percent of them."

"What if I travel to Perth with you, mate?" he suggested.

"I always drive alone, Manu. I can drive when I want, take a break when I like, and play my music. So, you coming with me won't work."

This guy was nearly as big of a pain in the arse as me. I finally relented, telling him: "I am heading straight back to Perth. That's a 55-hour drive, and there are no unscheduled stops. So, if you are coming with me, you must have all your plans in place."

We arranged to meet at a petrol station (servo) on the outskirts of Liverpool, a suburb of Sydney. I made good time getting through the city and suburbs in my trusty Ford Louisville and Jumbo Pantech.

I was in go mode and thought, *If my man isn't here, I'll buy a coffee and give him 15 minutes before I leave.* I pulled into the servo, and a brand-new white Lamborghini was sitting there. The hottest-looking Sheila I reckon I have ever seen climbed out of the driver's seat, and Manu joined her. After the introductions, Manu gave her a big kiss, and she left.

"Holy shit, who was that?" I asked.

"Oh, she's the girl who works for the movie director I mentioned."

"Wow, she's a stunner. OK, are you ready to roll?"

"Yes, let's go."

We were heading south down Sesame Street towards the Wagga-Wagga turn-off, as the truckers call the Hume Highway. We are then heading west for about another 50 hours.

"Can we stop and get batteries for my voice recorder?" asked Manu.

"Yes, no problem. When we get to Perth, we ain't making unscheduled stops. I told you that." I replied.

Manu asked if it was okay to jump into my truck's sleeper cab and quickly went to sleep. About nine hours later, he woke up.

"Where are we?" he asked.

"We are about 100 clicks out of Adelaide, and our Kangaroo count is eight. Sorry if bowling them over woke you up."

He fired up his phone and told me in an excited voice.

"Mate, it's Kylie Minogue's birthday tonight. She's in Adelaide, and we are invited to her party."

"Stiff shit, we are heading west, no unscheduled stops," I replied.

After a really long drive, we eventually arrived at my house. Manu stayed at my home for a few weeks, interviewing me, and left to fly back home.

Several months later, a movie script arrived and looked pretty good. I was very impressed with Manu's work. He left it to me to have it registered somewhere in the movie world because it was a story based on my life. I never followed up. I was too busy looking forward at the time, planning my next steps towards building my land speed car.

I did revisit it a few years later, about 2005. Still, just about that time, the movie "The World's Fastest Indian" was released with Anthony Hopkins playing Burt Munro. I thought *This wasn't the time for two land speed movies* and put it away again. That script is still gathering dust in my office. Sorry, Manu.

At the time of our meeting, Manu had just started his TV and movie career, and he has gone on to be a famous actor in the USA, making some great movies and TV shows.

-20-
How to Build The World's Fastest Car

In late 2008, knowing we needed rocket power, I managed to hook back up with a fantastic young and dynamic rocket scientist from Invercargill, New Zealand (the birthplace of Burt Munro) named Peter Beck. Peter had been introduced to me by Juan Manuel Lozano Gallegos (The Mexican Rocket Man).

Peter was self-taught, loved what we were trying to do, and offered some expertise and advice over the phone and email. So, I decided to visit him and made arrangements to fly and meet with him at a technical facility he had rented near the centre of Auckland, New Zealand. We hit it off immediately, and I got a guided tour of some of his rocketry innovations. I explained that we were building a car in which we wanted to reach 1,600 + km/h (1,000 mph), and his eyes lit up.

He told me about his new in-house trajectory modelling capability. He said he would conduct preliminary calculations into the performance capabilities of our car. Ackers had put together a design for the latest iteration of *Aussie Invader 5R*, which I sent to Peter.

Peter was also in the process of establishing Rocket Lab, a new company that needed to make its way. Peter could little afford the luxury of offering cutting-edge information, his time, technology and expertise for free, but that's precisely what he did.

I had given Peter calculations from our great mate Ackers on the shape and drag coefficient of our proposed design. A few months later, in February 2009, a beautiful document landed in my computer's inbox from Peter. It laid out trajectory modelling for *Aussie Invader 5R*, which was a revelation to me. For the first time, I had a plan of how to create the world's fastest and most powerful car right here in my hands.

This document provided the information we needed to build our car, containing estimations of propellant load, speed, acceleration, Mach numbers and other forces involved. It was a work of art and the big sledgehammer we needed to crack a bloody tough nut.

As you have just read, there have been several false starts and roads to nowhere. When we started to build this car, we had been designing and planning it for over ten years. In truth, we knew now rockets were the only way to go, and they packed an enormous punch for their size. I was bloody excited about the future and what we would build.

The report from Peter established we needed a rocket engine to provide around 62,000 lbs of thrust. Although hard to directly equate to horsepower, in this scenario, it was approximately 200,000 horsepower (about the power of 200 Formula One cars). So, this car would be five times more powerful than *Aussie Invader 3*. I thought, *Bloody brilliant.* I was excited, and rightly so. Now, we just had to work out how my team and I would build it!

Peter soon became more interested in our project and produced a brilliant technical report on our predicted wheel and aero drag, thrust requirements, propellant payloads, and more. We became great mates, and I was fortunate to be invited to his first rocket launch in 2009.

His first launch was from Great Mercury Island, just off New Zealand's North Island Coromandel Peninsula. This private island is owned by Sir Michael Fay and is a brilliant location and an ideal launch site. His first launch was spectacular, and since that day, his company has jumped ahead in leaps and bounds.

The thing about Peter and Rocket Lab's work is they have brought rocket launch costs down considerably. Until that point, rocket launches would cost tens of millions of dollars to get something into space. Peter's reusable, 3D-printed Electron rockets could launch small satellites for a fraction of that cost. In addition, it meant universities, schools, and businesses could now afford to put their products, experiments and equipment into space.

Rocket Lab is now Rocket Lab USA, with launch sites worldwide and a staff of hundreds. Their satellite deliveries into low orbit trajectories are a regular occurrence. Sadly, for our team, Peter and Rocket Lab got too famous too quickly. They are now prohibited by NASA and other international rocket companies they work for from sharing any technology with others. However, we are so thankful for the performance prediction data Peter did for us, and it started us on our road with *Aussie Invader 5R*. Luckily for us, this was before the rest of the world discovered him as the great rocket guy he is. Thanks, Peter.

Aussie Invader 5R Explained

This section may be heavy going for some, but if it hadn't been written, I know many people would have asked why. The following chapter explains the car, its design and how it works as simply and accurately as possible.

To help with the following explanation, please refer to pictures of *Aussie Invader 5R* at the end of this chapter. I feel it is essential to read this chapter because it explains why *Aussie Invader 5R* is the way it is and why it has taken so long to build.

I would be rich if I had a dollar for everyone who asked me when the car would be finished or was going to run. I have had a lot of people suggest better ways to do things. I try to be polite, but if you know how to build a car to break the current world land speed record and achieve over 1,600 km/h, please be my guest and do it. I will happily hold your jacket and make the coffee whilst you try.

I am not saying my team and I are the only people who can do this, but this is a massive task. There are many things to consider, and not getting it right means you probably won't live to tell the tale. World land speed history is littered with people who attempted the record and didn't survive. Contrary to common opinion, I don't have a death wish unless it is dying next to a beautiful woman in bed when I'm 104!

I have served a 60-year apprenticeship and don't have all the answers, but I have quite a few. The UK's *Bloodhound SSC* project, with all its expertise, resources, funds and fantastic team, thought their car would be completed in 5 years. That meant it would have been finished in about 2014, and we thought the same. Both teams are a lot wiser and know differently now.

In a previous chapter, I met Darryl Greenamyer. He set the world low-altitude speed record for an aircraft in a modified F-104 in 1977 at 1,590 km/h. To put our land speed goal into perspective, we are trying to build a car to achieve a speed no aircraft has ever managed at a low altitude.

How much money do the aircraft industry and military spend on design and manufacture? It runs into hundreds of billions of dollars. My team and I are building this car in my home workshop with very limited funds.

Peter Beck's fantastic document outlined a clear path: the 62,000 lbs of thrust rocket engine would push the car to over 1,600 km/h in just 22 seconds. It was going to be an exciting ride. I had driven rocket-powered vehicles before, during my stay in the USA in 1980. Then I broke the drag racing record for a rocket go-kart, hitting 407 km/h (253 mph) over the quarter-mile in just 5.97 seconds. It was the most exciting thing I had ever driven. Yes, driving *Aussie Invader 5R* would certainly eclipse that experience, I have no doubt.

Rockets are far less predictable and less throttleable than jet engines, which will make *Aussie Invader 5R* a handful to drive. Saying that, I am not overly worried about driving this car. When I received Peter's fantastic report, I was a long way off getting my backside in the driver's seat, and by the time I did, I would know every inch of it. I personally would have built or overseen the construction, and I wouldn't be getting in it unless I was 100 percent certain it was right. Also, some of the best engineers in the world have worked on this project. They were my friends and wouldn't want to put me at any more risk than necessary.

To clarify, a rocket engine, unlike a jet engine, carries its own oxygen in liquid form. In this case, it would be white fuming nitric acid (WFNA). A jet engine, or an internal combustion engine, burns oxygen directly from the atmosphere. It means our car will have to carry fuel (furfuryl alcohol) and a serious amount of WFNA oxidiser. We aren't talking about a few litres or gallons. Both oxidiser and fuel would amount to about 2.8 tonnes of liquid propellant. Most of which would have to be pushed through the engine in 22 seconds, a big ask.

We designed the car to keep it as simple as possible, with the least number of moving parts that could fail. We decided to use a pressure-fed propellant system to push the fuel and oxidiser into the engine. We were not going to use mechanical or electrical pumps, as most rocket engines do. The other thing that was a real headache was that we would be firing our rocket horizontally (along the ground). Ideally, liquid bi-propellant rockets are designed to be fired vertically (straight up).

Peter Beck had worked out that we needed to slow down the acceleration of our car. Why try and build a car to go as fast as possible and then slow it down? It wouldn't affect *Aussie Invader 5R's* top speed, just how quickly it got there. Peter had identified that we didn't want to exceed 3.2 G when accelerating, and it wasn't about protecting me, the driver. I had driven cars that had accelerated with higher G-force than that.

If the car accelerated too quickly, the free-spinning solid aluminium wheels, each weighing around 140 kilograms (310 lbs), wouldn't be able to spin up quickly enough. This issue would mean the wheels could all be spinning at different speeds and losing traction with the ground. Each wheel would act like a big gyro and skid along the desert surface. If this happened, it would pull the car all over the place, making it impossible to steer. I had experienced what happens when solid wheels lose traction on a land speed car in *Aussie Invader 2*. It went sideways at well over 800 km/h, and I didn't want to repeat that experience.

The way to slow the car's acceleration down was to increase its mass (weight). Peter had determined that we needed the car to weigh a minimum of 6.3 tonnes dry (unfuelled). It meant *Aussie Invader 5R* would weigh just over 9 tonnes when fully fuelled. However, even with the car's considerable weight, our rocket engine has enough power to keep the car accelerating at an almost constant rate, right up to about 1,600 km/h, without exceeding 3.2 G.

Whenever I talk about us trying to keep the weight of *Aussie Invader 5R* up, people also naturally assume that this is to keep it on the ground. However, the only thing that keeps our car on the ground is its aerodynamic performance. This is through its nose cone design, tail fin, canards (winglets just behind the front wheels) and the "V" shaped underbelly. With the fully fuelled car's weight of just over 9 tonnes and its engine producing 62,000 lbs or 28 tonnes of thrust, you could put the car on its rear end and on half power, and it would still go straight up in the air!

Once the car hits the start of the timed and measured mile, we will reduce the engine's power slightly because, at over 1,600 km/h, the wheels would rotate close to their 10,000 rpm limit. At those speeds, each wheel would generate a massive 50,000 G loading on the wheel's rim, with the wheels wanting to literally tear themselves apart. That means if you fixed a one-kilogram weight to the wheel's rim and spun it at 10,000 rpm, that one-kilogram weight would effectively weigh 50-tonnes!

It was all starting to make sense to me, and I had a clear path to start the build. Ken Warby had said to me many years ago.

"Just make a start and deal with the 'opportunities' as they arise."

There was going to be a mass of "opportunities" that would arise, and we had many years of serious work ahead of us.

The speed of the build was definitely going to be subject to available funds. But, even if we had $10 million on day one, some things we were out to design and build had never been done before. So, they would take a long time to develop and test regardless of money.

The design structure we had come up with was simple. We were going to use a 12-metre-long high-grade steel tube, referred to as the "mainframe," which was just under a metre in diameter. The mainframe was rolled from a flat sheet of 10 mm thick steel and seam welded, with boundary layer rings (slight bumps) rolled into it at 300 mm intervals. The mainframe itself weighs a massive 2.5 tonnes. This weight was also a great start in helping us keep the car's weight up to the minimum 6.3 tonnes dry weight magic number we needed.

As for the length of our mainframe, why 12 metres long? We had to be able to transport the car interstate and internationally. We needed it to fit into a standard large transport container. So, taking the Art Arfons approach, who built his *Green Monster* car to fit his transport truck bed, we adopted the same thinking. The mainframe of our car, with its rear wheels on, fits snuggly into a large transport container. The front wheel pack and nose cone could be removed and put into a smaller container, along with other necessary parts, tools and equipment.

Sometimes, answers to the most complex problems can be the simplest. Nature has spent millions of years working out *Aussie Invader 5R's* design for us. Some of the toughest and strongest creatures on the planet are insects. *Aussie Invader 5R* borrowed its construction from their example, having its skeleton (mainframe) on the outside. Our design was the reverse of most race cars, which get strength from an internal chassis covered with a thin skin. Our insect-like shell is a 10 mm thick bisalloy tube perfect for protecting and securing all the rocket pressure vessels and internals.

The mainframe would also support our propellant delivery system, which we called the Orbital Propellant Module (OPM). An explanation for this name comes later. Finally, the super strong mainframe would protect and support hundreds of other critical components and me, the driver.

We had some great support in sourcing the steel and rolling it into a tube, and we needed custom-made jigs to support the mainframe in our workshop. These jigs allow us to rotate and move the 2.5-tonne tubular mainframe so that we can work on the underside of the car as well as the top. The jigs and the tube were made and sponsored by great local Perth companies Di Candilo Steel City and Advanced Electrical Equipment.

One of the most critical parts of *Aussie Invader 5R* is the design and construction of the nose cone. The nose cone sets up the airflow over the whole car, which is critical for the car's aerodynamic performance and stability. The nose cone is angled down one degree to give us downforce. The faster we go, the more downforce we create. Downforce is a delicate balancing act. Too little and the nose could lift, and the car would end up somersaulting down the track. Too much and wheels will dig into the ground and "mine" into the hard-baked desert surface. Aero Jacks fabricated this nose using the latest composite materials, the same products used in constructing their MX Aircraft.

Aussie Invader 5R has a "V" shaped underbelly running the length of the car. The "V" shaped underbelly was designed to help deflect the ground-generated shockwave when it approaches the speed of sound (transonic) and faster. John "Ackers" Ackroyd had studied cars like Craig Breedlove's *Spirit of America - Sonic Arrow* and the *Budweiser Rocket* car, producing an excellent report for us on these vehicles. Unfortunately, both of these machines experienced considerable instability when going transonic.

Craig's car went up on one wheel and did a 180-degree U-turn at over 1,050 km/h, and luckily, Craig was uninjured. However, when the *Budweiser Rocket* car in 1979 went transonic, the shockwave bouncing down the car lifted the back wheels off the ground. The car then ran for about 250 metres on its nose wheel, with both rear wheels completely airborne.

The shockwave coming off the nose and fuselage of an aircraft can dissipate around it through the air. The shockwave from a car on the ground doesn't have that advantage. The portion of the shockwave that deflects off the nose downwards will hit the solid ground and bounce back up. It will then proceed to bounce down the length of the vehicle, creating lift, precisely the same as when a car hits water at very high speed and aquaplanes. Our car's "V" shape underbelly will allow the deflected shockwave to escape either side of *Aussie Invader 5R*, reducing the potential lift and pounding drag.

This lift effect applies to all the car's surfaces close to the ground, such as axles and their supports. These also need to have the smallest cross-sectional area possible to limit this transonic/supersonic lift effect as we approach and exceed the speed of sound. So, again, there is a conflict between streamlining and surface area, and we must get the balance right.

We know our rocket engine has the power to blast us through the transonic region in a very short time. This is ideal, as the transonic phase is very dangerous. This is because some of the car's surfaces are subsonic, and some are supersonic, which can make the car very unstable. So, the quicker you can blast through it, the better.

No car has really experienced travelling supersonic. Yes, *Thrust SSC* hit Mach 1.02 but was only there for a very short time. We will be travelling there for a lot longer. We hope the further we go into the supersonic region (past the speed of sound), the smoother the ride will get, but who knows? I have been told that conventional steering may no longer be effective or work in the supersonic region. Aerodynamic forces will control the car, and hopefully, it will keep going straight!

Our rear axle is a 125 mm diameter bisalloy hollow round bar. This axle is super strong, so we don't need axle support struts that create massive aero drag. *The Blue Flame* team in 1970 discovered that the aero drag from their rear wheel axle supports alone could be as much as 24 percent.

The front wheel assembly bolts to the front of the mainframe, as does the 3.5-metre detachable composite nose and encases the front wheels. The nose angle of one degree down was calculated after a huge computational fluid dynamics (CFD) study by Dan McKeon. Dan is one of the best CFD gurus, having been a Formula One aerodynamicist and a ballistics expert.

Just behind the nose cone and front wheels are two floating canards (winglets), one on each side. These will assist in trimming the car and keep Aussie Invader 5R and me hopefully on the ground. Our brilliant team member and engineering genius, Paul Martin, designed these. The canards are needed because the car's weight and centre of gravity will constantly and drastically change as we burn our massive propellant payload.

The canards work on the same concept as some of the latest jet fighters. They "float" on a common shaft mounted on bearings across the centreline of our car, just behind our front wheels. Because they float, they set themselves into the oncoming airflow as the car gains speed. As the propellant loads drop and the car's centre of gravity moves rearward, the front will automatically become lighter. Because they are in the forward air stream, the canards apply pressure and load the nose downward. The same applies when the nose is too heavy or is pushed down excessively. Then, the canards adjust themselves into the airflow and assist the front of the car to "unload." This weight transfer prevents the front wheels from "mining" or digging into the ground.

The car was going to be long, just under 16 metres. Most of this length was to contain the Orbital Propellant Module and nitrogen pressure-fed propellant delivery system. This system forces the 2.8 tonnes of propellant into the engine.

The car has four wheels, two at the back with 2.3-metre track width and two at the front. The front wheels are side by side on a common axle, 30 mm apart, with each wheel spinning independently. This configuration means *Aussie Invader 5R* would qualify as a car for record purposes.

Each wheel is machined from a solid piece of 7050-T7451 aerospace aluminium. The alloy for these wheels is very expensive and was kindly sponsored by Calm Aluminium in

NSW. The wheels are 900 mm in diameter and 198 mm wide. They rotate on a quad-bearing pack designed and manufactured specifically for us by SKF Bearings.

The cut-out for the driver's cockpit area is supported by a roll cage made to FIA standards. It uses four longitudinal hollow round bars supporting the mainframe at its opening. This prevents it from bending at its weakest point, the driver's cockpit. The roll cage was professionally heat-treated and welded in place. We managed to secure the services of LF Performance Products in Perth to make our roll cage. These guys do some first-class race car engineering.

Many land speed cars, including *Spirit of America - Sonic Arrow* and *Thrust SSC*, have their cockpits and driving position just behind the front wheels. Sitting there means you can see and feel what the front of the car is doing, but you have little or no idea what is happening at the back of the car. Often, the rear wheels are a long way behind you.

That would certainly be the case with our car if we sat at the front. If the back of the car is "snaking" or sliding, you cannot feel it straight away. By the time you know there is a problem, it could be too late. Sensors and systems in the car will help monitor this, but a lot is going on when you are driving. It is almost certainly too much to absorb in such a short time. Everything will happen so quickly. Often, a driver's feel for a car is far more accurate than sensors.

The best location for the driver is two-thirds down the length of the vehicle, just behind the centre of gravity. You can feel what is happening at the back of the car and see what the front is doing. As we aren't using a bulky jet engine with an air intake, which limits the choice of cockpit location, we have the luxury of this better driving position.

Our car has two throttle pedals, one for each foot. If my foot lifts off either pedal, the engine will automatically go through a shutdown sequence and abort the run.

This was to avoid what happened to Craig Breedlove in *Spirit of America - Sonic Arrow* when one of its rear wheels lifted at 1,050 km/h. As a result, the car did a massive U-turn, which threw Craig to one side, causing his foot to get jammed on the throttle pedal. It made it very hard to lift his foot off straight away, so it was still under power whilst doing the U-turn. Luckily, Craig freed his foot and stopped the car without further issues.

The tail fin on *Aussie Invader 5R* is a work of art. It is machined in two halves, a left and a right-hand side, that were later bolted together. These halves were originally two solid billet alloy blocks, taking over 800 hours of CNC machining. Its centre is a honeycomb construction, comparatively light but incredibly strong.

The tail fin has quite a small horizontal stabiliser bolted to the top of it. The horizontal stabiliser can be adjusted one or two degrees up or down with expertly machined spacer blocks. The rules do not allow adjustment of the tail fin during a run. However, this could be done between runs if load sensors and testing indicated it is necessary.

The tail fin and horizontal stabiliser are held together with about four hundred bolts and screws, which took two of my team members and me over a day to assemble. Each bolt is a specific size and custom-fitted to its location. A picture later in the book shows this. In addition, we had several pages of plans to bolt the two halves of the tail fin together.

The Orbital Propellant Module (OPM) feeds the propellants into the rocket engine. It is a central part of our car's unique design. We designed a system using seven, six-metre-long aerospace aluminium tubes to make a liquid bi-propellant engine operate in a horizontal plane. These tubes have pistons that are pushed down the length of the tube when high-pressure inert gas is applied to them. The pistons force the propellants into the engine's injector, where they are atomised. When the propellants meet in the engine, they create an instant hypergolic reaction (chemical ignition) and a massive amount of thrust.

The tank system we designed could refuel satellites in a zero-gravity environment, like space. That is why we have named this our Orbital Propellant Module. Who knows, we may be able to give something back to Peter Beck for all his help.

This configuration replaces conventional cylindrical tanks, which were initially planned but rejected. The weight of these vessels, at the required pressure rating, proved far too heavy. Even the best lightweight materials, like Nitronic 40 constructed tanks with baffles and surge doors, were too heavy. So, we had to come up with a lighter-weight, anti-slosh solution. Otherwise, we could have up to 2.8 tonnes of propellants slamming side to side, front to rear. That amount of liquid, moving about under acceleration, braking or steering, could spoil our day out big time.

The pistons in the OPM have ring magnets in their crowns, and we have a series of sensors running down the side of each tube. These will track the movement of the pistons so we can monitor propellant usage. We can also tell if all the pistons are moving evenly. By increasing the pressure on the pistons via regulators, we can speed up or slow them down. This will adjust the amount of propellant being forced into the engine over a given time and vary the engine's power and, subsequently, the car's performance. Once again, we had to design and manufacture the OPM ourselves, as we couldn't find anything that did what we wanted.

One thing that is in no doubt is that *Aussie Invader 5R* is going to travel fast, bloody fast. By the time it exits the measured mile on a full-power run, it should be travelling around 1,600 km/h. Getting to the measured mile from the start line will only take 22 seconds. In that short time, the car will travel about five kilometres before entering the mile and kilometre speed traps.

Once it enters the measured mile, I will be throttling back slightly, reducing power so as not to push the wheels beyond their maximum design speed. Travelling at 1,600 km/h, the car and I will cover the measured mile in approximately 3.5 seconds and a kilometre in just over two seconds.

Once I exit the measured mile, my thoughts will turn to try and stop this beast as quickly and safely as possible. However, this will take a lot longer and a lot more track than getting it up to that magic 1,600 km/h speed. We will need about 13 kilometres (8 miles) of track to stop the car.

This is because if I were to shut the engine off as soon as we exited the measured mile, we would encounter two massive issues:

1. I would pass out because the car and I would experience an extremely high negative G-force.

2. The wheels would almost certainly lose traction, skidding over the desert/playa surface and making the car unstable.

Stopping our high-speed car requires the perfect timing of our five braking systems.

Firstly, the engine will do a timed and controlled three-second shutdown when I step off the throttle. This will allow our car to transition into deceleration mode, allowing our wheels to gain traction from their 10,000 rpm and 50,000 G nightmare.

Once the engine is shut down, our car will naturally slow very quickly, as the aero drag will be enormous. I will activate the hydraulic air brakes at about 1,250 km/h (775 mph). These are situated at the rear of the car on either side. The air brakes will take about four seconds to fully deploy. When they are completely extended, the car will slow very rapidly.

The fully extended air brakes will experience about 7-tonnes of force at those speeds. Their job is to disrupt the airflow and rapidly slow the car so the parachutes can be deployed.

We believe this air brake design is unique to *Aussie Invader 5R* and was designed by our engineering guru, Paul Martin. Paul has worked for McLaren and some other great companies and helped McLaren develop their first supercar in 1991.

Paul designed these air brakes with a series of holes in both the upper and lower fin edges. These holes (disruptors) increase the air brakes' efficiency by about 30 percent over conventional air brakes.

The air brakes' angled fin edges also direct the airflow away from the car and hitting the underside of the horizontal stabiliser. If this happened, it would create a lot of lift, making the back of the car very light.

Both air brakes operate through a single hydraulic ram via bell cranks. This ensures that both brakes deploy or fail to open in unison. It is better to have no air brakes than only one open, as it would be a massive issue for me and the car, making it very unstable.

Then, two parachutes are deployed. Both parachutes are fired out the back of the car via drogue guns, which use a pneumatic charge to try and pick up clear air so they unfurl correctly. The high-speed chute is deployed at about 960 km/h (600 mph). This chute slows and stabilises our vehicle by "tugging" the back of the car very hard. It will straighten her up if necessary. It will feel like someone hitting me in the back with a sledgehammer.

The low-speed chute is deployed when our speed reaches about 640 km/h (400 mph), slowing the car further. When our speed is down to about 320 km/h (200 mph), it will allow me to apply our high-speed disc brakes fitted to the rear wheels only, bringing the car to a complete stop.

In an emergency, should the parachutes or air brakes fail to deploy, we have our "Fred Flintstone" brake. It is a hydraulic steel ram with a flat metal plate (foot) on the bottom of it. In an emergency or "runaway" situation, it can be hydraulically forced downwards by the driver. It will bury itself into the hard desert surface to stop the car. This is definitely a last resort, as it will do some high-speed "ploughing" and be very rough on the car, me and my visibility.

As an added safety feature, this "Fred Flintstone" brake can hook up with a buried catch-cable submerged near the end of our track. This would stop us before we reach any upcoming mountain range or lake. Similar to how they stop aircraft when landing on an aircraft carrier.

This hydraulic ram's primary use is to lift the front of the car for maintenance and when she is being turned around. We lift it up on the ram, putting the "jinker" (big trolley) under the front wheels, but it also works as a fail-safe measure.

Claiming a new world land speed record depends on our car being turned around and headed back in the opposite direction from her first run within one hour. Then, the average of both runs is calculated for the kilometre and mile record.

One of our concerns with our car is its pure brute power. Trying to make our car run within the FIA rules, which were primarily written over 100 years ago, might prove very hard. The rules were designed for petrol-driven cars that ran a fraction of the speeds we expect to reach.

The FIA has recently changed one of the rules, which will help us, but we will have to see if we can comply. If we feel we can't, or it is just too restrictive as far as safety is concerned, we may run under the Guinness World Records rules. This would involve one flat-out run over the measured, timed kilometre and mile distances.

We understand that many purists will say that these are the rules you must work within. However, we don't feel they reflect current progress and thinking. For example, very few sporting world record asks you to back up a record by running it within an hour in the opposite direction. Instead, you can monitor windspeed or gradient; if it is not within the accepted limits, the record won't stand.

ROSCO THE FASTEST AUSSIE ON EARTH

1. Bi-propellant rocket engine with 62,000 lb/f. 200,000 hp.
2. Vertical & horizontal stabilisers.
3. The air brakes are deployed at 775 mph. 7 tonnes of force.
4. Aerospace-grade aluminium wheels. 4 x 140 kg. 10,250 rpm max limit (1,050 mph).
5. Propellant actuator valves.
6. Adjustable propellant regulators 300-600 psi.
7. High & low speed chutes deployed at 600 mph & 400 mph.
8. Composite filament wound blowdown tanks - 4,000 psi.
9. Electronics & hydraulics service bay (details not shown).
10. Propellant feed lines from OPM to the rocket engine.

AUSSIE INVADER 5R OVERVIEW

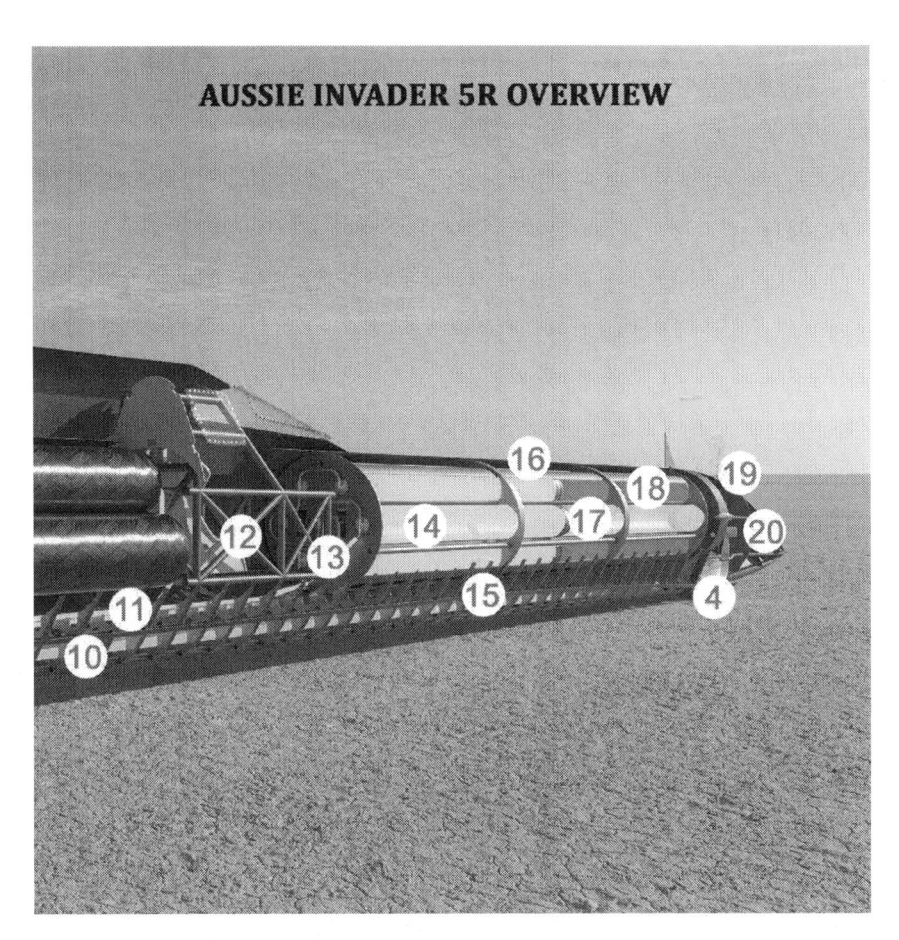

11. Gaseous nitrogen fed to OPM.

12. Driver's cockpit & roll cage (detailed view not shown).

13. Fire & breathing systems.

14. Gaseous nitrogen pushing pistons along OPM. Pistons force propellants into the rocket engine. Hypergolic reaction.

15. "V" Shaped underbelly to deflect shockwave.

16. Orbital propellant module (OPM). It is 6 metres long & holds 2.8 tonnes of propellants.

17. 3 x fuel tanks (gum spirit).

18. 4 x oxidiser tanks (white fuming nitric acid).

19. Carbon fibre nose cone with avionics & radar.

20. Canards (winglets). Self-levelling to balance the car.

Our good friend and Rocket Lab founder Peter Beck, with one of his Electron rockets.

Peter and I together at one of our many meetings in NZ. He is a very clever young man.

Peter Beck has taken Rocket Lab global, launching Rocket Lab USA on the NASDAQ.

In 2015, Beck received the New Zealander of the Year Award in the Innovator of the Year category.

In 2019, he was appointed adjunct professor at the University of Auckland. Rocket Lab and Peter were awarded the Pickering Medal by the Royal Society Te Apārangi in 2020.

Aussie Invader 5R at the Avalon Airshow in March 2023. Heather Jones and David "Spider" Guy of the Pilbara Heavy Haulage Girls Group kindly sponsored truck transport and logistics.

-21-
Build Events and Milestones – Part 1

The last chapter was quite a lot to take in, but it was necessary to explain what we were trying to achieve and the complexity of the task. The following few chapters explain how we did it.

Going through the car's build and everything we did would make this book a very tough read. A lot of the work is very repetitive and uninteresting. Jobs are performed until we are happy with the results. Sometimes, designs change, and new ideas get incorporated. It's a fluid process, and it is outcome-driven. We know what we want and where we want to be, but sometimes, we don't know the best way to get there, but we eventually find it.

This book is about my life and my passion for being the fastest man on Earth. The last 14 years have been devoted to physically building a car to do just that, which is less interesting than you might think. However, what is interesting about the day-to-day construction and what makes this journey unique is the people I have met along the way. The next few chapters contain some of those people, their stories and key milestones we have achieved when constructing this unique car.

-ooOoo-

As I've always said to my team, sponsors and individuals find it hard to put money into something unless they can see and touch it. That's the same with this car. So, we have always tried to keep the construction moving forward, sometimes quickly, sometimes slowly, but month after month, we have moved forward. The exception was when we had a run-in with the Australian Tax Office (ATO) in 2015.

The team and I had always known that this would be a very long journey when we started out. But not as long as the 20 years it has taken so far when you include the planning and false starts. COVID and other world events have certainly played a part in slowing things down in recent years, but we are nearly there. We understand that it is the nature of the beast we are trying to tame. I have always been told, "If it was easy, everyone would do it!"

If anyone wants to break the world land speed record from now on, it has to be someone with very deep pockets. A billionaire, multi-national company or even a government-backed project, I doubt it will be an individual through raising sponsorship anymore.

By talking to Andy Green and Richard Noble, I knew they wanted us and Australia to break their record. It would have given them something to go after. Breaking your own record, which your country has held for many years, does not capture people's imaginations. Striving to take it back from another team or country when it's been lost that's what gets people fired up. We have always promoted our friendly sporting rivalry between Australia and the UK, which benefits both teams.

I felt very sorry for Andy and Richard when the *Bloodhound SSC* project had to be wound up, as they are both good friends. It was great of Ian Warhurst to finance the *Bloodhound SSC* project to try and keep it running and attract other sponsors to get it finished. Unfortunately, at the time of writing this book, the UK's *Bloodhound SSC* project is still mothballed.

Around 2009, at the start of the construction of *Aussie Invader 5R*, I got a call from the current fastest man on Earth, Andy Green. He invited me to join him and his lovely wife, Emma, who were both coming to Australia to check out some possible land speed locations. Andy was looking for a suitable playa (dry desert-baked surface) to race their newly designed *Bloodhound SSC*.

Their car was soon to commence construction, and I was excited to have them here. I considered his offer, the toughness of the outback, and the extremely remote locations and vast distances involved. I also decided that three is a crowd, and Emma may not like an Aussie who swears and eats with his hands. I wished them a great adventure but stayed home working on our *Aussie Invader 5R* project. I had big hopes of beating our British friends and rivals to the finish and running our car first.

A few years before this call, we were blessed that whilst Andy was on a joint RAF/RAAF initiative on the east coast of Australia, he made time to visit us in Perth. He met my family and had time to look at our *Aussie Invader 3* car. Obviously, we did some bench racing and talked speed.

I think Andy Green is probably the best driver of this type of vehicle I've ever seen. He's calm and knowledgeable, and as I said in the past, he was the only person who could've driven *Thrust SSC* to that record in 1997. For most of us land speed guys, that car was undrivable.

Raising The Projects Profile

Right at the start of the construction of *Aussie Invader 5R*, when we were trying to get sponsors, we needed something to explain and show our vision. We needed a good website, but I needed help getting our latest website up and running. It was many months late, and I was frustrated as we needed something to show and excite people.

At the time, *Aussie Invader 5R* was just a 2.5-tonne, 12-metre cylindrical steel tube sitting on a stand in my home workshop. It wouldn't look like a car for quite some time, which was a big problem. The one thing I had going for me was I had a proven track record of building land speed cars. I wasn't someone who said they would build a car, never to get it off the drawing board.

I have met so many people who told me they would take my Australian land speed record or how they would build a car faster than mine. To date, none have materialised. Saying it is one thing, but doing it is another. It is so bloody challenging, time-consuming, and costly.

In 2009, we recruited someone with website experience into the team. We met in Perth and spent several hours chatting, drinking coffee and feeding parking meters. This team member was an enthusiastic hot rod builder with website experience and spent the first month working on the website every day. What had yet to be delivered over the last six months suddenly became a reality in a few weeks. Now, we could really excite people with our vision.

It had been nearly ten years since we had started planning *Aussie Invader 5R*. We had seen a lot of designs and engine configurations, but now the talking had to stop, and the building had to start. After completing the website, our priority was to get eyeballs to it and raise the project's profile to get some sponsorship money flowing into *Aussie Invader 5R's* build.

My wife Cheryl had done much of this in the past, but as I was working full-time on the project, Cheryl was tied up trying to ensure we had an income. First, we needed to eat and pay the bills; after that, every spare cent went into the car. We still had years of debt we had to repay from the previous land speed record attempts. We didn't know how long it would take us to complete the new car.

These days, it's a challenging task to raise sponsorship. Gone are the days when there was just one person who could make an executive decision on financial spending or sponsorship in most larger companies. Everything has to go through many layers of management and decision-makers. It is almost impossible for one person to make that decision now. That is why many of our sponsors and contributions come from small to medium-sized family-owned businesses, and we thank them all.

The Build Process Begins

We had our 2.5-tonne steel tube (mainframe) sitting in the workshop. So, Pete Taylor and I carefully cut out the space for the driver's cockpit and roll cage, located just behind our car's centre of gravity.

Over the coming months, we made significant progress. The roll cage was in, and the bulkhead and "top hat" section behind the driver's cockpit were welded in place. The rear axle support box structure was also welded to the mainframe.

The car was coming together nicely, and after less than a year, we had something that resembled a land speed car from the outside. A lot of parts like the tail fin, wheels and nose were only temporary mocked-up pieces, but they added to the car's appearance so people could understand the shape and size of this beast. In addition, we now had a website helping visitors to understand what we were trying to achieve.

Mike Annear was working hard on our computer animations. Of course, in those early days, the systems weren't as advanced as they are now, but still, it was 500 times better than my folded pieces of paper and poor drawings.

Later in the project, Mike Annear moved away to the East Coast for work. We got some brilliant 3D modelling and CGI visual animation help from a Perth-based company, Unique 8 Design Studio. Clint Davis, who worked at Unique 8 then, helped us again personally. He created all the fantastic CGI visuals and cutaway images you see of the car on our website (aussieinvader.com) and in this book.

Flooding of Our House and Workshop

In March 2010, about a year after our build started, disaster struck in the form of mother nature. Perth receives a month's worth of rain in an hour, with a massive hail storm. Unfortunately, we were not spared. The workshop and my home were completely flooded. Luckily, the workshop and car were unscathed, but my home faired less favourably. The flood took out most of my furniture, and the house was a bloody mess.

Most rooms needed replastering, and a new kitchen and bathroom were required. We were insured, but the project had to take a back seat while we sorted our house out. The good news for myself and Cheryl personally was about three months later, our house was 99 percent complete. We were able to move back in after several months of living away from our home and workshop.

The front suspension and steering setup was now taking shape, thanks to the work of our long-time suspension guru, Dr Ian Sutherland. The rear axle was also now fitted.

The best news was that our design engineer, John "Ackers" Ackroyd, was heading our way after several months of delaying his trip. His input and advice were always appreciated, and it would give us a chance to get his opinion on the car's progress.

At the end of 2010, the parachute tubes were installed, and the first carbon fibre driver's cockpit canopy was mounted. The rear external panelling was in place, which didn't look like a lot of work, but some of these tasks were massive.

During the year, the team sold our vision and project to anyone who would listen. Alex Blain came on board to help us. Through Alex, we managed to secure the services of Clarity Communications PR Agency to work with us on a pro bono basis. At Christmas, a miracle sponsor joined forces with us, Kentin Engineering, and their work was outstanding.

By early 2011, the "V" shaped underbelly support structure was coming together. With 36 support plates running the length of the car, each meticulously welded in place. Each support was laser cut and had its particular place in the line, as they were all slightly different shapes. These were once again brilliantly cut by Di Candilo Steel City. Rowe and Sons from Maddington in Perth also rolled and shaped all the external panels to cover the "top hat" rear section and "V" shaped underbelly.

By the end of 2011, we had most of the front suspension in, and the nose cone support was in place. The car was now off its rotating jig and was supported on some of *Aussie Invader 3's* spare wheels at the back. The front end was supported on a purpose-built stand.

RACE Programme and Schools

In March 2012, team member Alex Blain and other team members had been working on the concept called Regional Australian Community Education (RACE). We wanted to involve schools and education authorities in our project through Science, Technology, Engineering and Maths (STEM) subjects. This world needs clever people to overcome our problems, so young students wanting to be scientists, engineers, mathematicians and entrepreneurs are critical. But, unfortunately, we couldn't run this programme ourselves, as we didn't have the money or time, and our focus was building the car. So, we approached the WA government and education authorities and were told to apply for a particular grant, which we did, and it was refused.

The Bloodhound Education programme was going from strength to strength in the UK, spreading worldwide. This was a fantastic initiative and one of the reasons the *Bloodhound SSC* project got UK government assistance in the first place. But, unfortunately, in Australia, we had no such foresight or luck.

Around this time, Brett Boughton joined our team. He was an engineering and physics teacher from Perth's Willetton Senior High School. He was a teacher with exceptional enthusiasm. Often, 75 percent of his class would go on to study engineering at university, many through scholarships.

Brett was awarded the prestigious Engineers Australia National "President's Prize" at Parliament House in Canberra in 2010, along with another teacher, Paul Hogg. This prize was for their work at Willetton Senior High School building electric vehicles.

The education department and the government were not interested in supporting our plans. So, we decided to take the bull by the horns and run our own educational workshop with Brett's help. Brett got permission to bring his engineering year 12 class to our workshop north of Perth. Each student was invited to come along with their parents. We held an open day where Brett had created about seven or eight different engineering tasks for the group to design or perform. The students were split into groups of four and given the tasks. These included designing the air brake operating mechanism, working out the propellant loadings for the car under specific criteria, creating a mechanism to open the cockpit canopy, and several other tasks.

They were given about two hours to look over the car, write down questions, take photos, and speak to the team members and me. The local television station came down and recorded the event. The students were asked to produce reports and models, and they would later return and present their findings. It turned out to be a massive hit with the students. They loved it. The students worked on real problems with something they could see and touch. This wasn't theory; this was cutting-edge engineering. Their work was outstanding, absolutely first class, and the RACE concept was deemed a great success, with everyone enjoying it.

Unfortunately, we didn't have the time to continue something like that. My team were all volunteers, and we needed to get on with building the car. We certainly didn't have the people or finances to make it happen again without government help, which sadly was never forthcoming.

During the first few months of 2012, we had pneumatics for the canopy and the steering fitted. After that, we took delivery of a full-size, double-sided stand-up image of our *Aussie Invader 5R*. We could now go to events or shows with it, showing what the finished car would look like.

In July 2012, CALM Aluminium sponsored and delivered six blank high-grade 7050-T7451 aerospace aluminium blocks for our wheels. These wheels were the culmination of many years of work by Ackers, myself and the team. They were expertly machined by VEEM, one of WA's top engineering companies, and known for their precision work in Defence, Marine, Transport, Mining, Oil and Gas. We desperately wanted to take at least one of our new 1,000 mph wheels to the Sydney Motor Show for our launch.

The Sydney Motor Show

At the 2012 Australian International Motor Show in Sydney, we officially launched our bid for the world land speed record and our 1,000 mph wheel to the world's media. We appeared at the show with just one wheel, a life-size stand-up image of our car and our engine's ablative rocket nozzle for display. We had very little to show except the desire and passion for achieving the Holy Grail of land speed racing.

Despite our lack of a completed car, our team and the project received tremendous media interest in Sydney. A day after our launch, we realised just how much, when interviews and press stories appeared all over the world. Over the coming weeks, about 300 news stories appeared worldwide on our project and car. We had Clarity Communications assess the impact of these stories, and they said our project had reached a potential audience of over one billion people.

I had an interview on the BBC, which didn't go quite to plan. My knockabout humour and general political incorrectness seemed to throw the female BBC presenter when I called her "Darling". Of course, she took to social media to make a fuss. Oh, dear, old habits die hard.

In 2013, we saw the wheels and bearings fitted so the car could stand on its own. That was a significant milestone achievement for us. We could see the car's proper stance and clearance with the wheels on for the first time. The first proper nose cone and some air brake components and mechanisms were fitted. The car had never seen daylight but did when we pulled it out of the workshop and turned it around with a forklift. It's not easy when the car is nearly 16 metres long. We stopped the traffic outside our workshop. God knows what the drivers thought as they patiently waited for us to complete this task.

Lake Perkolilli Race Centenary and More!

In November 2014, I was invited to attend the 100th Anniversary of the first motor racing event in Western Australia. We had been doing a lot of work on *Aussie Invader 5R*, so a few days away was a great idea.

This event took place at the original remote dirt lake, where the event had run 100 years before. It was in our state's east,

Lake Perkolilli, near Kalgoorlie (a gold mining town) in WA. It was first used as a racetrack in 1914, and it amazes me the stamina those racers must have had back then. Water would have cost as much as beer, and the tracks to get to this site wouldn't have even qualified as goat tracks. These people were true motor racing pioneers, with cars and motorcycles racing on a massive oval red dirt track in our outback. A great book has been written on the racing history of Lake Perkolilli by Graeme Cocks, called Red Dust Racers.

I drove seven hours with another team member to Kalgoorlie in a people carrier sponsored by our long-time friend and local car dealer, John Hughes. First, we were to attend a show of all the cars, followed by a day's racing at Lake Perkolilli. Amazingly, some of the cars and motorcycles at this event had raced at the first meeting 100 years before. It was incredible to see these cars at this venue, exactly as they were a century ago. It was like going back in time. Then, unfortunately, the heavens opened, and the actual racing day was washed out. However, two days of practice had gone ahead and been a brilliant success.

Due to the actual race day being cancelled, we found ourselves with time on our hands and decided to have a couple of beers in town. We ended up in the Grand Hotel, and I chatted with the publican, "Smitty". During the conversation, I retold the story of the jet-powered dragster racing up the main street some 30 years earlier. To my surprise, "Smitty" produced a photo from behind the bar of *Aussie Invader 1*, ready to make one of its runs.

"I still have nightmares about this, and everyone I tell this story to doesn't believe it ever happened," Smitty said.

When I told him I was the driver, he was astounded. In exchange for some signed merchandise of our latest project, we talked him into letting us have the photo... exciting times that will never be repeated.

Visit from Gina Campbell and a 50th Anniversary

In late December 2014, we were honoured to have Donald Campbell's daughter, Gina Campbell QSO, pay us a visit to check on our progress of *Aussie Invader 5R*. Donald Campbell was a legend who motivated me from day one.

Over the years, I have kept in contact with Gina, who holds a water speed record herself. On several occasions, she has visited me and my cars in Perth. This trip in 2014 was as a guest at the Melbourne Motor Show. At the same time, Gina decided to make the trip to the scene of one of her father's greatest triumphs at Lake Dumbleyung whilst here. This coincided brilliantly, as it was the 50th Anniversary of her father's record-breaking event.

In 1964, Donald Campbell achieved a rare double. On 17th July 1964, on dry salt flats at Lake Eyre, he broke the world land speed record when he set an average speed of 649 km/h (403 mph) in his *Bluebird CN7*. However, he wanted more, so he shipped his *Bluebird K7* speedboat to Australia and, later that year, went after the world water speed record.

His quest eventually took him to Lake Dumbleyung, 280 kilometres south of Perth. On 31st December 1964, he clocked an average of 444 km/h (276 mph). This was enough to break his own water speed record. It was his greatest achievement, and what timing, by the skin of his teeth, he had become the first person to set a new world water speed record and land speed record in the same year... 1964.

The Shire of Dumbleyung in WA holds Donald Campbell's name in very high regard. In 2014, a special New Year's Eve gala ball was held in Dumbleyung to mark the 50th Anniversary of this historic event.

Myself and the *Aussie Invader* team were invited to the gala ball along with Gina. There was to be a grand unveiling of a full-size replica of Donald's boat, *Bluebird K7*, for Dumbleyung. Again, the town pulled out all the stops, putting up the guests in their houses, and we partied late into the night.

In the afternoon before the Gala Ball, everyone travelled out to the Lake, where the record was broken, to see the monument built by John "Jack" Fewson in 1984. It is one of the best I have seen.

There is a large piece of granite standing upright overlooking Lake Dumbleyung with a small angled hole through it. On the ground, in front of it, is a brass plaque with an outline of the Lake. On that brass plaque in the middle of the lake is a miniature replica of Donald's *Bluebird K7*. As the sun rises, a beam of sunlight travels through the angled hole in the granite, moving across the lake. At precisely 3.43 p.m. on 31st December each year (the exact time when the record was broken), the sunlight shines through the hole, hits the replica brass boat, and lights it up. Stunning!

We started 2015 with some momentum, but it was a funny year. There was a lot of work and activity with little to show for it. This was because our attention had turned to the internals of the car, the driver's cockpit, electronics and batteries. We also received delivery of our composite wound pressure tanks. These were rated at more than 5,000 psi and were needed to hold our gaseous nitrogen. These tanks would push our propellants into the engine via step-down regulators. By adjusting the regulators, we could vary the amount of propellant forced into the engine and its power.

Fitting these was a very tough job, and it saw me crawling in and out of the car on 40-degree days. I was inside a 930 mm tube of 10 mm thick steel, not the best place to be on a bloody hot day. I was doing this for weeks and lost a lot of weight in the process.

Peter Madsen – You Couldn't Make This Up!

Late in January 2015, we were getting a visit from Peter Madsen, a Danish rocket scientist. His visit was prompted by his work with a rocket company in Denmark called Copenhagen Suborbitals. Peter and I'd been chatting for several months about rocket technology and if he could help us with *Aussie Invader 5R*. He was here primarily for a holiday with his partner Sirid, and they would initially stay in Perth. I wanted to take the opportunity for him to see our car and discuss its propulsion system. Then, he and Sirid were off to explore our beautiful state of Western Australia.

Cheryl and I picked him up from Perth International Airport, and he immediately came across as a bit strange. He walked off the aircraft in a thick black one-piece jumpsuit. Everyone else was in shorts and T-shirts. This was the height of the West Australian summer, with temperatures hitting 40 C and above. Anyway, I offered to take him to buy some shorts and T-shirts, as he came with very little luggage. He declined and proceeded to travel throughout Western Australia in this thick black jumpsuit in stifling heat.

The first thing he did once he was in our car was to start telling my wife, Cheryl, how I would kill myself in this car so we didn't get off to the greatest start. I was going to invite him to stay with us for a few days, but I'm glad I didn't. He seemed very intense and a little strange. So, we took him and Sirid to their digs.

"Once you are over your jet lag, give me a call, and I will take you to see the car," I told him.

He called two days later, and I picked him up and took him to our workshop. But, speaking to him, he seemed a bit of a loose cannon, quite difficult to deal with and not what I had expected. So, I decided to leave him to his own devices for the rest of his trip.

I also discovered that he had left Copenhagen Suborbitals about six months previously. However, he hadn't mentioned that or that he had started a new company and rocket venture called RML Spacelabs.

He borrowed my ute and travelled around WA. He was caught trespassing on a mine site, where he had strayed onto private land. He was questioned by their security about being there. Then, the security guy noticed the *Aussie Invader* signage on the truck. He was asked if he had anything to do with the *Aussie Invader* project. He told them he was our rocket engineer, and they laid out the red carpet for him and his wife. He and Sirid got a guided tour of the mine site, which I only learned about later.

Roll forward nearly three years, and we see on the news that Peter has been arrested for the unexplained sinking of the submarine he had built. He was also questioned about the disappearance of Kim Wall, a Swedish journalist. Kim was last seen alive aboard his submarine, where she was writing a media piece on him.

Once Madsen had been arrested, he admitted that Kim Wall had been killed when he lost his grip on the submarine's hatch cover. He said it hit her on the head, causing a fractured skull, and she died. Navy divers assisting the police in searching for Kim found her head, arms and legs, a knife and pieces of her clothing in bags at the bottom of Køge Bay in Denmark.

It appeared Madsen had weighted them down with pieces of metal. Still, a police spokesperson reported no signs of any fractures to Kim Wall's skull.

The prosecution had found videos on Madsen's computer showing women being murdered and decapitated. They also found material on asphyxiation sex. Later, during the trial, Madsen changed his account of Wall's death and admitted to dismembering her body. Madsen was found guilty of torture, murder and sexual assault and sentenced to life imprisonment.

A psychiatric evaluation of Madsen described him as a narcissistic psychopath. In 2020, Madsen managed to escape his suburban jail in Copenhagen by taking a psychologist hostage but was quickly recaptured.

There is now a great Netflix film about the murder of Kim Wall by Peter Madsen called *Into the Deep: The Submarine Murder Case*. Chasing the world land speed record brings you into contact with many people. Some good, some great and some not so good, but it makes life interesting.

Mexican Rocket Man Visit

Around June 2015, I took a trip to Cuernavaca, Mexico, to see my old mate Juan Manuel Lozano Gallegos in Mexico. Juan is the "Mexican Rocket Man" and a very clever and highly respected rocket guy.

Juan builds and sells rocket belts. These were made famous in the early James Bond film Thunderball when Bond escaped using one. His company, Tecnologia Aeroespacial Mexicana (TAM), is unique in its engineering expertise, mainly using hydrogen peroxide in rocket engines. It is used in the oil industry to clean the sludge buildup in delivery pipes.

It's a type of rocket engine that mounts to one end of these pipes and, when fired, generates a massive amount of thrust, heat and steam. As a result, the pipes that are sometimes seventy percent blocked come out looking brand new. What great technology.

I stayed at Juan's house, and it was fantastic. We did a few tourist things but spent most of the time talking about fast cars and rocket engines. I once again took a small Stentor ICBM rocket out of the country to discover its secrets. It was not in hand luggage this time; it went baggage.

A telephone call many years ago with Juan was responsible for me hooking up with Peter Beck. Juan said a New Zealand guy living in Auckland was doing some great work with rocket engines. He suggested that I should be talking to Peter. Juan had told me that Big Brother in the USA scrutinises everything to do with rockets. "You'll never be able to take the technology out of the USA and back to Australia," he said.

I was back from Mexico in July, and for the rest of the year, we had a mass of work going on. There was work on the nose cone, air brakes and tail fin. All were being machined. This was with the help of many great companies and engineering experts, from Paul Martin, Newland Associates and Kentin Engineering. Calm Aluminium again came to the party and supplied some expensive 7000 series aero-grade aluminium for these pieces.

We were really kicking goals and progressing well; we had a lot of momentum to move the project forward, and then it all halted. We were devastated. This came as a big shock to us.

Lunch with John Ackroyd and Gina Campbell in Perth, 2014.

Gina Campbell QSO in Dumbleyung with a replica of Bluebird K7 in 2014. This was the 50th anniversary of her father's dual world record in Australia.

Build Events and Milestones – Part 1

Visit from "The Fastest Man on Earth" Andy Green MBE with my son Bryce checking out Aussie Invader 3 in 2000.

Richard Noble OBE at our home for a BBQ in 1999.

Peter Madsen, his wife Sirid and me in January 2015. In life, you meet all types of people, some good and some not-so-good.

Sydney Motor Show - October 2012 with our 1,000 mph wheel.

-22-

Mongrel Bunch of Bastards

One of the most upsetting events in building *Aussie Invader 5R* was our involvement with the Government's Research and Development tax incentive. This incentive we were invited to take up caused a major headache and didn't go to plan. In fact, it nearly killed us, setting the project back a long way.

In October 2012, I was giving one of my many talks about the car and the project whilst at the Sydney Motor Show. A Management Consultant approached me after my talk. He told me they worked with a qualified, experienced company in government grants and tax incentives.

The grant they thought we would qualify for was the research and development tax incentives scheme. So, we had them prepare an application about our expenditure on the car, as this scheme would allow us to reclaim 50 percent of our tax back. This was a lot of work for us, with form filling, amended tax returns, valuations of the car, detailed accounting of expenditures, etc. We hadn't anticipated doing this work, but the promise of money from the government to help us build our car was too good an opportunity to miss. We were funding the project as we always had done, hand to mouth. Once you start dealing with a government department, the Australian Tax Office (ATO), in this instance, they want to know everything. The application was finally submitted, and we waited to see if we were accepted.

A few months later, we got the nod and were told we would be eligible for a refund of about $450,000 over three years. It was absolutely brilliant, just the shot in the arm the project needed. We could now plan and commit to some of the more expensive jobs.

Roll forward to mid-2014, and we received the first payment from the tax office of $180,000 for the first two years. This was fantastic for our project, and work increased, and we were excited. In the last 30 years, I have yet to have a sensible reply to our requests for government assistance or funding. We were absolutely stoked.

Another year later, we were looking forward to receiving our next instalment of this grant. Part of this grant process is random auditing by the Australian Tax Office. The first we were aware of this was around October 2015. We received a demand from the ATO to repay the Tax Incentive money back within three weeks, plus interest and costs totalling $230,000.

We were at a loss to know why this had happened and what to do. For some reason, we didn't now qualify for this incentive. The project ground to an immediate halt. Everything was put on hold while we tried to clarify the situation. We struggled to know what had gone wrong and how to repay such a large sum. That money had long been spent on the project and even more research and development!

Aussie Invader 5R was 100 percent research and development, as virtually none of what we are doing has ever been done before or in the way we were doing it. We constantly broke new ground with technology, design, aerodynamics, computer modelling, etc. The project, which will fly the Australian flag on an international stage, was a perfect fit for

Prime Minister Malcolm Turnbull's innovation campaign, which he was "selling" at the time.

After about a month of heated meetings and discussions with lawyers and all the parties concerned, we were getting nowhere. I wrote to Malcolm Turnbull, asking him to look into it. My team and I weren't taking this lying down. We had been encouraged to apply for this grant. We had undergone a very tough qualification process, and the ATO and Austrade accepted it. They had partially paid the money we were told we were entitled to. We felt we were the innocent party, caught in the middle of some bureaucratic nightmare. Any checks should have been done before the grant was handed out, not a year later.

Prime Minister Malcolm Turnbull promised to look into it and get back to me personally. I waited and waited, but no response came. I chased him with calls and was promised I would get an answer, but I never did. In the meantime, we were getting threatening letters from the ATO, and they were appointing a liquidator to seize the car and any assets we had. Now I was very pissed and going to fight hammer and nail to stop my teams and the culmination of my life's work from being sold off for scrap.

In early 2016, we were paid a visit from the liquidators, and I wasn't going out of my way to welcome them. We started a GoFundMe campaign to raise money to fight against this injustice. We raised several thousand dollars and received messages from all over the world supporting us. These included messages from Andy Green, Richard Noble, and the *Bloodhound SSC* Team. We had a lot of support from many others, including local MPs and even officials in the Government!

A friend of the project, David Anderson, mocked up an excellent newspaper front page and article with the headline

"Liquidators to Move on Land Speed Record Car." This laid out the situation we found ourselves in and why we felt we were victims, and it was through no fault of our own.

The media seized on this story. It was widely reported internationally and wasn't a good look for Australia. Malcolm Turnbull was still talking about his "ideas boom" and strengthening ties between businesses, universities and scientific institutions. He had set up a $200 million innovation fund to invest in companies that develop technology from the CSIRO and Australian universities. Our story was starting to embarrass the Turnbull Government. Exactly what we wanted, as we needed action, not warm words.

At this time, I was so stressed I considered taking our creation down to our city's tax office and dumping her on their doorsteps on a Sunday night. As it happened, I couldn't convince any of my transport buddies to help me. So, we took the wheels off the car, which had been sponsored by Calm Aluminium, taking years to design and produce. Then, once the ATO had appointed the liquidator and they said they owned the car, I started demanding they pay rent to me for storing it!

Malcolm Turnbull was coming to Perth, so my chance to have another word in his ear. I was steaming, and when he arrived at this event, I got in and pushed my way to the front. I was seriously going to swing at him but was stopped by his security, as I looked pretty angry. He looked at me and said, "Hello, Rosco," I immediately responded. "When are you going to answer my bloody letters."

Security was trying to pull me away, but I wasn't moving. I wanted an answer there and then. He promised he would answer my letters. I left and thankfully didn't hit him, or I could be writing this from prison. I never did get a response from him directly, just a letter from one of his advisors saying the government can't get involved with tax matters. What a load of crap. The government is solely funded by tax money, and they pass laws to decide where it comes from.

After a month or so of the liquidators trying to sell the car, they got no takers. Well, except for a bloody idiot, who said he would buy it and then asked if I would finish it for him! You can imagine my reply. It was ladened with expletives.

In all honesty, the liquidators knew no one would buy *Aussie Invader 5R* with that amount of work still to do. My team and I were the only ones who completely understood her. The liquidators didn't want to spend weeks trying to sell bits of the car. I got the impression that they didn't want to see it sold.

So, we raised $5,000 and offered that to them, and they accepted it, and we bought our blood, sweat and tears back. I had spent my entire superannuation retirement fund with local lawyers. Soon after my super fund was depleted, two Sydney tax lawyers contacted us and offered their professional services pro bono. This was a fantastic gesture, and we are truly thankful for their involvement. We are still very grateful and appreciative of all the help we got from many people to save our project.

We were not alone as soon as the dust had settled on our rough treatment. An ABC's Four Corners programme produced a documentary called "Mongrel Bunch of Bastards." This show outlined how the Australian Tax Office had shafted us and many other battling Aussie development pioneers through this scheme. They were a law unto themselves, with a heavy-handed approach. They treated everyone like criminals when their own guidelines were blurred and unclear, and their implementation of this scheme was utterly flawed. This caused a lot of genuine people severe stress, leaving their dreams in shreds and losing their businesses, not to mention their sanity.

Aesop once said, "We hang the petty thieves and appoint the great ones to public office." He was so bloody right in this case.

When we break this record, the Australian government will be the first to start talking about Australia's innovation and technology, which has made this happen. It will talk about how we, as a country, punch above our weight. They will try and take the kudos for what my loyal team, supporters and sponsors have strived to achieve over many long years. We may just have to remind them of this story.

-23-

Build Events and Milestones – Part 2

This sorry chapter with the ATO was brought to a close and cost us dearly. In real terms, this had probably set our project back at least two or three years. It hurt our credibility with any potential sponsors and investors. It did untold damage to team morale and my mental well-being. The government and the Australian Tax Office should hang their heads in shame, but I doubt they will.

We had to start trying to build the car again. Unfortunately, all work had stopped over the last several months and had been winding down before that. Thankfully, many people and companies that believed in what we were doing started to work with us again. However, the damage to our reputation and project status was immense. Whenever you searched for our project on the internet, you would read stories of liquidation or our demise. Why would anyone invest in or sponsor us if they thought they would never see the project finished?

Luckily, some great companies did back us. In 2016, we saw the tail fin and horizontal stabiliser finished by Newland Associates (now Newland Precision Engineering). These pieces needed over 800 hours of machine time on one of the biggest CNC machines in Australia. The tail fin was a work of art. It was produced in two halves with a honeycomb interior. It was super strong and very light. Understandably, Newland Precision Engineering had to fit our job in between paying jobs, so it took many months to complete. This work should have cost us about

$200,000, but they did it in exchange for their name on the side of the car. Thank you so much, Newland Precision Engineering.

We shipped *Aussie Invader 5R* off to Parins Truck City in Malaga, Perth, for a slick paint job. Parins has supported our cause for many years. These people do brilliant work and set about painting our 16-metre-long beast and all her panels. Parins paint a lot of trucks, so our supersized racer didn't daunt them at all. They had previously painted *Aussie Invader 3* over 20 years before, and it still looks like she has just come out of the paint shop. PPG very kindly sponsored the paint for our slick paint job.

One of the nice highlights of 2016 was when Perth artist John Dixon said he wanted to paint my portrait for The Archibald Prize. This competition is an Australian portrait competition held each year in Sydney. The fantastic portrait entry of me was spray painted on the spare *Aussie Invader 2's* record-setting tail fin. Unfortunately, it didn't make the finals, and we donated it to John Di Candilo. John has supported our projects for a long time, sponsoring many tonnes of steel and other materials for our builds.

Most of the work in 2017 wasn't visible on the car, as a lot of internal work took place. However, we did get a new composite driver's canopy with side windows from Aero Jacks, and the canards had just started to be machined at the end of the year. This work was carried out again by Kentin Engineering, who machined all the challenging jobs we threw their way.

We had some fun experimenting with explosive charges on some private waste ground. These tests ensured our newly manufactured drogue guns could fire the chutes far enough away from our cars' slipstream to pick up good clear air. If the chutes don't function properly, we would have no chance of stopping our car within our designated track length. That would be very catastrophic indeed, so the drogue guns have to work reliably and consistently.

The canards (small winglets behind the front wheels) were installed, and the car looked almost complete from the outside. So, our attention started to turn to the propellant tank system we were developing. This meant we could accept a couple of invitations to some motor show events in 2018 to showcase *Aussie Invader 5R* for the first time.

It also allowed us to test our ability to transport our car by road. We had purpose-built shipping containers specifically for this, sponsored by ABC Containers. Again, REEF Group was on hand to get us to and from the shows.

Our first appearance with *Aussie Invader 5R* was in May 2018 for the Motor Pavilion show at our local Perth Convention Centre. This was closely followed by the WA Hot Rod Show and Street Machine Spectacular in June of that year. These appearances received a very enthusiastic response. UK photographer Max Read captured some great images of me and our car for our first outing. Glen Hoskins of GG Graphics also captured our second appearance. These photographs appear later in this book, with their kind permission.

To be clear, before we receive a mass of invites to local school fetes and smaller motor shows. Moving a 16-metre-long *Aussie Invader 5R* is a massive task. It takes about two days to dismantle the car and pack her into our transport containers. Then, we have to load the containers onto the back of two large trucks and ship the containers to where we are going. We then have to unpack and assemble the car again. Then, obviously, the reverse on the way back. It costs in time, transport, and insurance about $50,000 to move our car and ties up three of the team for about four days.

Filming a Documentary for Discovery Channel

In 2018, we discussed with a UK documentary producer to put together an hour-long special on our car. It was going to be part of the Discovery Channel's documentary series called *Impossible Engineering*. We finally agreed that we would film this documentary in early September 2018. So, we relocated the car to an aircraft hangar at Jandakot Airport near Perth. Jack Moshovis and his company, Aero Jacks, kindly loaned us his hangar to shoot this episode of *Impossible Engineering*.

This would be a great shot in the arm for the project, as this documentary series was being shown worldwide and on numerous cable and satellite TV networks. In fact, we would gain international attention for the project because this was a prime-time show, going out in 120 countries across five continents.

The documentary was well received and showcased some of our car's unique features, including our "V" shaped underbelly, air brakes, tail fin and rocket engine. It was a significant moral boost for us, thinking that interest was also growing in the project from outside Australia.

A Trip to NZ and The USA

In December 2018, crew member Barry Fitzsimmons and I went on a two-week trip to New Zealand and the USA with a few meetings and goals in mind. We left Perth and flew to NZ, putting the 16-hour stopover in NZ to good use. We managed to catch up with our great mate Peter Beck, the founder of Rocket Lab and, undoubtedly, one of New Zealand's greatest innovators.

Peter was an inspiration, as always, and we got a four-hour guided tour of his new mega-rocket manufacturing facility. It was mind-blowing. We visited his new engine test site and heard of his plans to develop more launch sites and his expansion ideas. But, of course, everything was secretive, so phones and cameras were handed into security on arrival.

We flew to Los Angeles, hired a car, and then drove to Mojave, California. We met with a small niche rocket company in the Mojave Air and Space Port. Close by was Richard Branson's Virgin Galactic facility and the famous Burt Rutan's Scaled Composites hangar.

We were discussing with this company a concept I had looked at many years previously when I had personally spoken with a German rocket scientist, Lutz Kayser. We were going to use pistons to push the propellants into our rocket engine. This company was developing a similar system but utilised this technology in a vertical design.

Later, it became clear we couldn't afford the cost of developing this system with an outside company. I felt our best option was to explore this ourselves. I was later vindicated when we developed and successfully tested our horizontal propellant system in early 2022. Yes, it had taken us over three years to develop and build this system; it was highly complex, and we had to start from scratch. We called it our Orbital Propellant Module (OPM), believing this could be used in a zero-gravity environment as a satellite refueller.

Barry and I tackled the next part of our trip, visiting some USA dry lake race locations we could use to run *Aussie Invader 5R*. So, we headed east to look at Diamond Valley in Nevada, where the late Steve Fossett had earmarked this as a promising land speed record site. At the time, the mighty North American Eagle Team had done a lot of work with the authorities to gain permission to use this site. Unfortunately, it was about 725 kilometres (450 miles) away, and Barry had kindly offered to take over all the driving duties, allowing me time to do my homework.

We arrived at the nearest town, Eureka, where I believed accommodation would be easy to find. Barry had suggested we should ring ahead, but I told him they would be happy to see a couple of new faces.

I said to Barry, "We will probably be invited to stay with the town's mayor." I was completely wrong! When we got there, all the town's accommodation was taken, and the mayor had died the week before. The nearest accommodation was 160 kilometres (100 miles) away, and the deer population on the roads was scary.

We decided to sulk over a beer and see if we could make friends with anyone who could put us up for the night. This worked, and we ended up in a partly restored house on top of a sleazy bar. It was heaven after thinking I would wake up next to Barry in the back seat of our car.

The following morning, we headed north to look at the Diamond Valley playa. Our first observations were concerning, with many cattle roaming the playa, and the side tracks would take a lot of work to secure. It also had very poor vehicle access. We spent several hours surveying this surface and discovered that the best length of the track was only around 16 kilometres

(10 miles) long. This was far too short for us, and I was disappointed with what we found. In addition, the number of ranches close to this site would make it difficult to control the boundaries, with animals and people possibly wandering onto the track.

We decided to scout several other options but didn't believe we would ever find a more suitable venue than the Black Rock Desert. Richard Noble and Andy Green set outstanding records there, but it is in very poor condition now. This Nevada location is now trashed and unusable for record attempts, being the home of the yearly Burning Man Festival.

Whilst we were so close to Utah, we decided to pay a visit to Bonneville Salt Flats, where some action was still happening. Unfortunately, we arrived in Wendover with a massive windstorm halting all runs on the salt. Nevertheless, we met with several teams, and I drooled over the Late Don Vesco's turbine-powered car, The Turbinator. That car set a new wheel-driven world record the following day, at 482 mph (776 km/h), driven by Californian Dave Spangler - a brilliant milestone for a great team.

We were rapidly running out of time in the States, and I told Barry we must visit Norton Sales Inc. and Joe Factor Sales. I had to drool over these stores' rocket parts and aerospace hardware. We visited both of these stores and reacquainted ourselves with the owners. These guys have been in their respective businesses for decades, and they knew their stuff. If only Australia had just a tenth of the gear these people sell, our car would have been running years ago.

On our last day before flying out, I mentioned to Barry that it would be great to shake hands with Jay Leno in Burbank. Of course, we were told this would be impossible, so my interest level immediately spiked. We made a few calls to contacts we had, and it worked!

Barry and I soon found ourselves that afternoon at Jay's Garage. We met with Bernard, Jay's General Manager, and Jay Leno himself. We were given a guided tour, and I was in heaven. He has a fantastic car and bike collection, with about 180 cars and 160 motorcycles!

The conversation naturally drifted to land speed records, and I mentioned Jay didn't have any land speed cars in his collection. He said he stuck clear of anything to do with land speed records. It was too risky, as the USA loves litigation, especially against people with a few dollars. He forever had to defend stupid claims against himself, just with the car show he did. Hence, land speed vehicles were definitely out. He and Bernard were fantastic hosts and great guys to go with it.

Help from Above

In late June 2018, we were introduced to a lady called Trish Bischoff by Dave Gutsell, who was part of the project. Dave would meet with friends most Friday evenings for a drink in the bar of the Duxton Hotel in Perth. Trish was a senior commercial airline pilot, a Commander of an Airbus A380 for Emirates, with over 22,000 flying hours experience.

Trish was staying at the Duxton after a long flight to Perth. Trish and Dave struck up a conversation, with Dave eventually turning it to *Aussie Invader 5R*. The conversation continued into the design and construction of our land speed racer, with Trish asking Dave whether the car had forward canards to assist in aerodynamic performance. Dave was a bit surprised by that question, not knowing Trish was a senior airline pilot with knowledge of aerodynamics.

Trish lived in Dubai, so Dave thought she might be just the person we needed to take the project further in the Middle East. He suggested that the next time Trish had a layover in Perth, it would be nice if she met with me and some of the team.

So, about two weeks later, a few team members and I arranged to meet Trish on her next visit. After a brief conversation, I asked Trish to join the team. With Trish living in Dubai and having time between flying duties, she might be able to help us. We asked her to explore if there was interest in sponsorship or running the car in the Middle East. Trish agreed and joined the team, putting in considerable work over the next year or so.

This led to a chance for us to attend the Dubai Expo with the car planned for 2020. Unfortunately, COVID saw that delayed until October 2021. Trish was also in discussions for us to present our car at the LA Motor Show in the USA. One of our long-time team members had moved to Houston temporarily, so they worked on this together. Soon, it became apparent that COVID and Western Australia's hard border restrictions killed off any chance of us attending anything internationally. We couldn't move, and neither could the car. Our hands were tied. We had to look for opportunities closer to home and within Australia to showcase our project.

COVID hit the aviation industry hard, so Trish retired early and moved back to Canada in July 2020. She joined her husband, Chris and started to build their fantastic dream home in the mountains. We will always be grateful to Trish for making things happen, even though they didn't work out as planned. Trish is still on our team and a great ambassador for our project.

The following two years were almost solely devoted to developing the Orbital Propellant Module (OPM). There was other work going on, mainly around systems and electronics. Still, everything depended on the OPM; it was a critical component of the car. As we were firing our rocket horizontally, it was paramount to get this system functioning correctly. It enabled us to get the propellants into the engine efficiently and safely.

As previously explained, we were going to push the propellants into the engine with what was equivalent to seven large syringes. This had many advantages over standard tanks, with all their baffling and surge issues. However, getting pistons to travel down the six-metre tubes in unison took a lot of work, as each tube would have slightly different tolerances.

A local company came to the rescue, Hardchrome Sales, and took on this complete operation. However, we found a few sticking points once we tested the system with actual pistons and seals in place. So, we designed our own honing tool to smooth these out. It took weeks to get all the pistons travelling perfectly in unison down these six-metre-long tubes, but eventually, we did.

We also had to develop a way to monitor the exact location of the piston in each tube. If the last fuel or oxidiser piston reached the end of their respective tubes before one another, the engine's combustion would stop. We searched worldwide and could not find anything suitable to do this monitoring. So, once again, we had to design our own system. We developed a special ring magnet that fits into the crown of each piston in the OPM. A line of sensors runs along the outside of each tube and tracks the magnet's path.

Setting The Record Straight

Outside the project, we had a massive shot in the arm from the FIA, whose rules govern world record attempts. We were invited to present via video link at the FIA's annual meeting and discuss our future record attempt, even though a date hadn't been set. This meeting was on the 1st of September 2021. Another team member and I discussed where we were with the project and our immediate plans for the assembled FIA members.

We had caught their attention because one of our team members had submitted a paper to the FIA earlier in the year. We had requested a rule change on the timing trap locations for the measured, timed mile and kilometre on safety grounds.

They had discussed and agreed to accept our proposed change that governed our Group C Unlimited Record class. Without going into great detail, currently, you have to run the same measured, timed mile location in opposite directions (e.g., North and South) within an hour. This was to alleviate any gradient or wind advantage. We had put forward an argument on safety grounds that allowed us to run our car over two different measured, timed miles, one northbound and one southbound. It wasn't a significant change that could undermine the records that had gone before, just a sensible one.

Cars going the speeds we were anticipating would finish such a long way down the track. It was almost impossible to comply with running the same measured mile. Our car takes about 5.6 kilometres (3.5 miles) to get up to speed to enter the measured mile, but it will take about 13 kilometres (8 miles) to stop. It would take a big chunk of the hour we are allowed to turn our car around and tow it back many kilometres to begin our return run. It left almost no time for us to perform the necessary safety checks between the two runs. This puts the driver at even greater risk than necessary in an already dangerous environment.

When attempting a record, we could now be timed over two designated measured miles, one north and one south. Each timing trap was about a third of the way down the two tracks that would be side by side. We can't use the same track in the opposite direction. Once used, the track would look like a plough had gone over it due to the wheels and ground effect shockwave churning up the desert playa surface.

This rule change meant we could start our return run from roughly where our car had stopped on the first run. All we had to do was turn the car around. This was a significant safety improvement for us and any future team attempting this record. Thank you, the FIA.

Initial Engine Pressure Test

February 2022 saw the final assembly of our propellant module in the car, and we were set to test it. We were fortunate to access a large vacant factory unit in our city's south. This generous offer allowed us to tether our car to big concrete anchor blocks to stop it from moving. We had the car's rocket nozzle pointing out of the factory unit through one of the big open doors.

We were replacing the chemical propellants with de-ionised water, many tonnes of it. We were going to pressurise the system with gaseous nitrogen and blast the water through the rocket engine's injector. The tests would gradually build up to full operating pressure, with a large jet of water spraying out of the car's rocket engine.

Many different tests were performed, and the tests were very successful. One of the main things we wanted to establish was our car's four onboard gas storage tanks capacity. We wanted to know if we could hold the required gas volume to perform two complete propellant system discharges/dumps. This is needed to guarantee that once we are ready to go for the record, we have enough gaseous nitrogen onboard to allow for two high-speed runs. The one hour between runs is insufficient to enable us to recharge our nitrogen storage system.

One of the other advantages of using this propellant module is that once we start to burn our propellants, the pistons push forward. The diminishing weight is transferred to the front wheels as the car gets lighter. If the load sensors find the front is too heavy, we can reverse the piston direction and push the propellants towards the back of the car. This allows us to fine-tune our centre of gravity when we reach higher Mach numbers.

Over several days, we performed our tests, and it was a great success, as the systems all worked well. However, we found a small hose leak, where the hose was mated to one of our propellant lines. This is what this testing was designed for, so we could discover any issues and fix them before using volatile chemicals.

The problem was with the hose's threaded fitting, and it could not be fixed where we were. We needed a new hose, so testing was cut short, and a new hose had to be custom-made and sent to us. Unfortunately, the hose swap could only occur once the car was back in our workshop, and now we will have to schedule a time to conduct further testing.

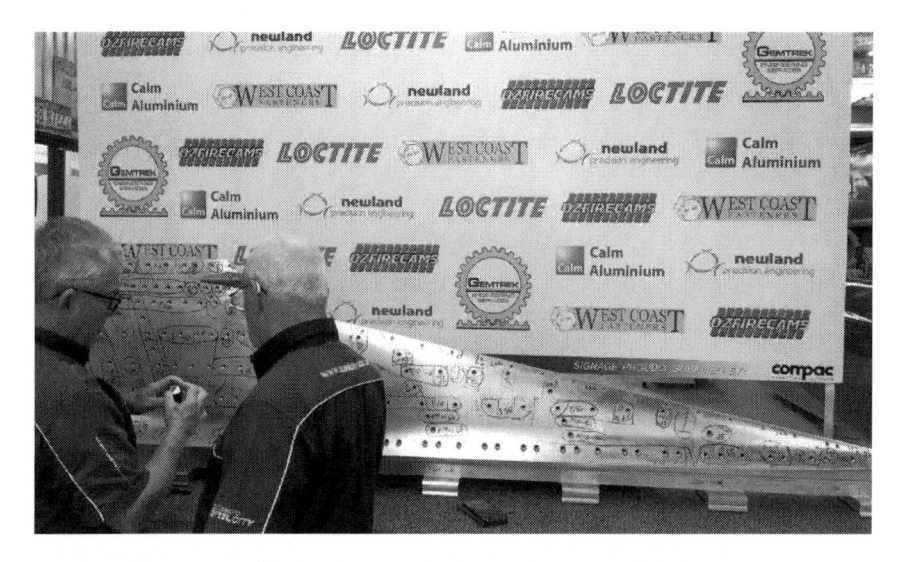

Bolting together the two halves of our tail fin in 2016.

Archibald Prize entry in 2016 by John Dixon painted on Aussie Invader 2's record-breaking tail fin.

Build Events and Milestones – Part 2

Picture discovered in 2014 of me racing Aussie Invader 1 up Brockman Street in Boulder, WA (taken around 1990).

On my trip to the USA in 2018, I visited Jay Leno's garage and got a personal tour. A bucket list experience.

Aussie Invader 5R's first public outing at the Motor Pavilion show. May 2018 at the Perth Convention Centre.

Aussie Invader 5R's second outing in June 2018 at the WA Hot Rod Show and Street Machine Spectacular. The picture was taken before other entrants had set up.

Build Events and Milestones – Part 2

Filming of Impossible Engineering documentary episode about our car - The 1,000 mph Car in September 2018.

*Canards were machined in 2017 by Kentin Engineering.
Designed by Paul Martin, our guru engineer.*

*In February 2022, we conducted pressure tests of our Orbital
Propellant Module.*

-24-
Aussie Invader 5R in Pictures

It's said, "A picture is worth a thousand words." These images show the work and design that has gone into *Aussie Invader 5R*. They are not in any particular order.

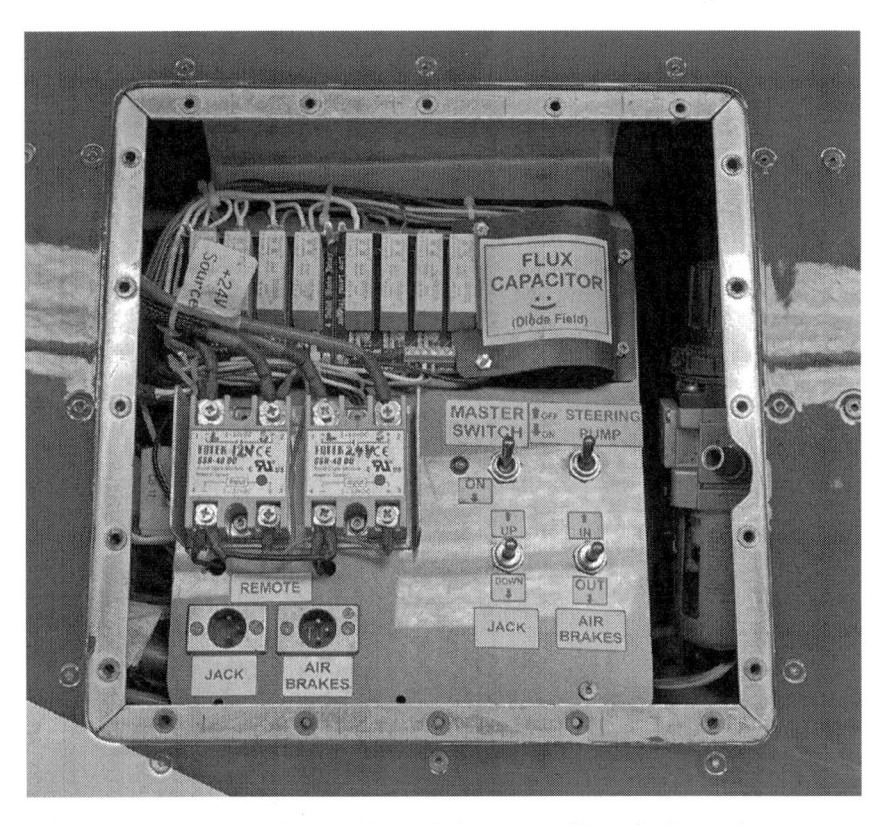

What's under the skin? A lot of clever stuff, including electrics. Hopefully, we will manage more than 88 mph. ☺

We are happy to have our car on display at the Perth Convention Centre in 2018 for its first public outing.

Aussie Invader 5R in Pictures

In the early stage of the build, with the car upside down on our jig, allowing us to weld the 36 "V" shaped underbelly supports.

Kentin Engineering's mind-blowing rear axle set-up.

Rear axle and brake set-up.

Aussie Invader 5R in Pictures

Fabrication legend Brad Stacy is welding up our roll cage.

The rocket engine injector plate atomises the propellants, producing 62,000 pounds of thrust.

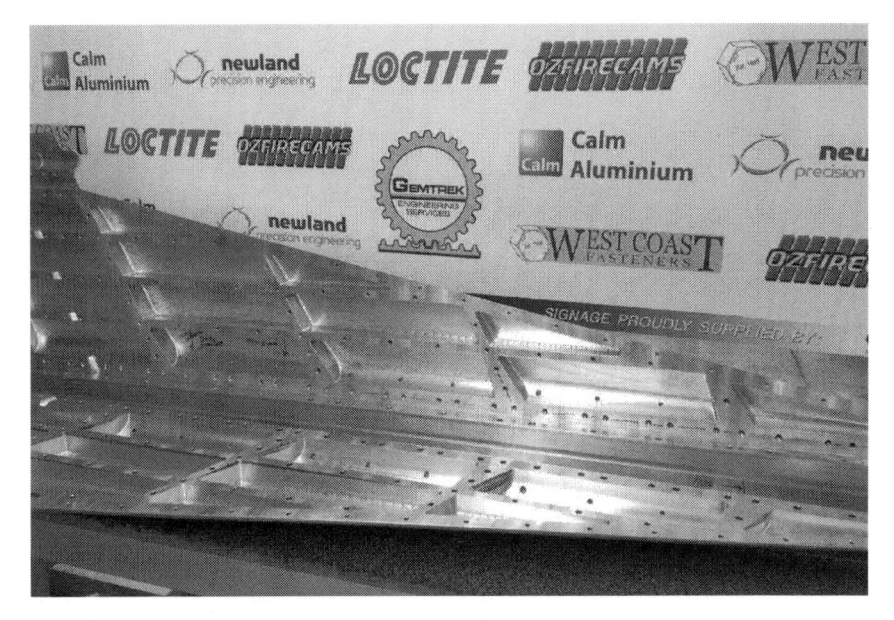

Two halves of the tail fin. Brilliantly designed by James Sutherland and machined by Newland Associates.

Tail fin bolt configuration. It took days to assemble.

Aussie Invader 5R in Pictures

Another work of art. The horizontal stabiliser took many hours of CNC machining by Kentin Engineering and Gemtek.

The air brakes and tail fin.

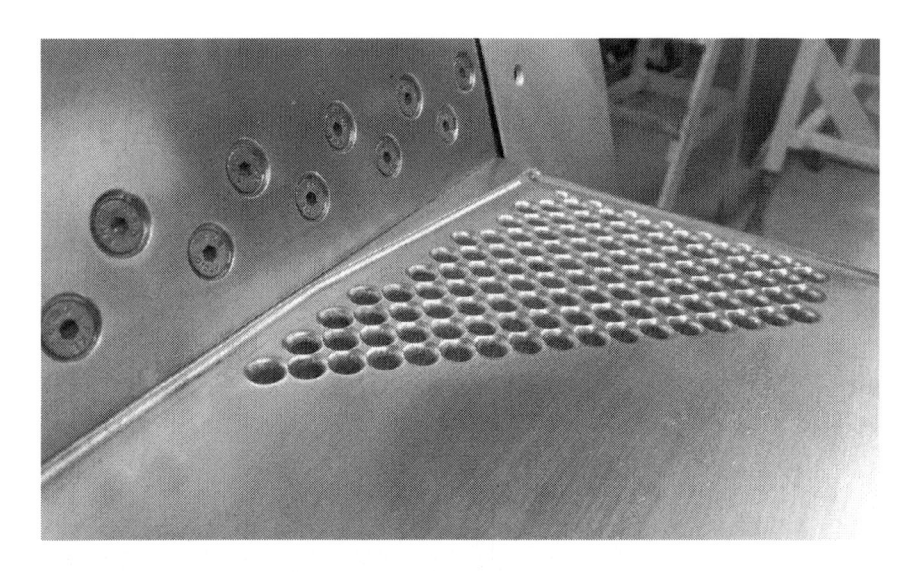

The air brake disruptors increase the air brake efficiency by 30%. Designed by engineer Paul Martin and expertly machined by Kentin Engineering.

The "floating" canards (winglets) are finished and ready for installation. Brilliantly designed by Paul Martin and machined by Kentin Engineering.

Aussie Invader 5R in Pictures

Barry Fitzsimmons and Chris Demunck working on the car. Rear view of the car with the air brakes deployed.

The front suspension and steering, with the canards installed.

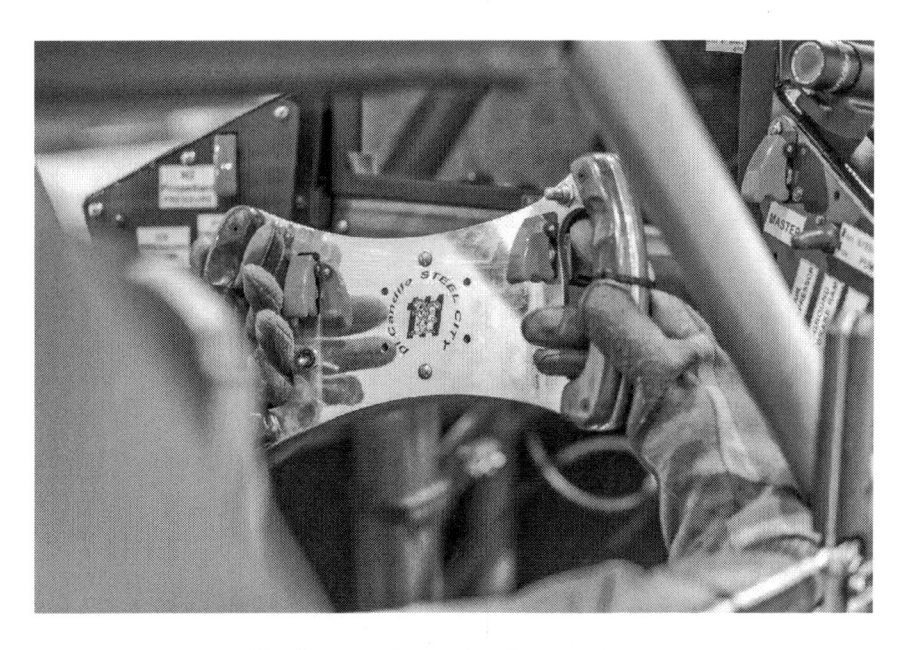

Early steering wheel prototype.

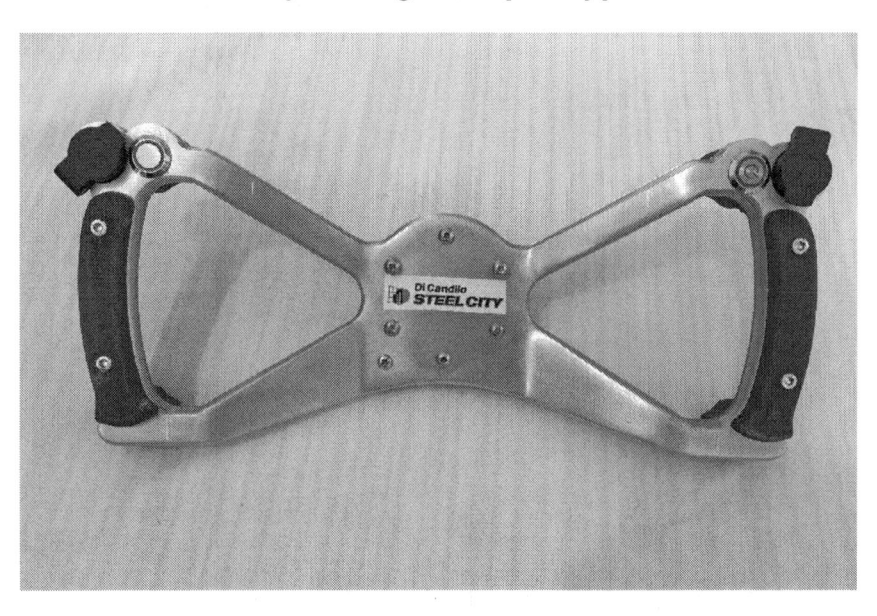

Later steering wheel design – RMS Machining.

Aussie Invader 5R in Pictures

SDR Engineering machined drogue guns and bolts used to deploy braking chutes.

The team is waiting at the Impossible Engineering shoot for filming and interviews.

Great shots of Aussie Invader 5R taken by G & G Graphics.

The Orbital Propellant Module (OPM) is on its stand, ready to slide into the car and connect up all the propellant lines.

The front view of the Orbital Propellant Module, with pipework to take the fuel and oxidiser to the rocket engine.

The OPM pistons (without their seals). A ring magnet allows the tracking of each piston as it travels down the OPM.

The rear of the OPM, with gaseous nitrogen (N2) feed lines. The N2 pushes the pistons down the propellant tubes.

-25-

The Woman Behind The Man

I saved the best for last! Cheryl has been my rock for the last 38 years. She describes herself as "The woman behind the man," but we are partners. We are two people working to achieve a goal. Without her support and dedication, I would not have achieved half of what I have accomplished.

I met Cheryl in 1984 in Victoria Park, Perth, when I was lost and went into a dry-cleaning shop to ask for directions. Cheryl was their bookkeeper but had volunteered to cover for someone who was ill that day, and we started chatting. Funnily she recognised me, as she had just read an article and seen my picture in the local paper. The article was about me wanting to break the Australian land speed record in my jet dragster, *Aussie Invader 1*.

Cheryl was into speedway and racing, having come from a racing family. I asked for directions to the local newspaper office and if she would like to go for something to eat.

I said, "Lunch or dinner will do," but the charm must have been slightly off that day as she turned me down. But, not daunted, I got her to reveal her name and roughly where she lived.

I tracked her down and went to her house that evening, only to find she had just left to go to the speedway. So, I shot there and waited at the bar. I thought *She'd probably get a drink. I'm bound to see her here.* Sure enough, she turned up at the bar with her girlfriend. Cheryl was amazed to see me and thought it was all a coincidence, not knowing I knew exactly where to find her. We chatted, and I asked her out again. She said she would go, but only if we went as a foursome, with my mate and her girlfriend. We went out and got on really well, and both wanted another date, so we went out again, this time alone.

The next date after that didn't go so well, as we had arranged to meet on Cheryl's birthday at a Kings Park restaurant in Perth. Cheryl was going to introduce me to some of her friends, but I was a no-show. She thought I had stood her up and was pretty upset after telling her friends they would get to meet me that night.

I had been in a motorcycle accident and was laid up in bed. I had ripped a lot of skin and flesh off my backside while riding motocross. I called her the next day and apologised, explaining why I didn't show up. I invited her to visit me in my Mullaloo home, as I was pretty banged up and couldn't drive. So, I was stuck in bed nursing a very sore and stitched-up backside.

The only issue was Dianne, my second wife, and my 5-year-old daughter Tenneille were at home. I was still married to Dianne at the time, but we had separated, with Dianne and Tenneille in the process of moving out. I had got them another place to live, but it wasn't ready yet. The positive thing was we were on really good terms.

Cheryl did say later that she had questioned whether she should come over, given the situation. She only had my word; it was as I'd explained. I also thought *Cheryl might feel it was all a bit too hard and not come over*. On the other hand, I'd been upfront and honest with Cheryl, explaining that I was getting divorced, so it wasn't a complete shock.

Dianne opened the door, welcomed Cheryl, and introduced her to Tenneille, who brought her into the bedroom where I was laid up. Dianne and Cheryl hit it off straight away. I didn't get a look in after that. Dianne cooked her a steak sandwich, and they chatted like old friends; the rest is history.

Cheryl helped her move a few months later. Dianne and Cheryl had boys over the next three or four years, so they shared babysitting duties. They got along like sisters and still are best friends today, 38 years later. I, on the other hand, have ended up with two wives. Only one I can sleep with, but two that nag me!

After a month or so, when Dianne and Tenneille had moved out into their new home, Cheryl moved in. We agreed to live together for a trial to see how we would get along. Luckily, Cheryl loved what I was out to achieve and my passion for wanting to build a land speed car. Finally, I found someone who shared my passion for racing and has done so all through our marriage.

Cheryl continued bookkeeping at the dry cleaners, which she did for 28 years. I had various jobs, selling insurance, real estate salesman, roof plumber, heavy vehicle fitter, mechanic, steel fixer, and even a hotel bouncer. In addition, I was racing *Aussie Invader 1*, my jet dragster, on the weekends at race meetings and speedway shows. Luckily for me, Cheryl, with her bookkeeping skills, started looking after all my finances, which desperately needed sorting out.

Until then, I paid cash for everything and did not keep my receipts. Cheryl showed me how to structure debt and how we could achieve things without having the necessary money upfront. She organised my life, looked after appearance bookings and race promotions and assisted me in looking after the race cars, trucks and trailers. I thought *This one was a keeper.*

Cheryl and I had our son Bryce, born in April 1987, over the long Easter weekend. I had a drag racing meeting with Ken Warby over east. I didn't want to miss Bryce's birth, so I saw him born and spent a day with them. I then managed to fly out, leaving them together in the hospital to rest, and I went away racing. I picked them up a few days later.

Bryce attended all the drag racing and speedway shows across Australia from a baby to his teenage years. So, he grew up with the world of motor racing in his veins. When Bryce couldn't attend school, he did remote learning. What he learned travelling with us has made him the great man he is today. He runs his own tourism business, skippering boats and flying helicopters in the Kimberley region in our state's north.

Cheryl and I got married, but neither of us was particularly bothered about it. Cheryl wanted her surname to be the same as Bryce's before he went to school, which I understood. We had a celebrant come to the house to marry us with Bryce and my daughter Tenneille present. We didn't make this a big family affair, with just three close friends as witnesses. This upset the families on both sides, but we didn't want a big wedding. We had both been married before, and a big wedding just wasn't that important to us. We didn't feel it was wrong to want a low-key ceremony with very little fuss.

Twenty minutes before the wedding, I was pouring concrete for the large pillars of our new workshop that we were building next to the house. My Best Man arrived looking smart in his suit. He said, "You're getting married in twenty minutes. Get in the shower, put on a good shirt and a jacket." I did and was on time, not keeping the bride waiting, to everyone's relief.

Our honeymoon was off racing again with two crew members, Keith and Jen Lovatt. Cheryl, Bryce and I appeared at Bunbury Speedway, then at the Albany Airshow, for a jet dragster demonstration. This was our life, and it was hectic, but we loved it and had great fun.

We have had 38 really great and exciting years together. We are happy and do not have many disagreements. Cheryl would have wanted more holidays, which I can't argue with. My dedication and obsession with achieving my goals have made me a workaholic. We have travelled a lot with the race cars, to motor shows, events and general appearances.

Cheryl has been bloody fantastic. The record attempts were at another level, and Cheryl and Pete Taylor were a great team. Their organisational skills and ability to keep things running in a crisis have been critical to our success.

In the later years, when we should be feet up and enjoying life, she is working to see we have money to live on whilst I work to finish *Aussie Invader 5R*.

Cheryl and Bryce have given up a lot of family fun times with what I have wanted to pursue. Without their understanding and support, I couldn't have achieved what I have.

Cheryl refers to herself as "The woman behind the man," and this picture sums it up well.

The Woman Behind The Man

Cheryl with Aussie Invader 2 at a motor show. Always working

One of our sponsors, Neways Gala Ball L - R Steve "Suggie" Sugden, Cheryl, me and Pete Taylor.

Cheryl, Bryce and I unveiled Aussie Invader 3 in 1995.

One of our many press conferences together.

The Woman Behind The Man

The Australian record in 1994 – An excited Cheryl and Bryce.

Cheryl and I are at a motor show with Aussie Invader 3.

-26-

The Final Chapter

So, there you have my story so far. It has been an interesting, crazy and fun ride up until now. Although this is the final chapter of this book, my story's actual final chapter is yet to be written.

At the time of writing this memoir, *Aussie Invader 5R* is well over 95 percent complete. It is a truly incredible and remarkable car, and the engineering that has gone into it is mind-blowing. We have had some of the world's best minds and experts help to get us where we are today.

The fact that *Aussie Invader 5R* has taken so long to complete shows how challenging and costly a project like this can be. However, this car would never have been built without the belief of many people, sponsors, supporters, 1000 MPH Club Members, and my fantastic team's dogged determination, dedication, desire and guts.

One such incredible supporter is Nigel Grant from the UK, who works extra night shifts filling shelves. Nigel sends $500 monthly to help us achieve our goal and record. You are a true inspiration, Nigel. Thank you so much.

We have in the past experienced disappointment when attempting to break the world land speed record. For a record attempt to be successful, you need a great car, the right weather and a lot of luck, with everything coming together on the day. Each part of *Aussie Invader 5R* will need to perform for about 60 seconds; that's all. It sounds so simple, but it is so bloody difficult to achieve. No one has ever gone this fast on the ground. We have complex parts on this car we think will give us trouble, and they will probably work fine. In reverse, we have experienced in the past simple parts, costing cents, that fail and cause a massive problem.

David Tremayne is a UK motor racing journalist and author who writes extensively about land speed record attempts. He has written over 50 motoring books and famously said, and I quote…

Attempting the World Land Speed Record is a bit like two-stepping blindfolded and barefoot along a 100-foot-high barbed wire tightrope whilst carrying a glass of nitroglycerine and simultaneously delivering a political speech.

A bit like it, but a damn sight more difficult.

To re-iterate this point further, when I was going after the Australian land speed record in December 1993, Formula One team McLaren was holding a press conference at its headquarters in Woking, UK. Its owner and head, Ron Dennis, announced it had been secretively developing a jet-powered vehicle to break the world land speed record and sound barrier for the last couple of years.

McLaren showed a mock-up of their car named *Maverick* and announced they wanted to go after Richard Noble's 633 mph record from 1983 and capture the sound barrier as well.

Maverick was being designed and built by McLaren's MAV (McLaren Advanced Vehicles) team, hence the name Maverick, with millions having been spent to ensure it got off the drawing board.

Its design was similar to Craig Breedlove's *Spirit of America – Sonic Arrow*, having a single jet engine and using McLaren's know-how, with light composites, aerodynamics and efficiency from Formula One to achieve its speed rather than brute power.

It was looking at an attempt in 1998, but the project soon stalled. It was never officially announced why the plug was pulled on it. At the time, McLaren was riding high and had no shortage of money or expertise. Not continuing with the project after such a public announcement possibly shows a realisation of the challenges of such a car and project.

-ooO0oo-

Although *Aussie Invader 5R* has some very complex parts, it is mostly sound and solid engineering. For our inspiration, you only have to look at Man's greatest engineering achievement, the Moon landing with Apollo 11. *Aussie Invader 5R* is more Apollo 11 than it is Formula One. This car has some very cutting-edge parts, but it is mostly just well-thought-out and executed belt and braces engineering.

I am very concerned that at 72, I may never get to put my bum in the seat and drive this car in anger. I desperately want to know what the world's most powerful car actually feels like to drive. I would love to have been telling this story as the fastest man on Earth, but I am not. I am frustrated at the time it has taken to get to this point and the lack of financial sponsorship we have attracted.

This car could have been finished and run several years ago if we had secured appropriate funding. Saying that, I am truly grateful for all the expertise and product sponsorship we have had from some great companies and people in Australia and worldwide.

The shortfall in financial sponsorship certainly hasn't been through lack of effort and the number of doors we have knocked on. My team and I have, and still are, busting our balls to make this happen, but there seems to be a reluctance to support projects like this now. Government and big business don't seem to think this type of project is relevant today, but I beg to differ.

I agree that feeding the starving, curing disease, and many other global goals are far higher priorities, but projects like this give hope. The hope is that man can overcome impossible odds and develop practical solutions to the complex problems we face in this world. Moreover, projects like this can unite a nation and put smiles on the faces of many people.

To see someone or a team achieve something that most people thought was impossible or beyond their capabilities. That's what inspires others on their journey, challenges and life's goals.

These personal challenges don't have to be breaking the world land speed record; they could be a lot simpler, but to that person, it is "their" world land speed record. So, it is always worth backing projects that push man, machine and technology forward. That is how the human race has progressed by striving for the unobtainable.

To me, a 1,000 mph car is the pinnacle of land speed racing. But unfortunately, a lot of companies are solely interested in investing in measurable returns. The nature of what we are trying to do is complex and not easily measurable. Nevertheless, we believe the rewards will be there for the people and companies who back us and put their faith in our project and projects like ours.

At the time of writing this, we need about $3 million to finish the car and get us to the start line of a prepared track, which is very expensive. Everyone working on the project is unpaid, with some helping and contributing for a few months and others for years, with their only pay being beer, coffee, food and my stories at times. What they have in return is the knowledge they are doing something unique and being part of a team for a once-in-a-generation project. I want to thank everyone once again who has helped us, big or small, to get us to where we are today.

People question my ability to drive this car with that amount of power. I am getting to the time it might not be possible, but that time certainly hasn't come yet. I have driven *Aussie Invader 3* at 1,027 km/h (638 mph), and I have accelerated in cars with greater G-force than *Aussie Invader 5R* will have. In addition, I have over 50 years of practical motor racing and land speed experience to draw on. So, the prospect of strapping myself into this land-based missile does not worry me, well, perhaps a little. If it didn't, you are either foolish or will probably end up dead.

People have also asked me, "Do you have the reactions to drive a car like that?" My response to that question is always the same. "The last thing you need is reactions. By the time you've reacted to it, it's half a kilometre behind you."

At 1,600 km/h (1,000 mph), you are travelling at 445 metres or about four and a half soccer pitches per second. So, once you press that button, you are going along for the ride. You can control a few things, but most will happen regardless, so be prepared to hold on and hold on bloody tight!

Yes, you can put a young, fitter man or woman in a car with 200,000 horsepower and the ability to accelerate from a standing start to 1,600 km/h in just over twenty seconds. However, do they want to press that big red button, and are they prepared to hold on? That is the question. If you are not hundred percent committed, you won't feel comfortable being there. That is where my experience comes in. I can still drive this car and have the will and passion to see this project through.

As a young man growing up, I faced many challenges and tough situations. My whole life has been built around getting me to this point, and the young, hard man with a fighting spirit still lives within me. I will do whatever it takes to get that chance to prove it.

Part of the reason for writing this book is to help raise funds and the profile of our project. So, rather than lend a copy of this book to someone, tell them to buy a copy, or better still, buy several copies and give them away as presents. I hope they will enjoy reading it as much as I did telling my life story.

Thank you once again for your continued support to help Australia break the world land speed record, and me not just be the fastest Aussie on Earth but become the fastest man on Earth.

Rosco McGlashan OAM

-27-
Awards, Honours and Appearances

I am very grateful to be the recipient of many awards and honours throughout my life and racing career. Most of these achievements and awards would not have been possible without Cheryl, the many *Aussie Invader* team members, supporters and sponsors along the way.

- Awarded the Order of Australia Medal in 1997 by the Queen of England for my services to motorsport and for setting a new Australian Land Speed Record.
- Given the "Premiers Award" of Western Australia by Richard Court MLA in 1999.
- Given the "Key to the City of Perth" by the state's Premier Richard Court MLA in 1999.
- International Jet Dragster Competition Winner 1998, 1999, 2001.
- Entered in the Australian Roll of Honour by Governor General Sir Michael Jefferies in 2001 as "The Fastest Aussie on Earth."
- Confederation of Australian Motor Sport Award 2001.
- Letters of Endorsement for our project from Australia's Prime Minister John Howard (1996-2007) and Defence Senator Robert Hill.

- In 2012, I was inducted into the RAC Walk of Fame, one of only seventeen West Australians to be included.
- Entry in the Who's Who of Western Australia.
- WA Museum Boola Bardip dedicated a section to my land speed record and cars.
- Awarded a Tae Kwon Do Honorary 1st Dan Black Belt.

Many television documentaries about my land speed record achievements are shown worldwide via Discovery Channel and several other paid and free-to-air TV channels.

Impossible Engineering dedicated an episode about *Aussie Invader 5R* called *The 1,000 MPH Car*. It can be seen on the Discovery Channel and many other TV channels.

I was included in US Rocket Legend – Bob Truax's life story documentary called *Bob Truax: The U.S. Navy's Rocket Man*.

Hundreds of hours of broadcast-quality vision belong to the team, not to mention countless newspaper and magazine stories about our achievements.

-ooOoo-

Over the years, I have made many personal appearances in support of many charities and given many talks supporting good causes. In addition, I am a registered motivational speaker with International Celebrity Management Australia.

These are a few charities and community organisations I have supported and appeared for at their fundraising events.

Awards, Honours and Appearances

- Patron, Making Life Better Group in Perth, Western Australia.
- Patron, Kids Cancer Support Group in Perth, Western Australia.
- Starlight Children's Foundation Perth, celebrity visitor.
- Rotary and Lions Clubs, regular guest speaker.
- Ronald McDonald McHappy Day, celebrity server.
- Make a Wish Foundation, celebrity workshop visits.
- Roads aren't Racetracks, my own Road Safety Foundation.
- Royal Flying Doctor Service, celebrity supporter, Northern Queensland.

What Peter Brock Said About Me

I was very honoured to have Australian motor racing royalty Peter Brock say this about me. It was for a documentary of my land speed record attempts called *Encounters with Speed* by Storyteller Media.

"I'm Peter Brock, and I've been around the motor racing world for more years than I care to remember. The Australian motor racing scene is always very interesting, with a lot of innovative people and a lot of ideas that come to fruition based on the good old tried and proven method of having a bit of a go.

One person I would like to introduce you to is someone who gives it a red-hot go, and that person is Rosco McGlashan OAM. He's a real character and dedicated; he's like a dog with a bone. He's got an idea and wants to have the world land speed record. And you know what, if his determination is anything to go by, he might just get there. One thing for sure, whatever he does, he's going to make a bit of news, create some headlines, and if Rosco gets there, he's going to make Australia proud."

Awards, Honours and Appearances

Cheryl and I were presented with keys to the City of Perth by Richard Court MLA in 1999.

Getting a driving lesson from Captain Starlight whilst visiting children in hospital.

Helping out at Princess Margaret Children's Hospital.

Inducted into WA's RAC Walk of Fame in 2012.

-28-

Special Thanks and Acknowledgements

I want to thank the hundreds of people and team members who have helped me throughout my career. I started to try and list them all, and the task became too enormous. Hundreds of people have helped, from my first V8 bike through my drag racing days and then all the land speed cars.

Aussie Invader 5R has also had hundreds of people help construct it so far. It would be unfair to try and list everybody because I would undoubtedly forget some essential people in its construction. So, please let me say, "Thank you so much to everyone who helped to get us where we are. We couldn't have achieved what we have without your help."

-ooOoo-

Special thanks go to Pete Taylor. His meticulous recordkeeping and attention to detail in recording facts in our many record attempts have helped considerably in writing this book. Pete worked with me for over 30 years. He was critical to the many record attempts we made and in helping build all of the *Aussie Invader* cars. Pete was the Team Manager and worked alongside Cheryl with logistics on the many trips and record attempts at Lake Gairdner. Thanks, Pete.

-ooOOoo-

A big thank you must also go to Keith and Jen Lovatt, the best husband and wife support crew ever. They worked with Cheryl and me for over 30 years, supporting our jet dragsters and land speed attempts.

-ooOOoo-

A big thank you to my sisters, Jill and Gail, who helped with their recollections of our early childhood, ensuring the events in this book are as accurate as possible.

-29-
Author's Note

My wife, Kaye, was the one who got me to write this book. She had said for two years that she wanted to get Rosco to start recounting these incredible stories. This came from several meals Rosco and I had eaten with our wives, and one or two of these great stories always came out.

Rosco told me he was taking a break from building *Aussie Invader 5R* for a few weeks. He and his wife Cheryl would travel extensively around Western Australia in their newly acquired camper van. Cheryl had wanted to undertake this trip for a long while, getting Rosco to agree, now that was another matter. So, in true Rosco style, he had torn himself away from building *Aussie Invader 5R* because he felt he could search for suitable places to test the land speed car later.

Kaye and I suggested that Rosco and Cheryl use this opportunity to record some of these great stories on their phones while on their long drives between destinations. These were the fantastic stories I had heard over many years, always leaving me wanting more.

Once Rosco and Cheryl had started recording these stories and stopped at their next location, they could send them back to us. Then, Kaye and I would begin typing them up. We knew Cheryl was also very keen to tell the incredible story of Rosco's life, which Cheryl had been an intricate part of for the last 38 years. So, Rosco now had no excuse.

Kaye and I started receiving a few audio stories. It became clear that over the last 14 years, my almost daily interaction with Rosco meant I knew many of the stories and their history. I also knew of the other vehicles he had built and driven. In fact, I knew a lot about his life, as I had worked closely with Rosco on building *Aussie Invader 5R* since its start in 2009.

I was the best one suited to writing these stories down. Each time a story was told, it was slightly different, not factually, but sometimes there would be extra details. These stories and their level of detail often depended on why they were being told.

Because I had heard them before, I could add the "missing bits." I had set myself a target of writing the book within six months, which was a big ask, as I had never written more than a few pages since leaving school some 50 years ago.

When we started, we didn't know if it would be 30,000 or 80,000 words. So, we would keep expanding the book until all the topics were covered and the stories were exhausted. I actually wrote the majority of this book in eight weeks. I couldn't stop myself; I got swept along with Rosco's incredible and compelling life story. Writing started about 2 a.m. most mornings and lasted until I was too tired to do any more.

Some of these stories were transcribed from recordings. But, I also "read between the lines" of what wasn't said but knew had happened. The recordings threw up a lot of questions, which helped to fill in the gaps appearing in a timeline of Rosco's life. These questions also confirmed and corrected dates and the order of events.

I would go back to Rosco regularly and say, "Tell me about...," which would lead to more stories or a detailed explanation. Even over the phone, I knew Rosco was rolling his eyes and a bit fed up with all my constant questions, but the

Author's Note

book suddenly took on a life of its own. More stories were being told, and more information was coming to light, which was a writer's dream.

Having been involved with the current project, *Aussie Invader 5R*, from the beginning meant I knew the history of the car's build and could write that section of the book without Rosco's input. This was great as Rosco was very time-poor, and another writer would have to start from scratch and take up a lot of Rosco's time. All I had to do was get Rosco to read and agree with what I had written.

Just as I thought I had all the stories written down and was bringing the book to a close, he said. "Did I tell you the story of me meeting the Dalai Lama!" I said, "Rosco, is there anyone you haven't met?"

Rosco has lived five lives already; I could have included a few more stories. But I didn't want to confuse people with even more to take in on Rosco's very full life. But, who knows, those other stories might appear when the record is broken, and I write another book about it.

If possible, I was trying to corroborate these stories with anyone connected with them. In most cases, the version Rosco told was pretty accurate. But you must remember that many of these events happened over twenty, forty or even sixty years ago. Therefore, everyone involved will have a slightly different recollection or version of events.

I have tried to ensure dates and years are as accurate as possible. Still, as you can imagine, no one lives their life expecting to be recounting it many years later. Rosco always looked forward to the next new thing, not thinking about the past and recording it.

Quoting an actual conversation was tough, but the essence of what was said and appears in this book, I believe, is correct. This is a memoir and not a biography, which is entirely different. It is a series of memories (stories) as Rosco recalls them. Others may recall a slightly different version, but this is his memoir and his version of events.

I know Rosco was initially reluctant to go over his early life as it was tough and painful. I would like to feel that once we started, it helped him understand why he is the person he is today.

There was a time in his life when he could have spiralled downwards, but he chose to escape that life. He became the driven, inspirational and motivated man I know today.

Hindsight is the world's most exact science, and I'm sure we would all do things differently if we had a crystal ball to see the future. I am sure Rosco is the same, but I marvel at his dogged determination to succeed. He often says to me, "It's hard to beat someone who never gives up", and he certainly lives by those words.

If you liked this book, please go to the Amazon website or where you bought it and leave an honest review. It really helps us promote the project.

Mark J Read

Author and proud member of the Aussie Invader team

Email: mark@aussieinvader.com

Website: AussieInvader.com
Facebook: AussieInvader
Instagram: AussieInvader5R
Twitter: AussieInvader5R

Manufactured by Amazon.com.au
Sydney, New South Wales, Australia